Robin Wight

The Day the Pigs Refused to be Driven to Market

Advertising and the Consumer Revolution

Hart-Davis, MacGibbon London

Granada Publishing Limited
First published in Great Britain 1972 by Hart-Davis, MacGibbon Ltd.
3 Upper James Street, London W1R 4BP

Copyright © 1972 by Robin Wight

ISBN 0 246 10592 5
Printed in Great Britain by Willmer Brothers Limited, Birkenhead

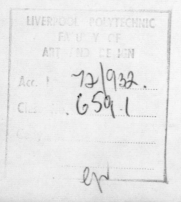

The Day the Pigs Refused to be Driven to Market

Contents

To Julia

Acknowledgements

Many people have helped with developing the arguments of this book, though none of them – of course – should be held responsible for anything I have written.

In particular, I would like to thank (in alphabetical order) Tony Crowther, Max Forsythe, Winston Fletcher, Terry Grimward, Derrick Hass, Robert Lacey, Raymond Lotthé, Chris Rainer and Laurie Rosenbaum. I am also grateful to Diana Cunliffe, Lindsay Clifford and Jill Retter, for helping with the research.

In addition, no one can write about the subject of business and advertising without being indebted to *Fortune, Business Week* and *Advertising Age* from the other side of the Atlantic, and *Management Today, Campaign* and *Ad Weekly* on this side.

The following sources have also been of great assistance to me in the writing of this book:

The Affluent Worker in the Class Structure by Goldthorpe *et al*; *America Inc.* by Cohen and Mintz; 'The Role of Crusader-Triggered Controversy in Technology Assessment' by Dennis W. Brezina, in a paper published by the George Washington University; 'Government and the Market Economy' by Samuel Brittain (an Institute of Economic Affairs leaflet); *Future Shock* by Alvin Toffler; *Managers and Their Wives* by Dr. J. and Dr. B. Pahl; *Abundance for What? and Other Essays* by David Riesman, and 'What One Litle Ad Can Do' by Leo Bogart, Stuart Tolley and Frank Orenstein, which appeared in *The Journal of Advertising*

Research, August 1970; *Occupation Housewife* by Helena Lopata; *The Greening of America* by Charles Reich; E. B. Weiss' columns in *Advertising Age,* and various research reports from J. Walter Thompson Ltd.

I am also glad to acknowledge the permission kindly given by many people to reproduce copyright material. This material is nearly always clearly indicated in the text, as and when it is quoted. But, for the record, the main copyright sources to which I am indebted are as follows:

Messrs Victor Gollancz Ltd. and W. W. Norton and Company Inc., for permission to quote from *The Feminine Mystique* © Betty Friedan 1963; The Marketing Science Institute, Massachusetts, for permission to quote from 'Effects of Television Advertising on Children and Adolescents' by Scott Ward; The Reader's Digest Association Ltd. for permission to include extracts from Table 64 in *Survey of Europe Today* © The Reader's Digest Association Limited 1970; the McGraw-Hill Book Company for permission to quote from *Aspirations and Affluence* by Katona, Strumpel and Zahn; the Institute of Practitioners in Advertising for the information on repetition of T.V. ads, reproduced from 'Advertising and the Public', a report on a survey on attitudes to advertising presented to the 6th National Conference of the Institute of Practitioners in Advertising, Eastbourne, 21 November 1969, by Dr. John Treasure, chairman of the conference; Penguin Books Ltd. and Random House Inc. for permission to quote from *The Greening of America* © Charles Reich 1970; Raymond A. Bauer and Stephen A. Greyser and Harvard University Graduate School of Business Administration, Division of Research, Harvard Business School, Boston, for permission to reproduce three tables from *Advertising in America : The Consumer View*; Stephen A. Greyser and the *Harvard Business Review*, for permission to quote from 'Businessmen's Attitudes to Advertising', *Harvard Business Review*, 1971; The Royal Swedish Ministry of Commerce for permission to quote from the Swedish Royal Commission on Consumer Policy; Andre Deutsch Ltd. and Houghton Mifflin Company for permission to quote from *The New Industrial State* by J. K. Galbraith; Calder and Boyars Ltd. and Harper and Row, Publishers for permission to quote from *Deschooling Society* by Ivan D. Illich; *Fortune* for permission to quote from 'More Power to Everybody' by Max Ways, which appeared in the May 1970 issue; Johan Arndt for permission to reproduce Figure 1 from 'Advertising to the Problem Solving Consumer' from Admap, October 1969; the Controller of Her Majesty's Stationery Office for permission to use Table 31 – Chief Leisure Activities, from *Social Trends* 1970; Oxford University Press for permission to quote from *Occupation Housewife* by Helen Z. Lopata; The Bodley Head and Doubleday and Company Inc. for permission to quote from *Culture and Commitment* by Margaret Mead; the list of new products 1971, reprinted with permission from the 6 December 1971 issue of *Advertising Age*. Copyright 1971 by Crain Communications Inc.

Finally, I would like to thank my editor, Michael Dempsey, for suggesting I write this book in the first place. And my wife, Julia for not divorcing me during the writing of it.

The Day the Pigs Refused to be Driven to Market

In 1948, in a world of ration books and Cold War, George Orwell inverted the 4 and 8 to create 1984. This was to be the date by which, encased in blue overalls and numbed by Victory Gin, we awaited like Pharaoh's lackeys the instructions of Big Brother.

In 1972 we are two-thirds of the way, in time, to this future. And though few today accept the trend towards Orwell's Big Brother in anything like the way it was accepted a quarter of a century ago, his basic assumption is still widely accepted.

That as individuals we are increasingly under control of the state or the corporate state as it has now become. The 'them' who stuff brown envelopes through our letter boxes to announce that our back garden is to become part of a motorway. The gentlemen in blue (sometimes not so gentle) who can hold us without a lawyer present pending a charge being made. The computers who can make us their slaves. And so on until one reaches a politico-technocratic tyranny equipped with all mod cons.

Perhaps the most widely accepted part of this vision is the control over our lives exercised by the mass media and in particular that part of it trying to separate us from our hard-earned pay packets: advertising and marketing.

First came Orwell, then Packard, then Galbraith to preach the same gospel. That the predestination of persuasion had replaced the free will of perfect competition. And growing fat on this mythology were the golden-fingered admen who, whatever private doubts they may have had to these immense powers, were not going to repudiate this unsolicited testimonial to their skills.

The predictable result was that no company felt complete without its high-stepping agency pumping out the hard hitting messages through the lines of N.B.C., I.T.V., C.B.S., or via the wide open spaces of the printed page. But instead of being White-Tornadoed into submission the recipients of this bombardment responded in a way that anyone who studied either the bombing of Dresden or had made but a cursory study of social psychology could have foreseen. The worm started to turn. All the time the whiter-than-white miracle was being promised, the consumer discovered a truth that was several shades greyer. For equipped with new learning sensors and gifted with a new electronic sight, the consumer now had eyes that could see through things that her parents' vision might have bounced off. Little by little this growing disenchantment has swollen into a quiet, silent, blood-less revolution that is on the point of transforming our society as profoundly as did the granting of adult suffrage a century ago. This revolution has had no marches, no manifesto, no real leaders and few formal followers. Its organization (where it exists) is com-posed of equal mixtures of enthusiasm and inexperience. Yet it has already the strength to humble the biggest and most powerful corporation in the world, and none that it has challenged has emerged unchanged.

This book is about that revolution. How and where it grew. The ideologies that fuelled its growth. The activities that formed its purpose. And the areas into which it can be expected to spread. It is a phenomenon whose existence will be traced both to profound changes within the structure of our society as well as to the unresponsiveness of the advertising industry to these changes. An unresponsiveness that has led them to worship false gods in a way that may yet involve the industry's ultimate self-destruction.

I am by no means the first reporter of some of the events described in this volume. Indeed, in one sense, there may be little that is totally new within these covers. (And that so many of the facts reported here have been ignored or brushed aside by the advertising community on both sides of the Atlantic is one of the strongest criticisms to be made against them.) Much of this volume, indeed, is no more than a patchwork quilt of ideas that have been freely drawn from many existing sources. But by their juxtaposition these ideas, for me at least, form a pattern that is not readily apparent while they remain separate.

These ideas cover many fields – sociology, economics, psychology, anthropology and even history – in which I am not qualified to encroach. But, in the full knowledge that a little learning is a dangerous thing, I have done so (if only to show these entrenched specialities that little breadth has its hazards, too). The price of this is that, no doubt, on some points of detail I shall have to stand corrected. (Though I have endeavoured to minimize this by using established sources as a handrail for my argument, and by having the benefit of the specialist advisers already thanked in my acknowledgements.)

But it is my hope that whatever slips time and my critics reveal, they will not be used as a subterfuge for ignoring the central argument. For if it *is* true that the pivotal relationship of our society, between business and the consumer, is being transformed in ways that have neither been fully recognized nor fully understood then those whose fortunes are built on that relationship – be they admen or businessmen – are heading for a fall. If this book helps in any way to break that fall and then helps to lead to the development of a new coincidence of self-interest between business and the consumer, it will have more than served its purpose.

I

Democracy of the Market Place

On 23 November 1969 a columnist in the *Chicago Daily News*, Mike Royko, put a coupon at the bottom of his column containing five names. Each of the names was, according to Royko, a potential presidential candidate in the 1972 presidential election. They were Muskie, Humphrey, Kennedy, McGovern, and Nader. Royko asked his readers to say which of these men should be the Democratic candidate in the 1972 presidential election. And the vote from the readers of the *Chicago Daily News*, the city that keeps the revolutionary figure Mayor Daley in power, was as follows: Muskie 7%, McGovern 2%, Kennedy 2%, Humphreys 0.5%, and Nader 89%.

The fact that a man who five years previously was an unknown young lawyer could rise to this level of public esteem, could attract forty times as many votes as a member of the Kennedy clan, purely on the basis of what he'd done for consumers, suggests that something is stirring in the American market place.

In the Japanese market place, too, a similar phenomenon is at work. Here, in a society that had been one of the world's most hierarchical, where respect for superiors was a watchword of life, a Japanese version of the Women's Institute boycotted buying colour T.V. sets until the manufacturers agreed to reduce the price by £25 a set. And having done that they joined with five other consumer associations to turn on the products of the world's third largest cosmetic company and started a boycott of that one too.

The third advanced society, western Europe, has not been immune from all this. Germany, Sweden, France, and even backward Britain have felt pressures from the bottom of the pyramid.

In Germany, for example, when Dash (known and loved in Britain as Daz) ran ads with housewives saying 'No, I won't swap my packet of Dash for two of another make' they ran into unexpected trouble. Hundreds of housewives contacted Dash offering to make the swap, and one indignant individual even offered to hand over one *ton* of Dash for two tons of Persil.

In Britain it was forecast that the Trade Descriptions Act would give rise to about 50,000 complaints a year. In actual fact there were 96,000 in the first year, 112,000 in the second, and 120,000 in the third. Complaints are currently running at twenty-six times the rate of prosecutions, showing that the consumer is already a great deal fussier than the law.

A fussiness which showed up in the Citizens' Advice Bureau statistics: between 1966 and 1969 compared to an average of 8% more enquiries received from harassed citizens, they received 20% more enquiries on consumerist issues.

The extent of this surge of feeling is shown in the fact that both the *Sunday Times* and the *Sun* (whose success has been entirely due to its ability to understand what makes the workingman tick) had detailed exposés in the first half of 1971 showing business failing to serve the consumer. The *Sunday Times*'s concerned the way companies were hiding the freshness of their food behind secret codes. And the *Sun*'s running over five consecutive days, showed how appalling was the servicing of many consumer durables. Both articles led to questions being asked in the House of Commons.

Are these sorts of developments, which every day become increasingly more frequent, simply fabrications at the media? Are they just isolated incidents that will blow over when the economies of the West pull out of their recession and everything on the money machine returns to normal?

Several people have argued thus. For instance, in 1967 the President of Campbell's Soups described consumerism as 'of the same order as the hoola hoop – a fad'. We will see in a later chapter just where this attitude got Campbell's Soup. And we'll also see how businessmen in America and elsewhere are now starting to sing a rather different tune.

The central point, in fact, to be made about these isolated incidents is that they're not isolated incidents at all. But that they betoken a very real shift of power in our society, away from the bastions of the Corporate State towards what will eventually emerge as the democracy of the market place.

This shift of power is part of a general crumbling of Authority that has been the star of stage and screen over the past two decades. Since demob started in 1945 trust in and respect for Authority, be it for Houses of Parliament or the House of Dior, have been on the wane.

How can one believe in a government if it's prepared to tell lies to the people it governs, as the American administration was shown to have lied by the publication of the Pentagon papers? How can a student believe in the impartiality of the press when the story he reads in the newspaper and sees on the television about, say, the Grosvenor Square riots bears precious little relationship to the events he participated in?

Nor is this distrust of the media just a long-haired student phenomenon. In a survey of people in *Who's Who* in 1971 it emerged that less than a third felt that any daily newspaper was truly impartial. The exception, with a score of 32% for impartiality, was *The Times*. That two thirds of the Top People could consider the Thunderer less than impartial is something that would doubtless cause its founders to turn in their revered graves.

But despite its loss of impartiality, the new mass media has played a key role in the destruction of Authority. (Whether as villain or hero depends upon your standpoint.) Profumo, for example, wasn't the first government minister to engage in sexual peccadilloes. But the media acted as a magnifying glass to enlarge, and perhaps distort, the affair into something of national proportions. The media, too, have helped to remove the dividing line between politicians and members of a government. Politicians have always been, in the eyes of the man on the Clapham omnibus, a rich band of brigands. But when a politician becomes part of the 'government' the mantle of authority used to be the mantle of respectability. Now continual exposure to 625-line close-ups has removed this credibility allowance, until a government has just become no more than a majority of two-faced politicians.

One study by the University of Michigan shows that distrust

of government has almost doubled in the last five years. And that the decline is steepest amongst the 'silent majority' of the American middle class, not the dissenting young (their opinion of government could hardly sink any lower).

In fact, although the absolute credibility of the media may well have declined, relative to other component parts of Authority it's probably risen. The *Who's Who* survey just referred to showed, for example, that more Top People thought the B.B.C. was 'very influential' than Parliament itself.

It's not just the constitutional pillars of society that have started to shake. Take those institutions that were fixed on the map as firm as the Rock of Gibraltar. Like Rolls Royce in Britain and the Penn Central Railway in the United States. Rolls was certainly the physical embodiment of the traditional principles of British industrial supremacy. And for those principles to go bankrupt was a shattering blow to all that was left of the old order.

So, too, have been the students' riots against their teachers, as at the London School of Economics or at Berkeley University in California. The relationship of teacher to pupil has always presented the teacher as the Authority. This is now questioned not only by physical revolution but by a more significant mental revolution. When high school students demand a say in choosing their teachers, they're going further than parishioners demanding a say in their choice of pastor (which, as any bishop will tell you, has transformed the selection of clergy in the Church of England over the last twenty years). For the students are effectively saying that they have lost faith in the traditional concept of schooling, where a licensed distributor of knowledge officially opens the eyes of the blind. The blind, as we shall see, are starting to have more knowledge than the official dispensers of knowledge.

And in the view of one observer (Ivan D. Illich author of *Deschooling Society*) this phenomenon 'endangers the survival of not only the economic order built on the co-production of goods and demands, but equally of the political order built on a nation state into which the students are delivered by the school'.

The social order appears equally endangered. Social authorities, from Emily Post upwards, are experiencing a different version of the anti-Authority phenomenon. A survey amongst a thousand Chicago housewives found that 54% of women who wanted to improve their newspaper would do away with 'Society

4

news' (à la Hickey or Jennifer's Diary). A typical comment was that of a young woman in the Park Forest suburb of Chicago: 'I don't hold the "Four Hundred" in awe any more. The average woman accomplishes as much good in her activities...'

It seems that the old idea of vicarious enjoyment for the plebs by reading of the bread and circuses of the rich no longer hold true. Even the formalized authorities like the Army are not exempt from the crumbling of hierarchy. Not long ago *Fortune* reported a Vietnam incident where a company of men, suspecting an ambush, had refused to go down a road. Mutiny for disobeying the orders of Authority? Not on your life. A few days later the deputy commander of the unit's brigade told the C.B.S. news that there would be no punishment: 'Thank God, we've got young men who question'.

What they were questioning wasn't just any particular authority, but the concept of Authority itself. As Professor Zinkin of Unilever told the 1971 Advertising Association conference (a group of men desperately trying to understand what was about to hit them). 'A revolt against authority itself isn't a new phenomenon. But in the past the successful rebel was the new authority. At the end of the revolution the rules were different, but the obedience of the ordinary man was the same'. It is this questioning of the *concept* of authority that marks the difference from earlier protests. The response to this is not a desire for independence. After all, who but the most ambitious recluse can be independent in our inter-connected world? No, the logical response to the opposition to Authority is not independence, but participation.

If authorities, of one sort or another, are a necessary part of life then at least one should have a say as to how they control you. So you find in a Brooklyn ghetto that poorly educated black parents, ignoring the sound advice of experts, demand control over their neighbourhood schools. So, too, the Roman Catholic Church, the authority of authorities, finds that from Texas to Holland it is confronted by demands for more democratic government. And in France, you find that more than fourteen newspapers or magazines have seen the formation of what they call 'journalists' associations', all designed to break the control of the publisher over the editorial.

Even in the traditional workers' associations, otherwise known as trade unions, one sees the shift of power to the factory floor as

5

a reaction against the central union hierarchy. A study in Britain (Goldthorpe *et al.*) found that though a majority of workers were involved in shop floor union activities, two fifths of all union members *agreed* with the statement that trade unions had too much power in the country. General de Gaulle was once more showing his perception in offering the people of France 'participation' after the students riots of 1968.

What participation essentially provides is a redistribution of authority. Look for example at the world of fashion. Who created the mini, the micro mini, the beads, the see through fashions, the unisex trend? Not some lisping fashion dictator of the Champs Elysées. All these fashions were started on the streets. By the same group who discovered low heels, long sweaters, and the cape – not to mention triggering off a rebellion against bras.

It's not just the young who have control over their fashion. Who turned down the midi, despite the blandishments of all the fashion authorities from *Women's Wear Daily* to *Vogue?* The corseted Madams of New York.

And at a national level, despite an apparent concentration of power by cabinet or presidential government, policy making now has more participants than ever before. No longer can a major new policy, like the Monroe Doctrine, simply slip into existence overnight at the whim of a president without consideration or consultation of others.

Today, the number of people who have some sort of a 'say' in decision stretches all the way from the White House, via the officers of the cabinet, via the bureaucracy of the Pentagon, via the columns of *Newsweek* all the way to the foreign policy study group of Hometown U.S.A. Not to mention the lobbies and pressure groups that can plug into any issue and so widen the distribution of influence over a still wider base.

As Max Ways shrewdly observed in an article for *Fortune* 'the people, an intellectual of abstraction that was useful in democratic theory, is being replaced by myriad concrete human beings who now have, as individuals and in groups, a real and active share of power.'

A recent study confirmed this of both Britain and America. Respectively, 62% and 75% feel that they, personally, can do something about *national* politics. (*Aspirations and Affluence,* Katona). Instead of the acceptance of the concept of 'superiors' the demand is now for equal relationships. It shows as between the

6

worker and the boss. And when in 1966 I.C.I. conducted a survey to find out why productivity was so much higher in America, their main finding confirmed this. It wasn't harder work that gave the American workers the edge. It was because America's hourly workers desire and expect to be personally responsible for much of their work. So there are fewer managers and supervisors.

The move away from authoritarian to participative management has lead to a dismantling of the assembly line and the development of workers' teams managing themselves. Philips, Volvo, and Saab are just three non-American companies who've taken big steps in this direction.

Five years after the I.C.I. survey, another side of the new boss/worker relationship emerged during the attempted closure in 1971 of four shipyards along the Clyde. When a similar thing had happened in 1933 to Palmers' shipyard in Jarrow, it's true there was a march on London, but that is all. When the Clyde management tried in 1971 to do what the Palmers' management had done in 1933, they found a different reaction. Workers took over the yards and held them to ransom in exchange for full employment. This sparked off similar uprisings by workers at Fisher Bendix and Plessey against being put on the dole. To do all this had probably never crossed the minds of the men of Jarrow, because they were still mentally touching forelocks, however much they hated those to whom they bowed.

This new equality of relationships even shows between husband and wife. 'Love, honour and obey' is a reflection of a Victorian ideal rather than a twentieth-century reality. Indeed one suggestion from sociologists is that many of the stresses of marriage, as shown by the 80% rise in divorces in America since 1960, are caused by the tensions of the shift towards a less unequal husband and wife relationship.

It is against this overall background in the home, the school, and the factory that the relationship of business and the consumer needs to be examined.

The first point is that, opposing the trend for redistribution of power in other areas, power in business has tended to concentrate. The largest 10% of businesses did 40% of all business in Britain in 1885. But three quarters of a century later they'd managed to collar 85%.

The Bolton Report on small firms showed how dramatically the small firm sector of the economy had declined in recent years. A

7

development that is an echo of America where in 1968 the nation's 500 largest companies had 68% of all sales and 74% of all profits.

Taking the automobile industry, three companies made 83% of all cars made in America. This compares with 88 independent car producers in 1921.

The phenomenon which changed the automobile situation was that in 1923 General Motors to put the pressure on the 'weaker' companies introduced the annual model change. By 1935 78% of these companies were out of business.

Once power is thus concentrated it is difficult to dilute. Morton Mintz and Jerry Cohen calculate in *'America Inc.'* that it would now cost a company $779 million to enter the automobile industry. But if the industry *hadn't* been restructured by the annual model change the price tag for entry would be only $55 million.

Against this, it should be said that both the Volkswagen and the Japanese companies have entered the U.S. car market without the difficulties implied by these figures. Nevertheless, unless one is talking of technical innovation like Xerox or a new sort of service industry, like package holidays, the trend to concentration makes it harder for outsiders to become insiders.

It's a situation, in fact, where the power of business appears to be on the increase (whatever brand managers struggling to shift 1% more product may say to the contrary).

In the Victorian period, or even at the time of the Rockefellers, this could happen without attracting too much critical comment. But now that the whole concept of Authority is under question, the institutions that make up the fabric of that Authority come into question as well. And as business' virtue is less believed, so the apparent power it wields becomes less sufferable. The old basis of the consumer/business relationship, caveat emptor, or buyer beware is seen in this situation as being grossly unfair. Caveat emptor recognizes no buyers' rights. It is built on the concept of buyers' self reliance. And in 1970, at the extreme it simply gives the housewife the right to bear one, two, or three thalidomide babies before she discovers that thalidomide is an undesirable product and punishes the manufacturer by refusing to buy any more thalidomide.

Even less dramatic cases like that around cyclamates in foods reflect a new situation. Once upon a time it was unlikely that any major company would introduce a product until its safety

8

was entirely beyond question. Now pressures on profits and the sheer complexity of the products themselves makes the consumer feel that this assurance has been removed. Trust, in fact, has been so far eroded that the findings of research by industry are no longer believed. It may well be true that, for example, to feed vast quantities of this or that additive to rats and deduce from the damage done that tiny quantities of the same substance are dangerous to humans makes a mockery of science. The important point is that this mockery is now more believed than science. (For example, the American experiments that put a question mark against saccharin involved feeding to rats the proportional amount of saccharin that a human being would only get if he or she drank 875 bottles every day of a typical saccharin sweetened soft drink.)

The implications of this erosion of trust between business and the consumer are important. For if Talcott Parsons is right in his contention 'that the vast volume of complex transactions that mark our society can only take place under conditions of general trust' then we have one more factor working to ensure that the old order changes.

If the consumer then tends to see business as stronger and wickeder than previously, how does she assess her own position *vis-à-vis* the corporate giants?

The Molony Committee, investigating the plight of the consumer in 1952, concluded 'the idea of consumer sovereignty is fallacious. In truth the producer is dominant and his voice is all powerful. His interests usually prevail over the welfare of the consumer'.

It's not just the sheer concentrations of business that fuels this feeling. It is the fact that consumers in the affluent societies find themselves smothered under a huge inventory of possessions, many of them too complicated to understand. This turns them into amateur buyers facing a professional seller, and in this situation the conventional wisdom that buyers can look after themselves collapses.

Of course, the consumer would mind this less if she was satisfied with what she was purchasing. But according to a study by the European consumer associations, one person in two is dissatisfied with the goods and services he buys and the ways he is treated as a customer.

On servicing of products, the last document by the British Consumer Council highlighted one cause of discontent. By 1969 the

9

average household was spending 59p a week just on servicing consumer durables, which was 30% higher than four years previously (compared to a rise of only 7% in the cost of the consumer durables themselves). And in 1967, a survey by the Gallup Poll for the Consumer Council showed that one new car owner in eight was dissatisfied by repairs to their cars under warranty. No wonder, then, that a further survey, this time by the *Guardian*, in 1963 showed that 80% of the British population believe that they should have organized consumer protection.

The concept that provided the focus for this nascent discontent was consumerism. In the same way that trade unions in the nineteenth century used collective action against industry, consumerism developed as the housewives collected defence mechanism in the twentieth.

Consumerism demands that an individual has a right to have an interest (in the legal sense) in a product even if he or she isn't a purchaser of it. It doesn't accept the concept of 'perfect competition' advanced in economic text books as representing a realistic analysis of the business/consumer relationship. It shifts the onus of responsibility fairly and squarely onto the shoulders of the management, and removes it from the market place. The fact that 'it sells' is no longer a sufficient justification for the existence of the product.

But consumerism extends beyond just the product itself. In the words of the Director Designate of the Consumer Council, Des Wilson, it is about 'the quality of the existence we scratch for ourselves, the values we obtain and the money we earn with the lives we are allowed to lead'.

The very existence of consumerism has two important implications. First, at one level, that consumers feel that the products industry provide them with are not performing 'as well as they should'. If people's expectations were less, the issues available to consumerists would be fewer too. But the increased wealth of society (where we start moving from being awe-struck by the existence of a fridge to being thunder-struck if it breaks down) and promises of 'good, better, best' by advertisers have interlocked to create what one Detroit car manager calls 'the phenomenon of rising expectations'. If it was good enough for my father, it doesn't mean it's good enough for me.

I will discuss in a later chapter the way advertising has worked to make people feel disappointed when their soap powder only cleans the wash and doesn't get it whiter than white. And in this sense, at least, the admen have very much triggered off the earthquake that now threatens their prosperous edifice.

The second, and wider, implication of the existence of consumerism is that it means business is out of phase with the real wants of the people, that despite the sophisticated models of marketing and lip service to consumer orientation, business is not supplying the people with what they really want. Nine years after the ending of the First World War came the first stirrings of all this. For if 1822 be remembered for the Tolpuddle Martyrs as a turning point in trade unionism, then 1927 bears a similar importance for consumerism. It was then that an economist called Stuart Chase teamed up with a mechanical engineer from the American Standards Association to write a book called *Your Money's Worth*. It soon became, apart from a best seller, the book most often stolen from the public libraries. It simply reported the results of tests made for the American government by the National Bureau of Standards. One of the discoveries that these made was that there was very little correlation between price and quality. For example, nine makes of sheets were tested: 'The make ranking eighth in quality ranked second in price. Of two makes whose quality was identical, one sold for two and a half times as much as the other. The make which ranked lowest in quality sold for 20% more than that ranking sixth' etc., etc. More than that, further tests showed that neither ordinary consumers nor even sales people could – not knowing the price – rank the sheets in the correct order of quality based on scrutiny and touch.

One of the authors of *Your Money's Worth* – Schlink – then teamed up with Arthur Kallet to write *One Hundred Million Guinea-Pigs*. This turned the spotlight onto advertisers as well as the products themselves, and out of the furore it caused grew the Consumers' Union.

It was not until thirty years after *Your Money's Worth* that a similar event occurred in Britain (now the time lag between consumerism in Britain and America is, hopefully, a good deal shorter). In 1957 a small group of enthusiasts, using a garage in Bethnal Green as an office, produced the first copy of *Which*. A first print of 10,000 copies was quickly exhausted. And since then the circulation has climbed at a rate of about 1,000 extra copies a week.

The fact remains, however, that neither in Britain nor America

11

have either of these consumerist groups increased their member-
ship beyond 2% of the population. Both of them are heavily
weighted towards the middle classes. A survey by the publishers
of *Which* in 1965 showed that their average reader was middle
class (middle manager status), between thirty-six and forty-five,
with two children, and his favourite paper was the *Daily Telegraph*. And a similar profile, with a graduate bias, shows itself
in the Consumer Union.

In 1965, the Consumers Association – who published *Which*
– tried to counter this bias by setting up a consumer clinic in
Kentish Town to reach the working classes. One reason why the
working classes have previously shown such little interest in this
desire to save money is that the sort of product examined by
consumer organizations wasn't the sort of product members of the
working classes normally purchased. Only a tiny minority of the
working class owned, for example, a car, a refrigerator, or an
automatic washing machine. (The sorts of thing on which *Which*
lavished its attentions.) Even those who did possess these products
of the affluent society saw their consumer durables very much as
possessions, rather than machines to do something. Until affluence
not only reached the working man but took the working man well
past the first flush of materialist excitement, consumerism was not
of any widespread interest.

But as well as the prevalence of more mature attitudes to
material goods, one other thing was necessary before the critical
mass of consumer concern was sufficient to trigger mass consumerism. It was that material goods became an integral part of
the consumer's life; that the consumer became enormously
dependent on the product's not failing. Until this moment, the
consumer's suffering was always mitigated by lack of his depend-
ence on the produce that had failed. But once he was living behind
what one writer has called 'the dykes of quality control' (Dr Joe
Juran) the irritation caused by even the tiniest hole in the dyke
could be tremendous.

It is for these reasons that consumerism developed most in the
most affluent societies. Even today, for instance, America has two
and a half times the gross national product per head of population of Britain. So it is not surprising that the consumer revolution
has progressed further on the other side of the Atlantic. It is not
surprising that Japan has a vigorous consumer movement while
India has virtually none. For until a society reaches a critical mass

of affluence the consumer movement remains restricted to having an influence only in direct proportion to its limited numbers. And that, quite understandably, is the amount of importance businessmen will regard it with. Of course, blue stockinged ladies will be overwrought that their dishwashers have chewed up their Spode. Of course, Hampstead intellectuals will feel that plastic daffodils are no substitute for a bigger packet of detergent. But in the market place, where the money's made, common sense – thank Heaven – still prevails. Did not the revered Molony Committee report in 1962 that 'it is difficult to avoid the conclusions that the consumer does not think she, or he, is illserved'? The main reason for this judgement, which contrasts sharply with the figures given in this chapter, was that '...our postbag from members of the public has been strangely small.' There was thus no 'cogent evidence of consumer dissatisfaction'. The assumption behind this learned opinion is totally educated middle class: that if you are dissatisfied with something you write to the manufacturer concerned. But the working class, less educated and less literate, are correspondingly less inclined to put pen to paper. And to deduce that the mass of consumers are satisfied merely because they haven't written a complaining letter to Mr Justice Molony is indeed a blinkered state of mind. More than that, it is rather a conceit. One tends only to write such letters if one believes that by doing so something will be achieved. But the man on the Clapham omnibus had very little reason to believe a letter to this august Committee would get the Electricity Board to repair his defunct cooker.

If the Molony Committee so misunderstood consumer sentiment then it's understandable that the average boardroom had no clearer idea of what was about to hit it. Indeed, the prevailing notion of a consumer society was that of a docile but affluent public, in the helpless grip of the hidden persuaders, buying exactly what business desired. So said another equally august figure, Professor J. K. Galbraith, and a lot of people chose to believe him. In this particular atmosphere, consumerism was thought to mean no more than the middle classes pursuing manufacturers in the same way that the upper classes pursued foxes, and of no more consequence. And a study by Sales Research Limited in Britain in 1963 gave further confirmation to such feelings. 'Despite the fact that as many as 11% of those who purchased an appliance in the preceding twelve months had listened to broadcasts or read the research reports for that appliance, only 1% deemed this to be the most decisive factor in brand choice.'

Why then should General Motors pay any attention when in November 1965 a young lawyer who was serving on a Senate enquiry into automobile safety published a book called *Unsafe At Any Speed*. Nader's attack wasn't so much on the *value* of a particular product, as on its *safety* (like Rachel Carson's *Silent Spring* two years earlier). And the Nader's charge, as will be seen, went beyond an unsafe car called the Corvair and onto the corporate ethos behind that unsafe car.

In one sense, of course, attacks on this ethos and its high priests who served it – the admen – weren't new. 'Nine tenths or more of advertising is largely competitive ramblings as to the relative merits of two indistinguishable compounds' had been Stuart Chase's verdict in the late twenties. In the fifties Richard Hoggart in the *Uses of Literacy* had attacked the advertising practice of appealing to baser instincts of humanity, like keeping up with the Joneses, for commercial ends. And J. B. Priestley wrote *Over The Rainbow* and coined the word 'admass' to describe the neon lit freeway draped, ad infested society called America. But none of these did anything to unsteady the citadel of capitalism. And their main effect was to give admen a desire to write poems and paint pictures to salve their creative consciences.

For the first three months after the publication of *Unsafe At Any Speed*, despite the fact that there was a hearing in progress in the Senate on automobile safety, there was no real indication that the fate of Nader's attack would be substantially different from the onslaught by earlier tribunes of the people. If one compares the number of major reviews of Nader's book in the five months after publication with the number of major reviews given to *Silent Spring*, *Unsafe At Any Speed* still has only *half* the reviews of Rachel Carson's book.

Dennis Brezina analysing fifteen articles in this period on Nader concluded that they 'emphasised primarily the series of events that transpired after General Motors admitted it routinely checked Nader's background.' This admission was made in March 1966, as a result of charges made by Nader in *New Republic* that he was being shadowed by private detectives. Once General Motors owned up to this the public furore began. After March 1966 Nader's name was on the front page of the *New York Times* eight times, compared to once for Rachel Carson. But the furore was about 'a big corporation snooping into the private affairs of a man who had almost incidentally written a crusading book' (Brezina).

This is a crucially important point in understanding Nader's impact. It was a direct result of the feeling by many consumers that their relationship with business was out of line with other parts of the fabric of authority, all of which, had been forced in the post-war years to redistribute their power at a grass roots level. Had Nader written the same book with the same facts in 1920 it might, like *Your Money's Worth*, have been a best seller and pinched from all the public libraries. But it would not have been the first blow that started to shake the corporate giants. Indeed it is probable that if General Motors *hadn't* behaved like a Big Brother, Nader's book would still have been limited in its impact (as the analysis of the newspaper reviews suggest). For until Nader represented the issue of the individual consumer against the corporate state instead of the issue of the unsafety of a General Motors' car, he was destined for no more than a second printing of *Unsafe At Any Speed*.

The media, of course, was the second factor that transformed Nader from a limited to a mass issue. The media did more than just supply the oxygen that kept the fire of controversy going. They magnified, distorted, and simplified the issues for mass consumption. And they spread the information at electronic speed to every home from Alaska to Arkansas. By doing this they gave chapter and verse to the inchoate, unfocused feelings amongst many Americans about big business.

Until this point, in fact, the word of business was by and large accepted against the word of the complaining citizen. But by taking the issue *outside* a specialist technical area (like automobile safety) and making it an issue which everyone could understand (the devious conduct of the biggest company in the land) and by providing evidence in every drawing room of America of this conduct (the televised cross-examination of General Motors' president at the Senate enquiry) the media changed the status of business overnight. Only since then has a company *had* to engage in corporate advertising to buttress its credibility.

General Motors' conduct in tailing Nader with private eyes had the effect, then, of turning this from a technical into a moral dispute. In a technical dispute, like *Silent Spring* or more recently Concorde, even parties to the debate obviously biased in one direction – like the British Aircraft Corporation – can make a *technical* argument on the credible position of their *technical* expertise. When the issue becomes a moral one they have no such natural reservoir of expertise.

When after this event, as in the case of air bags, the American car industry tried to resassert its technical expertise, it found that it had no longer the credibility to do this.

It is perhaps interesting in this context that though Nader and his followers have lambasted business since 1965, he's gone out of his way to underline the fact that he is criticizing more than imperfect products or imperfect advertising. Arguing for the need for structural change instead of solving individual consumer grievances – 'band aid solutions' – Nader pointed to 'car bumpers designed to withstand collisions of 2.8 m.p.h. This is calculated engineering design to increase sales of spare parts, giving General Motors more bucks for the bàng.' And a report issued by the American Insurance Institute for Highway Safety showed that a 5 m.p.h. impact on the rear bumper of a 1971 Chevy Impala will produce $447 worth of damage. Doctor William Haddon of the Institute commented 'vehicles are being made with an external delicacy that exceeds belief. You would not send a parcel post package wrapped the way a car is packaged'. And not just by co-incidence. As the British Consumer Council reported 'sales of spare parts and repairs have proved more profitable than sales of cars'. A £700 Mini built out of spare parts would cost £2,500. Another American report stated that application of known metallurgical processes would permit doubling the life of an automobile for an additional cost of $36 per year.

It is the state of mind that rules out such progress in a society that can send men to the moon that is the public enemy number one for consumerism. One of the assumptions behind this state of mind is that GNP is a fair measure of economic success, therefore the greater the cash turnover you can generate the greater your degree of progress. In fact, looking at the motor industry, the consumerist sees a parasitic sub-economy that generates cash turnover out of the malfunctions of the main motor industry. Worth $5 billion a year – which is almost the GNP of Brazil – and composed of everything from car repairers and spare part companies to traffic accident lawyers it represents a measure of failure not success. Yet by adding $15 billion a year to the GNP it appears as a profit in the national accounts, not as a loss. It may console the more patriotic of Americans, Nader has observed, to feel that by having a car crash they're helping the gross national product.

In another industry, a further instance of this is that both Canada Dry and Schweppes have started to market ordinary drinking water for those Americans who are fed up with having their bourbons tainted by the polluted variety. ('Finally. A great drink of water in Philadelphia', said Schweppes).

In the parasitic sub-economy, clearly one man's pollution is another man's market opportunity. A comment by a young South American to the educational reformer Ivan D. Illich puts the matter succinctly: 'First you tot up all that people eat, then you add to that their excrement': with such mathematical principles are gross national products calculated. Hence Nader's belief that only by dismantling corporate power can these distortions of the economic system by ironed out.

'The passion that rules Ralph Nader' said a hostile article in *Fortune* magazine 'is aimed at smashing utterly the target of his hatred, which is corporate power.' And though *Fortune*, as Defender of the Corporate Faith tends to be unable to see beyond its own top Five Hundred, the point would probably not be disputed by Nader. According to him, for instance, it would cost General Motors – who contribute 35% of the nation's air pollution by tonnage – about $150 million to develop a non-polluting engine. This is precisely *two-thirds* of what General Motors spent during 1967 to 1969 to change its dealers' signs to 'G.M. : Mark of Excellence'. All this is really an attack on corporate vandalism, a phenomenon which Nader would like to carry the same penalty as private vandalism. 'If we were as lenient towards individual crime as we are towards big business crime, we would empty the prisons, dissolve the police forces and subsidize the criminals.' In a vintage year, he observes, bank robbers steal $7 million. At the same time the automobile industry, by equipping vehicles with 'eye lashes which it calls bumpers' exposes car owners to repairs of around one billion dollars – or 150 times more than the bank robbers took. The strength of his feeling also emerged when, during a meeting of advertising men, someone asked him why he never mentioned the 'good things' done by businesses, like General Motors' offer to call in faulty cars. 'This is incredible,' snapped Nader. 'Would you write a letter to a burglar thanking him for not stealing from you?'

Nader's explanation of why business can get away with all

17

this directly relates to concentration of corporate power. By reducing the number of companies in any one market place, this phenomenon has tended to reduce competition in these market places to the detriment of the consumer. 'Companies either agree not to compete or to reduce the range of competition. Or they compete about packaging and advertising to avoid competing about the substance of the product they are selling. The only way business can plan for maximum certainty is to deny the consumer information for rational choice between products and to prevent just remedies for his grievances.'

The evil genius serving these ends for industry is, of course, Madison Avenue who 'is engaged in an epidemic campaign of marketing fraud. It has done more to subvert and destroy the market system in this country than ten Kremlins ever dreamt of' (*Fortune* May 1971). These rather sweeping statements contrast strangely with his detailed and painstaking analysis of the sort of business misconduct that will be described in chapter three. 'Misconduct' is perhaps the wrong word because several of the things Nader complains of (like the way tinned soup is prepared for photography) have been previously judged to be a fair practice.

The point about all these charges is not whether they are true but that they are increasingly believed. In the words of a Senate aide who worked with Nader often in drafting legislation 'Nader has become the fifth branch of government, if you count the press as the fourth.'

Nader himself remains unsatisfied. 'Very little progress, really. It's a push and shove situation.' And on a more general level he makes the comment: 'The level of the efficiency of citizenship action in most countries is about where physics was in the days of Archimedes.'

Writing in 1966 Eirlys Roberts of *Which* confirmed the gloomy picture. 'After thirty years in the United States and over eight years in the United Kingdom, it is not possible to say that consumer reports have any large, direct influence on manufacturers.'

Certainly, there have been false alarms in the past that the consumer Utopia had arrived. In 1963 – three years before Miss Roberts' conclusion – the *Daily Mail* gaily chanted 'you may not realize it, but we are in the middle of something which could be called the Revolution of the Consumer. We are all consumers now, and by golly we are fighting for our cause.' This brandishing-of-the-hockey-sticks outburst was an echo of the *Sunday Graphic* five years earlier that 'at this moment a quiet but major revolution is happening in British shopping. The customers – already a hundred thousand families of them – are beginning to hit back'.

Statements of that nature – contrasting sharply with those of consumer gladiators who actually went into battle with manufacturers – make one naturally weary of proclaiming a consumer nirvana. Yet what is undoubtedly true is that a structure of consumer power is growing, and growing fastest in those societies whose affluence is growing fastest, that is quite different from the middle class best-buying of the past.

Already in America this structure is powerful enough to chew up the largest company in the land, and is currently putting under the microscope the most powerful body in America, the United States Congress.

But before looking to see the actual achievements of consumer power, it seems sensible to look at its structure (or rather structures) in a little more detail and examine the various (and conflicting) theories that provide the fuel for its flames.

2

Power Grows Out of the Shopping Basket

A recurring theme of this book will be that more has happened between 1961 and 1971 than the passing of ten years.

Ten years ago the only formal structures of consumer power were the consumer associations. But by the end of this period a structure had grown up that was powerful enough in some countries not only to have senior members of government dismissed, take on and beat huge companies, but also to provide for the individual *as a consumer* the sort of support he had previously only had from trade unions in his role *as a worker*.

For all their appeals to the Hampstead gentry, the early consumer associations had fundamental limitations as power groups. Quite apart from their educated middle-class bias that I have spoken of, they saw their job as being to *educate* the consumer. To give him or her just enough accurate information to chose a good buy more easily, yet at the same time to stimulate the shopper into doing some of his or her own thinking. But their concept was not to *protect* the consumer (with the exception perhaps of electrical and engineering safety). The harshest strictures tended to be reserved for things like hormone creams and Queen Bee Jelly. Even when they did lash out it was on a limited scale. 'I suppose our biggest success was getting one brand of washing machines we criticized taken off the market', said Eirlys Roberts in 1962, of the early days of *Which*.

Nevertheless as a buying advice service to the middle classes they obviously represented something of significance. In Britain they spread into local consumer associations, and the flavour of their activities was perhaps caught during 1965 by a report in the *Sunday Times* that 'Oxford have done Trojan work in the greengrocery field'.

But in two other advanced societies, Japan and America, the gentlemanly concept of recommending 'best buys' was being replaced by a newer one: the concept of 'worst buys'. Rather than tell people what they should buy, the emphasis of this approach was to tell them what they should not buy. And tell them what they could buy *if* companies used all the technology available to them.

Nader's Raiders (who still only number 35 full time – on a budget that over seven years has been hardly more than the head of General Motors earns in one) in looking at automobiles, meat inspection, the food industry, the medical profession, Dupont's grip on Delaware, even land use in California, are as concerned as a *News of the World* reporter to find someone to *expose*. They act on the premise of vice, not virtue. For example, in the case of California land use they found that the land of snowy peaks and majestic redwood forests was in fact a despoiled waste whose wretched acres were either destroyed by pesticides, smoke, bulldozers or sold into ecological slavery by speculators. This sort of second generation consumerism has no time for the pedantic fairness of *Which*. It is openly propagandist. It argues that only thus does it have a chance to take on and beat the bureaucratic establishment that is its natural enemy.

Another consumer group operating on these hard-nosed principles is Banzhaf's Bandits. This began as an extension of the anti-smoking campaign run by a New York lawyer John Banzhaf III. Since July 1967 he has waged a battle against the tobacco companies with his group ASH (Action for Smoking and Health). And his students, using acronyms like SOUP (Society Opposing Unfair Practices), TUBE (Terminating Unfair Broadcasting Excesses), PUMP (Protesting Unfair Marketing Practices), SAME (Students Against Misleading Enterprises) have made brisk forays into the soft underbelly of American business. (Aided and abetted by sympathetic senators including Edward Kennedy).

Going East, Japan hasn't yet seen the emergence of an inscrutable Nader (although they do have a consumer motor pressure group) partly because the first generation consumer associations proved themselves more aggressive than their western counterparts. Using the technique of a national boycott Shufuren for

21

example has assailed everyone from rice growers charging excessive prices to canned food manufacturers whose labels conceal the truth. One reason why Shufuren can do this is that it has 6 million members, compared to *Which's* 600,000, and the Consumer Union's 1.3 million. More recently, a local women's association, Chifuren, has developed a technique which as well as attacking with words companies that fail to live up to Chifuren's standards, actually makes its own products to compete with such black sheep.

Besides all this, second generation consumerism in Britain still has an air of sweet reasonableness that's quite out of line with the ferocity of consumerists in other countries. For example, an article in 1970 written by a member of the Housewives' Trust on 'How to complain' began: 'Everyone who has to deal with complaints is aware of a hard core of professional complainers who are dishonest, mad, or have nothing better to do' (which puts Ralph Nader firmly in his place). The article continued by giving helpful advice about who to complain to. But the important difference about this approach is that, like the 'best buy' school of thought, it leaves action up to the individual. Whereas in Japan and America groups go into vigorous action *on behalf* of individuals.

One group in Britain which *may* fall into line with second generation consumerism in other advanced societies is the Consumers Union. This was formed by ex-members of the defunct Consumer Council as a grass roots militant body. It was only in response to the birth of this rival that the Consumer Association formed their own Consumers Campaign Committee.

But the major British approach is still a derivation, albeit a distant cousin, of the perfect competition school of thought, where the market place is controlled by the interaction of *individuals* (in this case well informed individuals).

It's certainly true that the role of the militant *individuals* in building a new structure of consumer power certainly isn't to be forgotten. Nader, after all, was an individual protesting about the designed-in dangers of the American automobile, before he was a group protesting about the designed-in dangers of American society. And other individuals, particularly students in America, have acted as militant consumers – if not quite as the perfect competition model suggests by purchasing alternative brands of the product they are dissatisfied with. It was students in California who were instrumental in making an issue of the Chevron

22

petrol advertising that the following chapter will examine. It was a mixture of individuals and consumer groups who filed the suit against Bristol Myers for alleged deception in their Exedrin advertising (of which more anon). It was an individual, Robert Choate, who took on the American cereal industry with his well documented allegations that two out of three breakfast cereals contained little more than 'empty calories'.

With a good enough cause, an individual can even dispense with the minutiae of documentation. A forty-year-old electrical engineer named Morty Batler, for example, incited the solid citizens of Long Island to boycott the commuter rail line to New York 'We get kicked around by the management, we get kicked around by the unions. Only with a massive boycott can we hit the railroad where it hurts, in their pocketbook.' (But as yet the Dartford Loop remains unassailed though the Northern Line has been under attack.)

Individual consumers don't, of course, have to stray beyond the law. They can fall back on the national, local and trade organizations as well as the Local Authority consumer advisory services in Britain. And in America there's an even more vigorous network of local consumer protection agencies in fifty cities and twenty counties whose activities make the efforts of some of our own bodies seem like a vicar's tea party.

The media, scenting this new interest amongst their readers and viewers, have cast themselves in a new role as champions of the consumer. The *Washington Post,* the *Los Angeles Times,* the *Christian Science Monitor,* the *Wall Street Journal* (with only the *New York Times* lagging) have recognized that consumer affairs are now front page news. In Britain, consumer guidance has emerged as another readers' service from the newspapers. The *Sunday Times* has its Consumer Unit, the *Guardian* has Checkout, and the *Observer* uses the Housewives' Trust.

Interestingly, it is not just the middle-class papers that have shown enthusiasm for this new cause. The *Sun*'s five day exposé of the bad servicing of consumer durables broke the ice. Then in October 1971 the *News of the World* followed up with a detailed brand by brand exposé of washing up liquids. And in February 1972 the *Daily Mirror* on two successive days ran major articles on 'The Great Label Muddle'.

This concern for their readers as consumers rather than worrying about the impact on their advertising revenue of an antibusiness stance, reflects not so much a higher degree of journalistic principle as a shrewd realization of where their bread's buttered. In the past all the mighty Thunderer was prepared to say was 'manufacturers should on their side show a greater respect for the intelligence of buyers and shoppers' coupled with the aside that no doubt the consumer organizations 'can do their jobs better as they learn it' (*Times* November 1958). Then in 1963 the *Sunday Times* (seven years later to be the sword-bearer of consumerism) took great delight in reporting that the electric kettle rated as 'best buy' by *Which* had failed the electrical safety cutout test for *Shoppers' Guide*. And in the same year, it ran an article *complaining* 'there are now in this country too many associations, committees and trusts – official and unofficial – to list all striving for the consumer' (to which has since been added the *Sunday Times'* own Consumer Unit).

In America, right up to 1965, it was the complaint of the Consumers Union that the press paid scant attention to their reports. Not so now. At one stage, in fact, B.B.C. Television was virtually broadcasting *Which* reports on their programme 'Choice' (until they decided that this was sailing too close to the wind of commerce. And A.T.V. turned Bernard Braden into a sort of television Consumer Ombudsman.

In America not only does one Boston station (WGHB) put out the Nader report – an exposé style programme from the Centre for Responsive Law – but 190 educational stations in 1971 carried the 'Great American Dream Machine'. This is a new sort of consumer programme which, far from ignoring the Consumer Union's reports, converts them into laugh-a-line jokes. For example, Morton's lemon cream pie was shown to be made from a recipe of 'good old monosodium phosphate, the same used in laxatives and cleaners...plenty of fresh whey solids...guar gum from the Texas grasslands' etc. 'But you will note', said the show's star Marshal Efron, 'no lemon, no cream, no eggs, just pie'.

The interaction of pressures from the media, individuals and consumer groups has led, as one would expect and hope in a democracy, to a response by government. Although *The Times* warned us all in 1963 that 'the consumer who relies on rules to stock his cupboard will eat a poor breakfast', rules on both sides of the Atlantic have been increasing. And even if the rules haven't changed, they have been given a much stricter interpretation.

Starting on the other side of the Atlantic it was President

24

Kennedy who first gave the number one citizen's imprimatur to consumerism. He promised that the consumer's voice would be heard at the highest level of government. A promise that was echoed in Nixon's pledge to give the consumer 'a permanent voice in the White House'. This of course, doesn't mean licensed business bashing on Capitol Hill. Someone, after all, has to pay President Nixon's election expenses and it isn't the consumerists. But one can see in both Congress and the government regulatory agencies the evidence of a new attitude towards the consumer echoing the shift of power in the market place itself. In the six years 1965 to 1971, for example, twenty consumer bills managed to get past the business lobbyists, the batteries of special interest lawyers, and eventually on to the Statute Book of Congress.

But of even more importance, in practical terms, have been the changes forced on the government regulatory bodies, particularly the Federal Trade Commission (hereafter referred to as the F.T.C.). The F.T.C. was created in 1914 to be an expert on monopoly and economic concentration. And for over half a century it lived in relatively peaceful obscurity, gradually choking itself to death with red tape. Over the years it became a convenient dumping ground for issues which no other government body was really equipped to deal with. So as consumer protection became an issue of government, it was the cumbrously organized F.T.C. who got the job. Just how cumbrous the F.T.C. was emerged in a study made after the rehabilitation of this department in 1970. It showed that there were forty-six distinct steps that had to take place from the time a complaint reached the F.T.C. until it was officially docketed for litigation. No surprise then that in 1969 a quarter of the deceptive trade practices being looked at by the F.T.C were over two years old. (A speed of response only rivalled by its sister organization the Federal Drugs Administration, which took almost twenty years to go from discovering dangers in cyclamates to making an outright ban on their use in food.)

This bureaucratic heaven had another failing that didn't endear it to the hearts of consumerists. It had been given considerable powers in 1914 which it persistently failed to use for the benefit of the consumer. For instance, from 1962 to 1969 F.T.C. fought a half hearted battle against Geritol, an iron tonic. It took three years for the first cease and desist order to be issued, and though this order was affirmed by the Court of Appeal in 1967, in 1969 a new Geritol commercial was on the air which the F.T.C. said

25

misrepresented the efficacy of Geritol no less than the commercial of 1962. But rather than ask for the fines of up to $5000 a day, which they were entitled to, they just asked Geritol for a 'compliance report'.

In fact, when the F.T.C.'s new head of their Bureau of Consumer Protection claimed the right to demand from an advertiser that he provide the F.T.C. with substantiation of his claims, his demand was based on the *original* power given to the F.T.C. by Congress in 1914.

To be fair to the F.T.C. however, if they had tried to use their full authority prior to the growth of consumer power that I have spoken of, no doubt all hell would have broken loose. One only has to look to the reaction in 1962 to the proposed law giving the F.T.C. power to issue a temporary cease and desist order (without going before a court) pending the completion of the proceedings. According to *Printers' Ink,* this proposal made 1962 'the year advertising faced death'. And a distinguished lawyer (in fact a former F.T.C. Commissioner) said of this proposal: '1962 was the first year a serious, well planned and politically powerful putch was organized to give bureaucracy the authority to stop an advertising campaign the minute it started and all without the formality of a trial.'

One can understand the wretched F.T.C. Commissioners' being so taken aback by this outburst in defence of 'free enterprise' and acting more than a little cautiously in the years afterwards. But this soft pedalling made them very vulnerable to a Naderite attack (with the alliance of the American Bar Association) in 1969. As a result, the F.T.C. was purged and given new leadership. As well as being rejuvenated in a way which, while not satisfying the demands of the Naderites, must have exceeded their realistic hopes (to the extent even of having the F.T.C.'s new chairman one of the members of the American Bar Association Committee which had attacked the ancient regime).

The fact that a *private citizen,* Ralph Nader, could have achieved all this – to be compared in Britain to having a senior civil servant fired and his Ministry reorganized – shows how far consumer power had grown.

It is likely that now the F.T.C. has started to change it will continue to move towards a position where it becomes an agency that functions as a *prosecutor* only, instead of being the body for the hearing of complaints as well. The complaints themselves could move to Trade Courts set out round the County Courts and working side by side with the Federal District Courts. Thus turning the F.T.C. into an ombudsman that not only acts on its own right but lets private citizens help it act as well. Already, for example, the F.T.C. has officially recognized the rights of groups of consumers, like SOUP to participate in its cases.

The stage beyond this is 'class action' where a private individual can take action against a company on behalf of all the consumers (pro bono publico) who have been deceived by the product or the advertisement. And fines are assessed not on the basis of how much the individual has suffered, but in terms of the *total* suffering incurred by *all* purchasers of the product.

In Sweden, this concept exists in the form of a Consumer Ombudsman who can take action in the market court to guard the interests of consumers. A move that is the latest in a long series by the Swedish Government, who have labelled the seventies 'the decade of the consumer'.

In the last ten years there have been fourteen different Royal Commissions dealing with consumer policy (compared to one in Britain). And there are currently eight government departments looking after various aspects of consumer problems. The last Royal Commission report in 1971 recommended that all but one of these institutions be swept away and a new Consumer Agency be put in their stead. Its job would be not only to enforce the truth-and-nothing-but-the-truth Marketing Practices Act but also to try and assess the needs of consumers. (This last point on the grounds that the imbalance between manufacturers and consumers makes it very hard for the *real* needs of the consumer to make themselves felt in a distorted market situation).

The Swedish view is really that it is old-fashioned to concentrate on preventing unfair competition between marketing companies when today's problem lies in the weakness of shoppers confronted by the marketing strengths of industry and commerce.

Yet on the other side of the North Sea, in Britain, the doctrine preventing unfair competition still prevails. This was not the intention of the Molony Committee, one of whose 214 conclusions and recommendations in 1962 was that a Consumer Council should be set up as a voice for the consumer. Such a Council was established in 1964, but the omens for its success in the future were clouded by a 1963 Conservative Party leaflet warning about the proposed Consumer Council turning into 'a small army of snoopers with a life baroness at their head'. This was from the Party some of whose members were already avid readers of *Which* and so protected to some extent by their own private watchdog.

A comparison with the early days of the trade union movement is of interest here. The early trade unions were supported by the more skilled and affluent workers. But the low paid workers in the sweated industries were in no position to help themselves. So successive governments set up trade boards and wages boards etc. to advance the ways of people to improve their own lot.

It was this equivalent group in present society, the poorer, more ignorant consumers, for which the Consumer Council offered some sort of help. It was these people, *not* the niggling middle classes, who paid too much for their food, their accommodation, and their credit. (And in the following chapter we will see the extent to which the brave new Council succeeded in protecting this group of consumers.)

The year before its inception, in 1963, it seemed that the Labour Party was going to offer the consumer even more vigorous protection than Mr Justice Molony had recommended. Their party's specialist in consumer affairs, George Darling M.P., drew up Labour's 'fair deal for shoppers'. As well as a Consumer Council, it included *compulsory* standards for a wide range of goods, a law to make advertisements prove the truth of their claims, guarantees to be approved by a public body (as a way to end guarantees that reduced the buyer's rights). But the Labour Government that came to power in 1965 did no more than introduce the Trade Descriptions Act of 1968. This, though hailed as the 'shopper's charter' has operated mostly on second-hand car sales and price-reduced packs in groceries. Important areas maybe, but hardly a radical facing up to the new relationship of buyers and sellers. And we shall see, it doesn't even give a misled buyer the right to a refund; he has to start a separate act for damages.

Three years after the Trade Descriptions Act the next government, a Tory one, decided that the proper function of government did not include the protection of the consumer (and this from a Prime Minister who as President of the Board of Trade had presented the first report of the Consumer Council to Parliament). The Consumer Council was duly abolished.

This action draws attention not only to the weakness of the consumer power structure in Britain, but also to the differences of

28

consumerist ideology behind the structure. Indeed, if you follow the consumerist thread running from the development of first generation consumerism to governmental consumerism to the democracy of the market place you can see how it goes through a hodge-podge of ideologies, often conflicting and rarely fully thought out. (But no less compelling to their believers for that.)

The classical doctrine of consumer sovereignty is that held by the present Tory Government and right-wing economists in America like Milton Friedman and Henry Manne. One might call it the Conservative ideology of consumerism. It makes a text book application of economic theory, arguing that competition between manufacturers, egged on by the carrot of profits, provides the best chance of a fair deal for the consumer. And that the individual himself makes this competition effective by distributing his 'votes' between competing manufacturers.

The first point of this doctrine, often expounded by Milton Friedman, is that the notion of social responsibility for companies is fundamentally at odds with the concept of a shareholders' financial incentive. The second point, an extension of the first, is that it's wrong of Washington or Westminster to force car manufacturers to abide by costly safety rules when the evidence is, given a free choice, consumers do not wish to pay for the safety extras. If the market isn't prepared to pay for a product, so the argument runs, there is no justification for its existence.

The second ideology for consumerism, let us call it the liberal one, is essentially an attempt to make this rigid Conservative ideology work in the conditions of an advanced affluent society. It pins its faith on distributing *information* about products to help the consumer make a rational choice and so combat the *misinformation* of mass advertising.

It is this doctrine that fuels magazines like *Which*, and British consumerism generally. By re-equipping the individual consumer with new-improved information (how the TV set is built, what an overhead camshaft does to improve a car's performance, which washing up liquid contains the highest proportion of active ingredients) the consumer becomes more vigilant and stubborn. And so manufacturers who wish to sell their goods in the market place are forced to respond to this different sort of consumer that confronts them.

But the first problem that arises with this model is that it is very difficult to get this sort of information distributed amongst important sections of the community. The need for this was part of the rationale for the existence of the Consumer Council. A way round this problem, to some extent, is information at the point of sale about the product's performance. So one has such things in Britain as the British Standards Institute Kitemark, the Design Centre Label, and the Teltag labelling scheme, all giving independent figures on the product's performance at the point of sale. The failure of many of these ideas (like Teltag) is something to be examined at a later stage. But the general point about the liberal ideology remains that it is probably restricted to helping those, like middle-class doctors and lawyers, who are least in need of protection – leaving the more misguided mass to purchase the items which *Which,* in its stiff-lipped way is 'not able to recommend'.

A more specialized comment on both the Conservative and liberal ideologies is that made by Samuel Brittain in *Government and the Market Economy.* His point is that due to the extension by the State into the market place, individual choice by the consumer is really only operative in the areas of food, household furniture, and leisure, and that 'what people want' can only be expressed for an increasingly wide range of products through the ballot box and not through the far more direct discipline of the cheque book. In this sense, then, there is less profit motive control than the Conservative ideology claims and less rational consumer control than the liberal ideology would imply. This modification of the model of consumer power argues for increasing market choice by reducing the 'Whitehall knows best' element, and as such it is probably closer to the Conservative ideology than to the liberal one. Which perhaps becomes clearer if we look at the next ideology in our spectrum, the neo-Marxist. This requires the state (i.e. the man in Whitehall) to discipline the corporate giants' ideology and make sure that the poor, misled, manipulated consumer gets his money's worth. Instead of producing too little for the worker, as Marx alleged, capitalism is now producing too much (hence the 'neo' prefix) and it is persuading the wretched worker to part with the contents of his hard-earned pay packet for things he doesn't really need.

The neo-Marxist ideology calls for shifting control of the means of consumption from the manufacturer to the state. And though it may seem odd, Ralph Nader's position in the ideological spectrum of consumerism is about here. True, he abhors – in a way that would bring joy to the face of Enoch Powell – the 'corporate socialism' involved in the increasingly interwoven relationship of large corporations with large government units. But, equally, he falls back on the government to do the job of keeping the shopping alleys free of corporate vice, in a way that any Marxist would applaud. The sidestep Mr Nader adopts to provide logical reconciliation for these two positions is simple. He concurs with Lord Acton that all power corrupts, and so to ensure that his all-powerful structure remains incorruptible he arranges for it to be insecure. This insecurity is provided by building up a cadre of 5,000 or so public interest lawyers. With their eagle eyes the government bodies can be watched extremely closely and, by use of the media, hammered like hell if – as with the old F.T.C. – they fail to exercise their powers or if they exercise them in the wrong way. Nader is thus advocating a radically different *use* for 'information' and a radically different *sort* of information to that implied in liberal consumerist ideology. And the information is obtained by radically different methods like 'total disclosure' and 'ethical whistle blowing'.

'Total disclosure' means just what it says. For example, a company making a deodorant and finding it has an irritating side effect on certain people should 'disclose' this information. 'Total disclosure' also relates to labelling of the product where, as we shall see, consumerists want very much more on the label than a brand name and an appetizing picture.

'Ethical whistle blowing' takes us back to the demand for more equal relationships between employer and employee, governor and governed. It simply means that when a consumer in the course of his role as a *worker* discovers something that is contrary to his interests in his role of *citizen*, and other citizens as well, then the demands on him as a *citizen* (to make public or inform to a consumerist body) overrides his duty as a *worker* (to say nothing out of loyalty to his employer). It was 'ethical whistle blowing' that provided the information for the I.T.T. disclosures by Jack Anderson, the Mai Lai massacre prosecution, that revealed the truth about the Apollo fire, and that made public the defect in the Ford Pinto engine which caused some of them to catch fire while the car was being driven. (It is revealing of the paternalism of British industry that this concept has been criticized here on the grounds that it is no more than an adaptation of the Communist technique of asking children to snoop on their parents. As if the relationship of employer to employee was the same as parent to child).

The sort of information that emerges from these new search-and-destroy techniques isn't just material for rational men to make best buys. It is first of all a countervailing force against the misinformation produced by business *and* government. And secondly it is a powerful lever in society that openly, at least, accepts rationality and fairness as a basis for decision. In such a society, information – as Nader has shown – can be the David that topples Goliath.

Nader's technique for achieving his 'unstructured power' is to make the concept of citizenship as daunting an obligation as it was to the Athenians. Citizenship is not a once every five years stuffing of a vote into a ballot box, it is a full time vigilance against corporate and governmental abuse. Not that all this abuse is a result of a deliberate human wickedness. The mere existence of a bureaucracy (which in Nader's eyes simply means where two or three are gathered together) cannot help but encourage lethargy and slovenliness in the carrying out of the duties of citizenship.

This revulsion from bureaucracy separates Nader from the social democratic form of consumerism, though he might well sympathize with its aims and intentions. The social democratic ideology, like suicide and free love, is a Swedish invention. And for all its sophisticated trimmings it is really just a hotted-up version of 'Whitehall knows best'. Having found the liberal ideal wanting, social democratic consumerism looks beyond the purchase decision in the shop – between this brand or that brand – to the *total environment* of consumption.

The latest Swedish Royal Commission on consumer policy expresses the matter thus: 'When appraising the household needs one cannot rely to any conclusive degree on the consumer's pretensions, expressed through the demand for products or in another manner. It is a well known fact that in many significant respects – in matters of diet for example – these preferences can be altogether too modest. As in other public sectors, the needs here must be formulated in terms of norms, based on the community's ambitions regarding the wellbeing of the individual.' Although this quotation loses something in the translation it is still a radical exposition of an extremely paternalistic concept of consumerism.

32

The crucial question is *how* the real needs of the consumer are discovered, if not by the exercise of their purchasing power in the market place. In Sweden this is to be determined by a Consumer Agency that comes fully equipped with a multi-purpose ombudsman. The Swedish Royal Commission report expounded how this Big Brother would look after the consumer's wellbeing: 'through household economy studies, and in other ways, one acquires in the consumer policy work a good knowledge of the essential household problems, and then the investigation leads one from that to the consideration and conducting of suitable measures'.

Social democratic consumerism, then, is really a way of saying that the liberal ideology doesn't work. And rather than wait for the slow and uncertain chain reaction from the consumer to the manufacturer to bring forth a better product, it simply says let's step in at the top as the spokesman for consumer aspirations and give the consumer what he wants even though he doesn't yet know that he wants it.

None of these five ideologies of consumerism are without their drawbacks, but then that is a nature of an ideology. However, the development of a 'participatory society' as described in the last chapter, strongly implies that it is the Conservative ideology that will be found to have the most drawbacks of the five. A consumer who increasingly wishes to participate in the decision process as to what it is she is going to consume will regard the take-it-or-leave-it attitude behind the Conservative ideology as less than helpful. And its supporters are likely to be restricted to those who see their future in the past.

The other four provide the opportunity for militant consumerists of every colour and creed to justify their existence (if they should so feel the urge).

As for the participating consumer herself, though she may only participate at one or two removes – through a consumerist group, through a Naderite group, or through a consumerist government department – it is her wish to participate that makes the activities of any of these three possible. Whether she understands her motives for approving of Ralph Nader in these terms is more than doubtful. (But, on the Swedish social democratic model, those who don't know their own needs can hardly be expected to know their own motives).

Of the approval by consumers of this new 'ism' there can be

33

no doubt. Who but a bigoted businessman can resist a concept that is trying to ensure a better deal for the housewife? And even the bigoted businessman in his alternative role as consumer (he has to live after all) may find some use for it.

A Harris poll in America revealed that 69% of people thought that 'it's good to have critics like Nader to keep industry on its toes'. Only 5% thought Nader was 'a troublemaker who is against the free enterprise system'.

Having thus looked at the *theoretical* reasons for the existence of the phenomenon of consumerism at this moment in time, it is necessary to see what are the *practical* consequences of its activities in the market place. And when one has read what is already happening in the Land of the Free, where the right to make a dollar at whatever cost was seldom questioned, one may wonder which countries, if any, will escape rule from the supermarket floor.

3

New Improved American Dream: Now with Added Truth

All of the following events have recently occurred in America.

A bread which had presented itself to the public in its advertising as a slimming bread was ordered to spend 25% of its next year's advertising budget saying that eating this particular bread wouldn't help you slim.

A promotional company was ordered to announce in its give-away sweepstakes the odds *against* winning.

A multi-million blue chip company had to run advertising defending its previous advertising, which was under attack from the Federal Trade Commission.

An iron tonic pill had to include a statement in all its television commercials to say that most people didn't need it.

A government consumer protection agency demanded that advertisements for identical products (for instance aspirin pain killers) shouldn't be allowed to *imply* that one identical product was better than another identical product.

A promotional company was ordered to pay out thousands more prizes in a competition after a more liberal interpretation of the rules by a consumer protection agency.

And over a five-year period, American car manufacturers were obliged to recall the equivalent of two years *total* production.

Events like these are becoming increasingly commonplace in the United States. And other advanced societies, taking their cue from the wealthiest nation in the world, have followed – at different speeds – along the same road as the U.S. 'America', declared Louis XVI's Finance Minister Turgot, 'is the hope of the human race, and may well become its future'. In the second half of the twentieth century Turgot's prophecy may well come true. The country that took capitalism to a new peak may be the one that shows us how capitalism is best disciplined.

According to Jean François Ravel in *Without Marx or Jesus*: 'the new American revolution' will be sparked by a new revolutionary method, originated and developed in the United States and labelled 'dissent'. Many of the examples of this chapter can thus be regarded as examples of dissent from the authorized version of the American Dream. Most of them come from America which, after all, has most to dissent from. But the important point to observe from the standpoint of the Eastern Atlantic is that *their* present is the best pointer to *our* future.

In the same way that Coca Cola civilized nations in the image of the society that first discovered this mystic concoction, so militant consumerism will reach us as part of a banded-offer from that same society in a new phase of maturity.

The examples are not meant to be comprehensive or complete (and if the thesis is right they will have been superseded by more militant examples by the time the book has travelled from manuscript to the printed page.) They are only meant to help put flesh on to the theoretical bones constructed in the preceding two chapters, and show that far from merely having an interesting academic debate about the structure of society, one is writing about a phenomenon that is travelling like Ajax's white tornado through the serried ranks of the capitalist world.

The first area that consumer power has chosen to show its strength is the area of the product that the manufacturer offers the consumer. And the first, and most predictable, area that consumer power should look at is the *safety* of the product itself. This is an area where even the most ardent believer in price competition will admit that the discipline of the market may operate, if it operates, fatally slowly.

Nader himself began on a safety issue: the General Motors Corvair; and sales plummeted by 89% following his attack on the safety record of this car. And in Britain *Which*'s constant cry has been about the unsafe wiring of electrical apparatus, and has even recently forced British Leyland to withdraw the Marina sports coupé on safety grounds.

Certainly, as the American National Commission upon Pro-

36

duct Safety revealed in June 1970, 30,000 people were killed and 110,000 permanently disabled each year 'as a result of incidents connected with consumer products'. On top of this it's been estimated that 700,000 children are injured each year by their toys: like a lawn dart that can pierce a child's skull, a toy oven that gets hotter than a real oven, and a balloon squeaker that can get sucked down a child's throat.

In grown-up products the motor car has come under the strongest safety spotlight. By the end of 1969 Naderite pressure groups had forced 28 safety changes on American cars. And by the mid-seventies all cars sold in America will have to be so built that their drivers can walk away from a *60 m.p.h. crash.* Moreover, if there *is* a safety related defect in a car, the car under the 1966 National Traffic and Motor Vehicle Safety Act has to be recalled. (And not content with having two out of every five cars made in America in the last five years recalled, Nader is now gunning for a recall of *all* fifty million cars made in America between 1963 and 1971 on the basis of an alleged defective valve in their brake systems.) The tyre makers of America also had to start a recall campaign when a test by the National Highways Safety Bureau found that one tyre in eleven failed to meet federal safety standards.

The differing impact of the consumer power structure in Britain and America is clearly shown up in the motoring area. In June 1971 (five years after the American car safety campaign started) the British Consumer Association launched their campaign to make British cars and roads safer. It included the demand that the wearing of safety belts – and not just the fitting – should be compulsory. This followed evidence from Australia that compulsory wearing of seat belts had led to a 16% drop in road casualties. But this demand has perished amongst all the press releases turned out by this well-meaning body. (Proving the truth of the old Chinese proverb that it's no use being a watch dog if you haven't got any teeth).

Another safety issue, enzyme detergents, echoes the extent of the difference of the consumer power structures on either side of the Atlantic. The evidence that enzymes in detergents were a potential health hazard emerged from medical studies on *British* detergent industry workers. But it was the *American* consumer power structure that first used this evidence to force Proctor & Gamble and Colgate in America to reduce the enzymes

37

in their detergents, and for Lever Brothers to announce they would drop them entirely. But in Britain Lever Brothers are still using enzymes in Omo and Radiant.

It may well be that the evidence against enzymes has been distorted. Certainly in November 1971 a Federal Drug Administration study gave enzymes a clean bill of health. If this verdict is accepted, then the strength of consumer power in America is even greater than if the case against enzymes is a fair one. Because it means, to repeat the point made in chapter one, that a company of worldwide reputation, like Lever Brothers, with massive resources, has less credibility as a dispenser of scientific judgements than the consumer power structure.

The scientific punch of consumerists also made itself felt in the case of monosodium glutamate (M.S.G.). Only three months after Nader had attacked the addition of M.S.G. to baby food, after a study by a St Louis psychiatrist, linking M.S.G. to brain damage in mice, the American baby food manufacturers agreed to stop using it. (Interestingly, the M.S.G. wasn't in the baby food to help baby. But simply because mothers who dipped their fingers in the tin preferred baby food that had M.S.G. in it).

The other additive to feel the crunch of consumer power, aided and abetted by the sugar lobby, was cyclamates. This one reportedly developed cancer in rats, and first in Britain then in America it became as unacceptable as monosodium glutamate in baby food. The success of the anti-cyclamate campaign in Britain probably owed more to the strength of the sugar lobby than to the consumer power structure. But, even so, it must have come as a rude shock to the companies involved (including Lever Brothers) to discover how little credence was given to their word. And that even if science supported them, consumers might still not.

In the interests of preserving their constituents' health, the tribunes of the people have even taken on the cornerstone of the American diet: the hot dog. 'America's deadliest guided missile' is how Ralph Nader described the apparently harmless frankfurter. The high fat levels in hot dogs, up to 51%, were seen as a unnecessary contribution to heart disease, cancer and strokes. And consumerists wanted a maximum fat level of between 25% and 33%. The industry reaction: 'We think the success of the product speaks for itself' (the Conservative consumerist ideology in action).

Even when federal controls over a particular food already exist, they may not be sufficiently well enforced. Take the Consumer Union's analysis of pork sausages which had been federally inspected. They found that one eighth contained 'insect fragments, insect larvae, rodent hairs, and other kinds of filth.'

Voluntary controls, beloved by the British, may not be any more effective. A check by public health inspectors in 1971 showed that 25% of all cartons of cream contained a level of bacterial contamination high enough to constitute a potential health hazard. And 8% – or 24 million cartons of cream sold every year – contained evidence of faecal contamination.

But in America consumer power has gone beyond demands as to the freshness (let alone the safety) of foodstuffs. It has started to question the nutritional levels of the products turned out by the food manufacturers. An American government survey in 1955 showed that 40% of American families consumed poor diets. By 1965, despite a dramatic increase in the wealth of the average American family, the proportion of families consuming a poor diet had *risen* to 50%. And this rise coincided with an increase in the sales of soft drinks, potato chips, cookies, ice cream, sweets and peanut butter. According to Dr Paul Fine, a New York food consultant, many Americans eat as many as ten meals a day, but still do not get adequate nutrition.

Nader blames the food companies for the downward shift in nutrition. An account executive from an advertising agency handling a cereal account put the company's point of view: 'Nutrition doesn't crackle or pop'. And when you're selling sizzle not sausages, that's quite a drawback.

This non-nutritional promotion of food has led to what another consumerist, Robert Choate, has called the current level of 'nutritional illiteracy'. It was Choate's analysis of nutritional levels in breakfast cereals that provided the evidence for this charge. Analysing sixty breakfast cereals sold in America (of which about fifteen are sold in Britain) Choate found that two out of three contained little more than 'empty calories that fattened but did little to prevent malnutrition'. And it was the least nutritious cereals that tended to be the most advertised. 'Your children's food habits are being formed by Madison Avenue cartoonists, not by nutritionists,' argued Mr Choate.

39

'Tony the Tiger, Fred Flintstone and Captain Crunch are the food educationalists of today. Ten times per hour, using wiles that mother never thought of, they advise your child to equate sugar with health and snacks with happiness.' In the beginning of 1972 the indefatigable Mr Choate provided still more evidence of the low nutritional content of many breakfast cereals. He went before a senate sub-committee to cite a study showing that rats fed on a diet of ground-up cereal boxes mixed with milk, sugar and raisins were healthier than rats fed on some of the cereals the boxes contained.

For food companies merely to improve the nutritional content of their foods would not satisfy the consumerist attack. They believe that whether or not nutrition has snap, crackle or pop, it is a duty of food companies to sell nutrition and not just the products themselves.

An obsessive interest in nutritional levels may be a new pre-occupation of consumerism. But that can hardly be said of the third aspect of the product that has felt the tread of consumer power, namely its value. Ever since 'Your Money's Worth' the backbone of any consumer association has been its reports on value for money. But three developments have given a new sharpness to these activities.

First, the shift of value for money tables from the pages of the consumer journals to the shop floor. This, going by the name of unit pricing, works by having special price tags on products indicating not just their absolute price, but their price per ounce. Thus doing away with a need for slide rule computations as to whether the jumbo size is better value than the economy pack.

The second new development in this area is the consumer boycott if they are not satisfied that they are getting value for money. This may be regarded as a militant method of responding to an unsatisfactory product as perfect competition says one should. Its greatest success to date has been in Japan, where the 20 million members of eight organizations of housewives started a six months' 'buying nothing' campaign against a major cosmetic manufacturer to try and break his retail price maintenance policy. In America, during 1966, faced by rising supermarket prices, several housewife pressure groups started a supermarket boycott. By the end of the year the index of supermarket prices instead of continuing to rise was down by one percentage point. And a percentage point on this index is worth several million dollars in shaved prices.

A third and most radical response to bad value for money is for the consumer group to bring out their own version of the product. The most successful example of this – apart from the British Co-op, which must be treated differently – began in 1925 when a young Swiss coffee planter, Gottlieb Duttweiler, returned from Brazil to Zurich. He found that he could make as much money in a few minutes from selling a kilo of coffee as a planter who'd spent five years cultivating the plant. This persuaded him that the retailer's profit margin was too large and he decided to go into business to sell things to housewives at a fairer margin. Using this formula, 46 years later the shop he had started called Migros had 784 branches and a turnover bigger than Tesco's (in a country with a tenth of the population). It also had its own political party and its own daily newspaper. And out of the profits schools, operas, and concerts are financed.

A more modest, though more recent, example is the Japanese consumer group Chifuren, who have applied the principle of bringing out your own version of the product to cosmetics. In 1968 they started to manufacture Yen 100 cosmetics (compared to prices of up to Yen 1000 charged per item by the big brands). By the end of 1971, it was selling at a rate of £2 million a year, a small market share in value terms, but because of Yen 100's low price, a good deal more significant in volume terms. Consumerists don't always make good businessmen and it may well be that Yen 100 won't have a permanent place in the Japanese cosmetic market. But if it does fade away it will only be after the expensive cosmetic companies have modified their prices in a way that probably would not have occurred but for this unorthodox way of demonstrating the extent to which the big brands were overpriced.

The new consumer power structure doesn't stop here, however. Its attack on the non-safety of many products is echoed by its attack on the impact of many products on the life of society as a whole. This is an area that is conceptually different from car or food safety, because at least one doesn't have to drive a car or buy any particular brand of baby food. But pollution isn't a voluntary matter. It constitutes compulsory consumption. Non-motorists suffer just as much as motorists from exhaust emis-

41

sions. Non-motorists have the same share as motorists of lead deposited in the atmosphere every year.

Against this 'silent violence' consumer power has made big demands. First, that the burden of proof be shifted from the victim to the polluter. So high are the 'risk levels' and so invisible the pollutants until it is too late, that a company should *prove* that its by-products are not harmful. Rather than merely wait as in West Virginia for the level of a respiratory disease amongst children and old people to reach four times the normal level, and so force Union Carbide to cut back their emissions.

This doctrine had not yet been established in law, but in the meantime consumer power has a good bash at some of the products whose quantity reduces the quality of our lives. Take the motor car. Consumer power showed itself in the fact that a motion was passed in the state senate of California banning the internal combustion engine after 1975. By a single vote a committee in the state assembly failed to go along. But to get a law banning the motor car inside a state which is literally built round the automobile would have been quite unthinkable a few years ago. Then in September 1971 the attack was focused on big cars with large horse power ratings. A consumer power group persuaded a U.S. Appeals Court to rule that television stations which carried advertisements for such cars must also broadcast information about the adverse effect of such cars on the environment. A sort of 'big cars can be dangerous to your health' on the lines of the warning on the cigarette packs. It was a parallel made by the judge in his ruling: 'Commercials which continue to insinuate that the human personality finds greater fulfilment in a large car do, it seems to us, ventilate a point of view which not only has become controversial but involves issues of public importance. When there is undisputed evidence, as there is here, that the hazards of health implicit in air pollution are enlarged and aggravated by such products then the parallel with cigarette advertising is exact.' And you know what happened to cigarette advertising on television in both Britain, Germany and America.

Another major product area in which consumer power has already shown its muscle in protecting the quality of the life is detergents. Consumer power in America wants them banned, arguing that their superior cleaning properties over soap powder is not worth their superior polluting properties. Their first jab was

42

to get the phosphate levels reduced. And they actually managed to get President Nixon and five U.S. government agencies to warn that phosphate in American detergents were killing American rivers. A year later, after the substitution for phosphates of Nitrilotriacetate was found to lead to foetal abnormalities in rats, the Surgeon General of the United States told Mrs America to return to her phosphates until a better ingredient could be found. A statement which had to be withdrawn in the face of consumerist pressures.

All the examples of consumer power in action so far concern the product itself. But the bulk of the remainder of this chapter is devoted to studying how consumer power has tried to affect the way this product is sold. Many of its most spectacular successes have been in this area. It's here above all that America comes into its own as the stamping ground for consumerists. That being said, it's also true (and worth remembering) that it's quite wrong to think of consumer power as something only pushing for fairer advertising and marketing practices. 'The problem of misleading advertising', says Nader himself, 'is nowhere near as serious as other problems in the consumer area.' Some of these problems have already been discussed. But advertising as a conspicuous and blatant expression of the corporate attitude *behind* the product is none the less an important area to look at. It clearly shows just how quickly, and with what effect, consumer power *can* act.

Let us begin with the advertisement on the pack, otherwise known as the label. In March of 1971 one of Banzhaf's groups, LABEL (Law Students Association for Buyers' Education and Labelling) presented a petition to Congress demanding a new food labelling law that required companies to list in order of predominance *all* the ingredients in their products (which means about seventy for things like Coca Cola). With a 58% increase in the use of additives in food from 1955-65, LABEL argued that people ought to know what they were getting – and for that matter, what they were not getting. Under the existing regulations for example a drink labelled 'orange juice drink' could contain as little as 50% of orange juice. Two months later a Truth in Food Labelling bill was before Congress.

An alternative strategy of consumer power is to put pressure on one of the regulatory bodies, like the F.T.C. and so force them to use their regulatory powers. The case of Firestone tyres is a typical example. Early in 1969 Nader criticized the F.T.C.

for not enforcing its 1967 guide lines for tyre advertising. Then in June 1969 the F.T.C. gave tyre manufacturers thirty days to get rid of advertisements which emphasized the speed and safety performance of their tyres, with the additional threat that any tyre advertiser who persisted in his misdemeanours would be 'challenged'. And just six months later the F.T.C. announced that it intended to try to stop Firestone using advertisements specifically saying 'Firestone tyres stop 25% faster'. The matter didn't end there, however, as we'll see when we look at the development of corrective advertising as a consumerist retaliatory measure against corporate deceptions.

Firestone is a large company, and consumer power exposés of misleading advertising have concentrated on the biggest, for the simple reason that they thus affect a greater number of consumers (which may be compared with the enforcement procedures of the British inspectorate of Weights and Measures, where two-thirds of the registered offices of the prosecuted companies were within the domain of the Weights and Measures inspector bringing the prosecution, i.e. a local firm).

One of the other big names who have come under the spotlight for misleading advertising practices as a result of consumerist exposés was Campbell's Soup. They filled the bowls of soup they used in press and television advertising with marbles to force the appetizing solid ingredients of the soup to the top. The prosecution in 1969 against Campbell's was actually the first for four years against a rigged TV demonstration (the last one had been in 1965 when the Supreme Court backed the F.T.C. judgement against Colgate for not using real sandpaper in a TV commercial showing that Colgate Palmolive Rapid Shave had so much softening power that you could even shave sandpaper).

From a prosecution once every four years, the F.T.C. rhythm now seems like one every four weeks (mathematicians will identify this as approximately a fiftyfold increase in activity). After Campbell's, Lever Brothers were next in line with their commercial for All detergent. In this an actor, wearing a stained garment stands in a giant washing machine and talks about the cleaning power of the product as the water rises and recedes, leaving the garment shiningly clean. The F.T.C. point was that the garment used in the commercial had been cleaned by a normal washing method, not by the instant immersion shown on

44

the screen. Five years earlier Lever Brothers would probably have acted like Colgate and fought the F.T.C. judgement in the Supreme Court, but in 1969 they meekly withdrew the commercial.

But despite this toughness it must be said that, in 1969, there was still little consistency of judgement between the various bodies whose job it was to control American advertising. Partly because there was (and still is) a mixture of statutory and voluntary bodies trying to do the job. One such voluntary body, the National Association of Broadcasters, in 1969 allowed on the air a commercial for Pall Mall cigarettes that had been specifically identified as being misleading by the Federal Trade Commission. 'Newest U.S. government figures show Pall Mall's 100s now lower in tar than the best selling filter king' said the commercial. Certainly Pall Mall had a tar rating of twenty against Winston's twenty-one, but Pall Mall also had more tar than forty-five other brands of cigarettes. Anyhow, a difference of 5% in tar is not thought by the experts to be of any significance. The only response by the N.A.B. to the Federal Trade Commission criticism was to order minor amendments to this commercial, which were described by the director of the New York office of the N.A.B. (who resigned over this issue) as 'meaningless'. This example is a good one in the sense that it has one of the basic ingredients of advertising which consumer power is attacking. Not untruth, which is rare. But the distortion of truth, which is more common.

For example, Colgate Dental Cream (with over a third of the market) ran an advertisement for some time based on tests which essentially showed that those who brushed after every meal with Colgate dental cream fared better than a controlled group which followed their ordinary brushing habits. Which is true enough. But it is probable that *any* toothpaste could have been substituted for Colgate (which was not the implication of the advertisement).

A few months after a consumer power group had argued this point before a senate sub-committee, a panel of scientists from the National Academy of Sciences (similar to the British Royal Society) reported that eight out of ten toothpastes were worthless in preventing tooth decay. Presumably this body could have made this charge any time in the last fifty years. But science,

45

only looking for what it expects to find, didn't see fit to reach these conclusions until *after* a consumer power attack.

Science is often involved in adjudicating misleading advertising claims because science is often invoked by the advertiser. For example, Milk of Magnesia rides along on the claim that it is 'the laxative doctors recommend most often'. Possibly true, but what is less true is the implication that doctors generally recommend laxatives.

The case of a pain killer called Exedrin was further grist for the consumer power mill. Exedrin is a pain relieving tablet made by Bristol Myers. A recent advertisement delivered by actor David Jansen, star of The Fugitive said : 'A study of hospital patients showed two Exedrins more effective in the relief of pain than twice as many aspirin'. What wasn't said was that the hospital tests were on mothers who had just given birth. And one of the doctors who did the tests said that post partum pains bore as much relationship with headache pains as apples to oranges. N.B.C. at first accepted the advertisement, until it was challenged by the makers of Bayer aspirin. Then the script was revised as follows: 'Isn't the way a pain reliever performs what really matters to you? Well, the performance of pain relievers on headaches is hard to measure, so a study was made of patients with a different kind of pain that medical science does use for comparing pain relievers. One purpose was to find out how many aspirin were needed to equal the pain relief of two Exedrin. The results of this particular study...*Two Exedrin worked better for relief of the pain tested than twice as many aspirin tablets.*' This revised script satisfied two of the big three television networks, but not N.B.C. And it didn't satisfy Nader's Centre for Responsive Law. They swiftly attacked the commercial on the Nader Report, their TV programme, using the testimony of another doctor to say that the results Exedrin had got from their tests *didn't* square with the result he'd got from similar tests. And they filed a charge in the courts against Bristol Myers for deception in advertising.

Such an action is harmful enough for the company concerned. But it becomes even more harmful when, as a result of consumerist pressures, a government regulatory agency takes action in the courts, as well. This was the case in October 1970 with Chevron F-310 petrol.

Chevron is produced by Standard Oil, which also produces

46

Mobil, Esso and Amoco. To promote F-310 Chevron's agency, BBDO, prepared an advertisement with a large balloon attached to the exhaust of two cars. One balloon was full of black gas (from the car without F-310) and the other balloon was full of clear gas (from the car with F-310). First of all, a group called the People's Lobby filed a $30 million suit against Chevron for this campaign. Then the F.T.C. applied for a court order saying that Standard Oil should not advertise again for one year for Chevron *or any other gasoline* unless it 'clearly and conspicuously disclosed' that the F.T.C. had found the current Chevron advertising to be false. Chevron's response, apart from fighting the F.T.C. in the court, was to run an advertisement defending their previous advertisements: an unusual development to say the least. (And in the advertisement, incidentally, they dropped the balloon test but printed the raw scientific data indicating a 13.9% reduction in unburnt hydrocarbons from switching to F-310.)

All these examples, Firestone, Campbell's, Lever Brothers, Colgate, Exedrin, and Pall Mall relate to what one conventionally means by 'misleading advertising'. But the coverage of that phrase is becoming wider all the time. It is being extended from the product not living up to the performance claim, to the product not living up to the *implied* superiority claim. This is a move with manifold implications, and one can see how the former can grow into the latter if we look at the case of mouth washes.

Ever since Listerine ran 'always a bridesmaid, never a bride' and Colgate invented their ring of confidence American (and British) cash registers have had their own ring of confidence as the millions tried to make their breath as pure as peppermint. Then in 1969 a panel of scientists told the Food and Drug Administration that there was no proof that mouth washes were effective germicides, and that there was no proof that they reduced mouth odour. A year later the F.D.A. gave the mouth wash companies thirty days to eliminate their claims that these products stopped bad breath, colds, sore throats or chills and stuck instead to claims like 'a refreshing mouth rinse'. So far a straight factual clamp down (albeit a little restricting for a company like Listerine, who in 1939 had said it cured dandruff; in 1944 that it cured sore throats; in 1958 that it protected you

47

against Asian 'flu, and in 1969 that it killed germs by millions on contact).

After the removal of these terminological inexactitudes a second point arose, made in this case by Congressman Rosenthal on the Nader Report in 1970: 'Chemically they (mouth washes) are all essentially the same thing'. And so the doctrine grew amongst consumerists that it was misleading for advertisers to state or imply that their product had unique or superior properties over rival products that were, in fact, identical or substantially the same.

In February 1971 a group of Banzhaf's Bandits called SAME (Students Against Misleading Enterprises) petitioned the F.T.C. to require manufacturers of products which are chemically identical to acknowledge this in their advertisements and not to make *any* claims or comparisons which might lead the public to believe the contrary. In one sentence, the keystone of a lot of modern advertising received a violent blow.

Because, as will be shown later, one of the vaunted skills of modern advertising has been to give to otherwise identical products 'added value' which would increase the consumer's pleasure while consuming the product. (Encapsulated in Charles Revson's statement that he wasn't selling cosmetics, he was selling dreams.)

One of the product categories immediately singled out for attention was aspirins. SAME reported the tests made in 1962 comparing Exedrin, Anadin, Bufferin, Bayer, and St Joseph aspirin. And reminded everyone of the finding that 'there was no significant difference between any of these tablets when we used two tablets per dose'. They contrasted this with Bayer's advertising : 'Bayer aspirin is the best aspirin you can buy'. Bayer also compounded their error by implying superiority as well as stating it specifically : 'Bayer aspirin is *pure* aspirin.'

Another superiority inuendo that was singled out was the type used in bleach advertising. All but one bleach (Purex) is said to contain 5.25% sodium hypochlorite and 94.75% inert ingredients. Yet Clorox, with the same formula as other brands says: 'No other bleach, liquid or dry, bleaches clothes cleaner, whiter than Clorox'. Of course, as a matter of fact Clorox is not actually *saying* that it bleaches better than other bleaches; just that no other bleach will get things cleaner or whiter, which may be true but the way the sentence is structured carries an implication that goes well beyond this literal meaning.

These criticisms by private citizens received the official imprimatur when the F.T.C. started action against Wonder bread for their claim that it 'helps build strong bodies twelve ways'. Their first charge was against the twelve ways. But their more significant attack was on the uniqueness implication. According to the F.T.C. : 'Wonder is a standardised enriched bread. All enriched breads are required by law to have minimum levels of certain nutrients. The amount and kinds of nutrients contained in the said Wonder bread is the same as that contained in most other enriched breads'. In short, that it is quite wrong for a product to imply superiority when its formulation is simply based on government standards. The extra irritation for the F.T.C. was that, for all the implied superiority of Wonder bread, it fell well below the maximum level of ingredients. For instance, it had only 38% of the maximum calcium; 57% of the maximum riboflavin; 72% of the maximum iron; and 83% of the maximum thiamin.

The final twist of the knife from the F.T.C. was this. That the question as to whether a product was claiming superiority rested *not only* on the words of the commercial, but also on research evidence of what consumers say about the advertisements. In the case of Wonder bread the F.T.C. introduced evidence showing a significant increase in the number of consumers who rated Wonder bread excellent or very good, as compared to other breads, in terms of nutrition. And they argued that an advertiser has an obligation to change his advertisements if surveys of this nature show that they are, with their advertising, creating a misleading impression. An impression which hitherto advertisers have paid agencies vast sums of money to create on their behalf.

It is interesting to note the response of the Continental Bakery Company (who make Wonder bread) to this attack. Apart from calling in the legal fire power of Covington and Burling (who themselves are now the subject of a Naderite investigation) they started to run advertisements defending their advertisements. 'An important message to every mother in America' ran the headline, and the copy argued that their advertising had for fifteen years been 'completely honest and factual'.

An advertiser having to run advertisements defending his advertising is something that we didn't see before the growth of consumer power. Equally new was the response of the consumer power structure to the evidence they unearthed of misleading advertising. In the past, it was simply exposed in a best selling book. But in the late sixties the response was different.

On 11 December 1969 Nader called on the F.T.C. to adopt a rule prohibiting advertisers from making any claims regarding safety, performance or effectiveness of a product unless competent scientific information was filed with the F.T.C. for public inspection. Article eight of the advertising code of American business might, if practised, be regarded as an endorsement of the principle behind Nader's demand: 'Advertising shall avoid the use of exaggerated or unprovable claims.' But the evidence presented by Nader showed that 94% of the advertisers whose claims he had challenged had been unwilling or unable to prove them. Then in 1971 two senators proposed legislation that would make the Nader proposal law, instead of just a regulation of the F.T.C.

As a result of all this the F.T.C. *did* start to demand claim substantiation. And even more important they decided that the onus of proof lay with the advertiser to substantiate his claim, rather than with the F.T.C. to disprove it.

Even more interestingly, they contended that it was an unfair practice for an advertiser to make claims when he had no data to support those claims, even if those claims happened to be true. So the General Electric Company found themselves being asked to show that their air conditioners reproduced the 'clean freshness of clear, cool mountain air'. And 18 tyre companies were given 60 days to substantiate claims for 75 brands.

Of course, the motor industry were not exempt from these compulsory disclosures of evidence. And when in October 1971 their answers started to come in, the consumer power groups found further ammunition for the charge that 'advertisers make vague claims which give consumers no real understanding of the product's performance; invoke clinical tests with little scientific basis to substantiate claims; and otherwise deliberately mislead and deceive the consumer' (Ralph Nader in 1969).

The 109 advantages that Chevrolet claimed stopped the Chevelle 'becoming old before its time' involved such items as an outside rear view mirror, automatic choke and padded sun visors, not to mention a number of safety and pollution measures required by law. And Ford, which had presented its cars as being quieter than pricey European cars, emerged a little battered as well. The quietness tests of 1965 had apparently matched brand new 1966 Fords with nine older foreign cars, including sports cars and a 1963 Daimler with 33,000 miles on the clock.

The F.D.A. has followed in the footsteps of the F.T.C. At the beginning of 1972 Commissioner Edwards announced a three-year study to probe the safety and effectiveness of 100,000 brands of non-prescription drugs. What spurred the F.D.A. to put all headache cures, anti-perspirants, laxatives and cold remedies under the federal microscope? The fact that on a sample survey of 400 non-prescription drugs only one in four were rated 'effective'. And the rest were in categories ranging from 'probably ineffective' to 'ineffective'.

Substantiation of claims is not the only response of consumer power. As the case of Wonder bread showed, it had also started to argue that the message of an advertisement is more than the words of the text. It's an argument that the advertising industry can hardly disagree with.

Ever since the theory of the brand image became accepted, admen have argued that one picture is worth a thousand words. Yet the main control of advertising has always been on the words. But with the nature of the television medium it is ludicrous to base one's judgement on the fairness of a commercial entirely or even mainly on its overt claims. One of the things every cub copywriter is taught is that if his commercial doesn't work with the sound off, it doesn't work. And so to go by the verbal claims is to go by the partial claims.

This is why one of the demands of the TUBE group was that a criteria for prescribing deception in advertising should be 'misrepresentation as to the *implication* derived from the totality of the deceptive advertisement' (my italics). Responding to this, the F.T.C. has held a series of hearings on the persuasive process of advertising. In the words of the F.T.C.'s hardline head of Consumer Protection, Robert Pitorfsky: 'Those forms of advertising which are essentially noninformational in character may raise questions as to their fundamental fairness, their conformity with the traditional economic justifications for advertising as sources of information upon which a free and reasonably informed choice may be made and the extent to which such advertising is designed to exploit such fears or anxieties as social acceptance of personal well-being without fulfilling the desires raised'. Under this analysis an advertiser who claimed his after-shave increased your attractiveness to the opposite sex, and who couldn't prove it in black and white, could look forward to prosecution.

Another area of advertising fairness to come under the consumer power microscope is advertising to children. In Britain, there are already specific controls about advertising to children. (Though in practice they sometimes seem most concerned with ensuring that the child does not exhibit bad table manners during the television commercial.) However, in America, not only have advertisements to children been subjected to hardly more control than advertisements to adults, but they have also been identified by business as a market in their own right, or rather a series of markets from teeny boppers to micro boppers.

And so the suspicion grew that advertisers were trying to exploit the ignorance and gullibility of children. It was Robert Choats who first pointed out that of the twenty most advertised cereals, fifteen were low in nutrition. And that the N.A.B. policy of policing toy commercials seemed to work more in the interests of the toy manufacturers than of the kids.

This following example of a commercial aimed at children was one of those presented by the TUBE group to the senate sub-committee. It is for a product called Johnny Lightning cars. The setting: several boys surround a race track. Dynamic music is playing in the background. Camera follows the cars and uses techniques that make the cars appear to slow down and speed up. Narrator: 'Here come the 1970 Johnny Lightning Challengers. New triple threat, three engine dragster – the speed hungry spoiler...the bug bomb...the powerful smuggler...the sand stormer...the explosive T.N.T....and many more new models. They are beautiful and they are fast. Race any cars against the new Johnny Lightning Challengers and see for yourself. Exciting new cars, alone or in sets, from Johnny Lightning'.

One would be forgiven for thinking that one was looking at an advertisement for a supercharged Detroit speedster. TUBE commented: 'The deception is caused by the impression, the speed of the sound track and the camera technique used. The cars seem to speed up while going around the arches and down the straightway... These techniques give the impression of greater

52

size, speed and ability of the toy. The total impression derived by the viewer is inconsistent with the actual performance of the toy.'

This is simply applying the F.T.C.'s doctrine of what a 'claim' is from grown-ups to children. For while a grown-up might easily realize that the television commercial was for a simple toy a child, it's argued, could easily be led to expect as much from his Johnny Lightning electric car as his Dad does from his supercharged Mustang. 'It's time', said one consumerist 'that there was some arrangement to ensure that children are not treated as markets for exploitation by every huckster with the money to buy TV time.' → *But children are not they still have things aimed at them*

For the advertiser to respond to these new consumerist passions with repentance and a new code of good conduct will not satisfy them. Having got the scent they won't, understandably, be satisfied with anything less than a good blooding.

The old penalty for false advertising in America was a cease and desist order to prohibit future deception. But the 'go and sin no more' concept is entirely unsatisfactory to a consumer group who – having caught a company out – believe that notwithstanding the cessation of the misleading advertising, the company is still benefiting in its present sales from its past misdemeanours.

It was SOUP and not the F.T.C. who first developed a coherent expression of a doctrine demanding corrective advertising. It was called in the F.T.C. hearing on Firestone tyres the 'rotten apple concept'. Very simply, if sales in year four resulted to some degree from advertising in year one then the deceptive claims in year one became the 'rotten apple' which leaves a deceptive impression contributing to sales in year four. The purpose of corrective advertising is to remove the benefit of those claims from the company by forcing disclaimers in year four advertising of the deception in year one advertising.

Advertising Age called such a doctrine a 'death sentence', and it certainly represents a vigorous reinterpretation of the F.T.C. powers. It was the legal eagles of SOUP who convinced the F.T.C. that they *had* the power to order 'an affirmative disclosure' by a company who was found to have engaged in misleading practices. This was in the Campbell's Soup case, though in this particular case they didn't feel the punishment fitted the crime of topping up bowls of soup with marbles.

53

In the case of Geritol, the punishment under the new F.T.C. represented a half-way stage between the old cease and desist order and the new corrective advertising. After five years of legal wrangling with Geritol, the F.T.C. forced Geritol to have the following statement in their commercials : *'The great majority of tired people don't feel that way because of iron-poor blood and Geritol won't help them.'* Ths was agreed by 1968, and it clearly implied the exact opposite to what most previous Geritol advertising had been working feverishly to suggest, and that had helped them sell 2 billion doses between 1950 and 1962. No longer was the absence of iron permitted to be linked to 'tiredness', 'loss of strength' or 'that run down feeling'. Instead 'builds iron power' was the name of the game for Geritol if they wished to advertise. But in 1970, the F.T.C. ruled that the word 'power' had to be deleted from this, leaving 'Geritol builds iron' with the disclaimer that most people didn't need their iron building.

Geritol, however, may consider themselves lucky escaping the full application of the corrective concept: the public admission in 25% of your advertising over a twelve-month period that your previous advertising was misleading. This was demanded in the Firestone case, when it was shown that Firestone had been making unjustified safety claims for some of their tyres.

The most interesting part of this case wasn't so much SOUP's attack, as Firestone's defence, supported by the Association of National Advertisers (representing about 90% of all advertising budgets). *The defence was simply that there was no significant residual çarry over of advertising from one year to another.* That there was no 'substantially persisting' communication of the advertisements' claims. This put SOUP in the extraordinary position of having to argue the case normally made by agencies to their clients about the long-term effect of advertising. It was the attorney from the Association of National Advertisers who argued 'taking into account thousands of advertisements and thousands of advertising claims, the general rule regarding advertisements is rapidly forgetting rather than memory'. It was the SOUP attorney who called Dr Darell Lucas of New York University to talk about the 'sleeper effect', an impression one receives which can become the basis for action at a later date when one has forgotten the source as a message. In addition Dr Douglas Greer was called to argue for the capital value of past

54

advertising campaigns. He actually calculated, against *opposition* from the Association of National Advertisers, that the value of Firestone's 1968 campaign in 1970 would represent about 35% of its 1968 expenditure.

This extraordinary role reversal by the advertising establishment is a measure of their blind desperation; the feeling that their only defence is to deny the power of the magical arts. Notwithstanding this extraordinary defence, however, the corrective doctrine is now established, and the F.T.C. have sought to apply to amongst others, Wonder bread, Ocean Spray, Chevron, Hi-C drink, and Profile bread.

It was in July 1971 that what had been called 'this Doomsday weapon' received its first trial workout. Profile 'slimming bread', from the same stable as Wonder bread, agreed to spend 25% of their next year's budget on this commercial: 'I'd like to clear up any misunderstandings you may have about Profile bread from its advertising or even its name,' said a trim young lady. 'Does Profile have fewer calories than other breads? No, Profile has about the same per ounce as other breads. To be exact, Profile has seven fewer calories per slice. That's because it's sliced thinner. But even eating Profile will not cause you to lose weight. A reduction of seven calories is insignificant.'

The advertising industry predicted that Profile was being forced to commit hara-kiri, but the agency who handle the account, Ted Bates, tested this commercial before it ran. Their conclusion, which will be examined in more detail later, is that the F.T.C. may have been doing Profile a favour in forcing them to bring out such flatly forthright and honest advertising.

A slightly different twist to corrective advertising has developed in Japan. In June 1969, the two giant Japanese car companies Toyota and Nissan, were virtually ordered by the Japanese Diet (Parliament) to run advertisements admitting that they had sold the Japanese public defective cars. Accordingly, Toyota went into the press openly admitting that they had to recall 617,247 defective cars, and Nissan confessed that they had to recall 395,300 defective cars.

The corrective doctrine in America doesn't just apply to advertising. Returning the fruits of your wrongdoing is only an application of American anti-trust law, that there is no reason why it should not be used against other aspects of the marketing process. Already, for instance, a version of it has been applied to consumer competitions. In this particular case, the F.T.C. argued that Coca Cola had not disclosed a key rule in their nationwide competition, and that *two* correct anwers might be required on some of the questions instead of the normal one. The F.T.C. demanded that the only way this unfair practice could be corrected would be for Coca Cola to pay a hundred dollars to every contest participant who misunderstood the rules and would have won except for this 'undisclosed rule'.

This new interest by consumerists in competitions and sweepstakes followed the disclosures to a congressional sub-committee that usually only about 10% of the prizes offered in the advertising for 'pre-selected winners' sweepstakes were actually awarded.

A latest development from America from the F.T.C. is 'counter advertising'. This is advertising by consumer groups against a particular point of view put forward by an advertiser which, while not being positively untruthful, may not be the whole story. For example, advertising claims relying on scientific claims that are themselves still the subject of controversy in the scientific world. Or advertising which does not reveal some negative aspect of the product. The F.T.C. cited the example of cars: 'In response to advertising for small cars emphasising the factor of low cost and economy, the public could be informed of the views of some people that such cars are considered less safe than large cars. On the other hand, ads for bigger cars, emphasising the factors of safety and comfort, could be answered by counter ads concerning the greater pollution arguably generated by such cars'.

But even then, when the corrected ads and the counter ads. are run, there may be still more to come. For in the case of Robert Choate's exposé of the cereal industry, the F.T.C. moved in with a demand that the cereal industry was an oligopoly acting against the interests of the public. And that Kelloggs should therefore be forcibly broken into two separate companies and General Mills into three.

Five years ago no American businessman would have believed that all this could have happened to the advertising industry in the Land of the Free. And five years ago they would have been right. Businessmen and other affluent societies round the world are beginning to feel the same forces biting into their own market place, as the examples from Japan show.

In some ways, in fact, Canada is even further ahead. The

situation an advertising agency faces north of the border as a result of the proposed Competition Act is approximately as follows. First, the agency lawyer has to okay the copy, then the company lawyer has to okay the copy. If either has got any doubts they can ask the advice of the people at the Ministry of Consumer Affairs. But that advice comes with the proviso that in the event of litigation the fact that the Ministry of Consumer Affairs advised them is no defence. The advertisement then appears in the press. Following that one of the government inspectors in one of Canada's five provinces, having seen the advertisement, decides to prosecute it – possibly on a hair splitting technical offence (for in Canada, the test of the credulous man is the test to be used). If the prosecution succeeds both the agency *and* the client can be sent to prison (the offence is a criminal *not* a civil one) even if they took all reasonable and due care to avoid creating a misleading advertisement.

In Sweden, which is almost as strict, there were half-serious forecasts that a certain petrol was going to be asked to produce a tiger from the tanks of cars containing this particular petrol. And woe betide them if they couldn't.

But in Britain? Will not the deep blue water repel these new invaders who threaten to change our society as much as the last successful invasion of English soil. Well, who better to follow in the footsteps of William the Conqueror than Nader the Raider?

4

‰ Will the British Ralph Nader Please Stand Up?

Good starter on permissible.

✗

'The great advantage of being in the same world as the United States', observed J. K. Galbraith, 'is that it reveals to other countries the pleasures and horrors that will afflict them only a few years hence.'

Will the guru of the affluent society be proved right? Or will three thousand miles of ocean protect us on this side of the Atlantic from the hatchet work that's going on in the American market place? Or will this new Inquisition arrive to perform their *auto-da-fé* on the luckless bowler-hatted brigade?

There are two broad reasons why those about to die far from saluting the new Caesar still sleep soundly in their beds, contentedly believing that militant consumerism is as American as pumpkin pie and likely to be just as localized in its popularity. First, that America – ever since the Boston Tea Party – has developed into a very different sort of society, and this particular eccentricity is no more likely to catch on here than prohibition in the 1930s. This is a point to be probed in a later chapter when looking at the development of the mass affluent society and the new types of consumer that it breeds.

But the second reason, why we are allegedly safe from this commercial potato blight, is worth examining now. It is the point of view that militant consumerism is a direct result of the excesses of American society, the biggest and best syndrome. And that as Britain – or for that matter France or Germany – has never engaged in these excesses, as our word has always been our bond and we have dealt fairly and squarely with each other,

58

the whirlwind will pass us by and go on to punish less virtuous lands.

Of course, one could examine this argument over a much wider spectrum than that of advertising. But for the same reason that we concentrated on it in the previous chapter it seems sensible to stay with it now. Believing still, that as the mirror in which business exposes itself, it is a fair reflection of how corporations actually see themselves.

It is perfectly true that the system of controls of advertising becomes stricter the further one gets from Madison Avenue. England is stricter than New York, Germany is stricter than England, and Sweden is stricter than Germany.

The British technique is to have a loose mesh of laws that would be entirely inadequate but for a voluntary adoption of a code of good conduct by the advertising industry, anxious lest the meshes become any finer.

About a quarter of all British advertising is an exception to this principle in that it appears on television, where it comes under the Television Act of 1954 and – by extension – under the Independent Television Companies Association (henceforth I.T.C.A.) rules and regulations. But the other three-quarters of British advertising is controlled by the voluntary adoption through the Advertising Association of a Code of Practice that in principle differs not a lot from the codes of practice of the American Association of Advertising Agencies (though its enforcement procedures are different).

The statutory background to the British advertising controls is a hodge-podge of sixty-one statutes covering relatively important things, from the buyer's rights in a transaction (the 1893 Sale of Goods Act) to prohibitions against the advertising of cures for pernicious anaemia or barber's rash.

The workings of this intricate mechanism are approximately as follows. A television advertisement has to be approved by the I.T.C.A. before it is allowed on the air. A press advertisement only has to be approved by the Code of Advertising Practice (C.A.P.) committee if someone, either a media, rival advertiser or member of the public, has complained about it. They do not act off their own bat. One should perhaps mention the supplementary control of print advertisements by the media owners themselves. But these control committees seem to work mostly to ensure that *either* no advertisements appear in their pages that

59

might possibly upset another advertiser, *or*, that no words appear in an advertisement that might possibly upset Mary Whitehouse. The statutory controls are enforced by the Public Health Inspectors (slightly) and the Weights and Measures Inspectors (mostly).

How good are all these policemen? According to the head of Young and Rubican, the agency that turns out those delightful Daz and Fairy Liquid commercials, they all work so well that 'as a result the rabid consumerist movement that is going on in the United States is unlikely to occur here' (Walt Smith). And if you listen to the advertising civil service you will hear further applause for their own good conduct. When Ralph Nader visited Britain in October 1971, they told him, with the suavity of a deb's escort, that all was well here and that we didn't need an 'American' approach to these matters.

In this they were echoing the sentiments of the chairman of the Independent Television Authority who told a meeting of the Advertising Association that, despite some over-exaggerated and misleading portrayals of quantity and quality of food products and a few examples of potentially offensive salacity, 'the ethical standards are high'. In fact, 88% of 6,000 proposed scripts were found to be entirely in line with the I.T.V. code without any alterations requested by the I.T.C.A. (the figure for the proprietary medicines was much lower, with only 66% acceptance of the first scripts). Interestingly, and this is a point I shall return to, there were almost three times as many scripts rejected on the grounds of taste as on the grounds of misleading claims. These 6,000 scripts turned into 4,000 new commercials and all but fifty of these could be accepted for transmission without further question.

In 1968 four of the commercials which this august body passed were for Shell petrol, showing the difference between Shell 'with the mileage ingredient' and petrol without this additive. In America this additive goes under the name of Platformate and has been the subject of a consumerist attack, on the grounds that Platformate is simply Shell's name for a type of mileage ingredient that is common to all petrols. And the implication from the advertisement – that the other petrol is another brand – is quite false. The other petrol is simply Shell without the mileage ingredient, something that you cannot obtain unless you drive a black car in a Shell television commercial.

Only *after* the attack on the Shell commercial in America did the I.T.C.A. ask Shell to modify their commercials in Britain. This they did by superimposing lettering on the screen telling viewers that the petrol without the mileage ingredient was not a proper petrol. But, alas, it was in letters so small that made this vital qualification relatively unnoticeable. Requiring no more change than this was in itself a surprising development as the head of advertising control at the I.T.A. has made the point that 'in television advertising there can for purely technical reasons be no small print like that seen in press advertisements to explain or qualify claims'.

Shell's purpose in making such a commercial was to persuade people that their 'mileage ingredient' wasn't just another phoney additive that did nothing, but something that actually improved the performance of the petrol. Which is fair enough (providing you don't accept the 'identical products' doctrine that was described in the previous chapter). Nevertheless, one could have expected a control system so much more advanced than the poor Americans' to have picked up Shell's questionable presentation of their product before the Americans picked it up themselves.

Or take the case of Ariel. This is a detergent containing enzymes that allegedly removes by presoaking a whole category of stains not removable by the normal washing process. And Ariel's commercial showed a stain, which ordinary detergents had failed to remove, being removed by soaking in Ariel. What wasn't shown, and what *Which* discovered, was that if you *soaked* your laundry in an *ordinary* detergent the result was just about as good as soaking with an enzyme detergent.

The failure of the advertising control bodies to enforce their own rules shows also in the case of Rank, Hovis McDougall's 'part-bake' bread. In 1970 £300,000 was spent giving the public the impression that this was practically the equivalent of real home baked bread. But a senior (an unnamed) marketing man did a little ethical whistle blowing by telling *Campaign* – one of the advertising industry's trade newspapers – that 'part-bake' was nothing of the sort. He claimed that part-baked bread didn't have extra flavour because the yeast had been killed, causing the loaf to sink and not rise; 'All you get is hot bread, and you could get that by shoving a normal loaf in the oven.'

If you wish to check the efficacy of the I.T.C.A. control system for yourself simply write to the I.T.C.A. at 52-56 Morti-

61

mer Street, London W.1 and ask for their seven leaflets on 'Notes of Guidance' for television advertisers. There you will find the rules and regulations for yourself and you will be able to judge whether they are being enforced.

In 'Notes of Guidance' No. 6, dealing with many medicine treatments and health claims you will find that *'nothing should be said or shown in an advertisement...to convey exaggerated impression of its (the patent medicine's) speed of action'*. How many times have you seen miracle cures where tired listless women were instantly transformed to smiling happy people? (Like 'Settlers bring express relief'.) Notes of Guidance No. 6 also contains this on 'pain': *'Care must be taken in referring to or illustrating heachache pain, whether visually, verbally, or in abstract, to avoid impressions of severe pain.'* (Remember all those wincing, unhappy faces prior to the merciful relief that popped out of the aspirin bottle when they were 'one degree under'?)

Keep on reading Notes of Guidance No. 6 and you will find this about mildness claims for detergents: *'Advertisements for soaps and detergents (e.g. washing up liquids) claiming to have a mild effect on the skin should not imply a positive cosmetic or therapeutic benefit'*. So how come Fairy Liquid have been able to spend twelve years sayings 'hands that do dishes can feel soft as your face with mild green Fairy Liquid?' And, why is Palmolive Liquid allowed to imply that it can be used to help manicure your hands?

Over the page from these particular rules are some more that you'd never have guessed at merely by watching the commercials that are allowed on the screen. For example: *'Anti-perspirants should not claim to keep skin dry either absolutely or for a specific period.'* Remember Right Guard's all-day protection? And remember how in the commercial for Sure deodorant a swathe of flesh on the back of the beautiful girl in the Turkish bath remained absolutely free of perspiration because she was wearing this particular deodorant.

Three more 'rules' in Notes of Guidance No. 6 may give you further food for thought. First, on laxatives. They *'should not be advertised for daily or habitual use'*. (What, then, was that All-Bran commercial doing with its copy line 'as regular as time itself' if not implying regular usage was beneficial to the consumer?) Second, on the subject of bad breath. *'It should not be claimed that a dentifrice or other product will completely destroy bacteria causing mouth odour or that it will provide long lasting freedom from mouth odour.'* (So be sure you don't misunderstand Colgate's 'ring of confidence' claim). Finally, from our brief trip around Notes of Guidance No. 6 (and remember we've got another six more notes of guidance to look at) you will find this comment on antiseptics and disinfectants: *'While germicides in effective concentrations can be an important aid to personal and household hygiene, they do not offer a complete protection against disease and over dramatisation of their effects should be avoided.'* But doesn't Domestos 'kill all known germs'? and how about Dettol's 'is yours a safe home, a Dettol home'?).

One final example, from Notes of Guidance No. 4, shows the often substantial gap between the rules and the commercials. Rule 5a states: *'Advertisements should not encourage children to make a nuisance of themselves to other people. Phrases such as "ask mummy to buy you" are not acceptable.'* But 'Don't forget the Fruit Gums, Mum' is?

Going from the square screen to the printed page you find that a different, and laxer, set of rules operates. This dual standard of truth has its justification in the fact that television is a more powerful medium than print and therefore regard for truth has to be that much more scrupulous. But a claim is either substantiatable or it isn't. And to allow an unsubstantiatable claim into a newspaper because a newspaper isn't as powerful a vehicle for it as a television commercial is somewhat strange. For instance Bio-Strath's Elixir isn't allowed to advertise on television because the I.T.C.A. medical advisers do not feel that the product has any significant nutritional value. Yet Jimmy Young can be found extolling its virtues all over the London Underground.

As well as a different set of rules, the print media have a different system to enforce their rules that makes them particularly vulnerable to consumerist attack.

The case of Sauna Belt Trim Jeans is illustrative of the general problems. Trim Jeans are a sort of inflated rubber pants, 'the amazing space age slenderiser so sensationally effective it is guaranteed to reduce your waist, tummy, hips and thighs a total of six to nine inches in just three days or your money returned'. When *Which* got twenty-one women to test these belts they found that more people *increased* their waist measurements with Sauna Belts than reduced them. More than this, the 1963 A.A. guide lines on this sort of belt said that these claims were 'unsubstantiable and entirely unscientific'. And the Code of Advertising Practice forbids advertisements for any slimming treatment not associated with a diet (the official ruling on this point is that these belts are *slenderising* treatments not *slimming* treatments so they fall outside this rule).

Sauna Belts wasn't a fly-by-night advertiser taking a column inch in the Saturday bargain page. Full page advertisements had appeared in many media including the Sunday glossies. But not only did the voluntary control system allow these advertisements to appear (similar versions had already appeared in America) but on their appearance the voluntary system can apparently take no action until a complaint is received. As the Director of the Newspaper Proprietors' Association, past whose vetting committee this had slipped, observed: 'You can't expect us to leap in and do something about it until we receive complaints.'

The complaints, of course, may not come in because the amateur buyer doesn't always know what's wrong. For example, when the Ford Capri was launched as 'the car you always promised yourself', the advertising included a photograph of someone sitting in the back seat with miles of leg room between them and the back of the front seat. But this was only possible because the front seat was pushed so far forward that only a wafer thin person could have driven the car from that position.

The point all these examples are trying to make is not that the majority of advertising isn't 'legal, decent, honest and truthful' (though there are many who dispute even that, as we shall see). The point is that *if* the majority of advertising is 'legal, decent, honest and truthful' it is more because of the restraint of the advertiser than the strictness of the controls.

Ninety-nine per cent of all scripts submitted to the I.T.C.A. may not be misleading. But as the Creative Circle (a group of senior creative executives in the advertising industry) sub-committee on the I.T.C.A. observed, 'every day new claims are made which contain new and ingenious weasels'.

The mere fact that there are so many prima facie breaches of the spirit of the I.T.C.A. rules, while a peppering of words like 'helps' instead of 'does' and 'relief' instead of 'cure' satisfies

64

the letter of the law, shows how much you can actually get away with if you want to.

Any advertiser who wishes to suggest more than is actually true on behalf of his product is aided by the way the advertising civil service determine what is or what isn't a claim requiring substantiation. This is done on the most primitive of pre-McLuhan communication models. Only overt, explicit statements – visual or verbal – are regarded as coming within the framework of adjudication. Anyone who has spent ten minutes studying the subject of communication knows that what is communicated by a persuasive communication is often very different from what is actually overtly said. Indeed there is now a research company in Britain, Eric Clucas Associates, who make their living out of telling advertisers what their advertisement is *really* communicating.

But this is not what interests the I.T.C.A. Lord Aylestone, the I.T.A. Chairman, observed on the Cadbury's Flake commercial – showing a young girl lasciviously eating in an obviously sexual manner the said Cadbury's Flake – 'If someone wants to see a blue movie in a thirty second chocolate spot, that's his problem'. For most people doubtless blue movies on television make a pleasant relief from the whiter than white movies. The point, nevertheless is clear; for the I.T.C.A. advertisements are only saying what they are saying. The unspoken language that says far more than words is not controlled.

Listening to Archie Graham, the I.T.C.A.'s head of advertising control, you'd imagine that Freud had never lived: 'To talk of implicit sexual references is nonsense. To the general public, this suggestion of symbolism of this kind is something sickening.' If Mr Graham was to read the in depth interviews done by many agencies for their own advertisements he would discover that far from this sort of symbolism being sickening, it is actually very real (and quite enjoyable).

The total *naïveté* of the I.T.A.'s approach to measuring what is communicated by a commercial was shown during a speech by Lord Aylestone to the Townswomen's Guild in 1971. Boasting about the lack of permissiveness of television commercials he said: 'The girl who sets up house in a television commercial is never without her wedding ring. Have a close look, and see!' The mentality that any tiny, almost invisible, prop of this nature makes any difference in communication terms, shows the pedantic

65

literalness in the television advertising controllers' minds. It permits claims like 'nothing acts faster than Anadin' which would offend against the new American approach. It allows all the detergent claims, like Radiant's 'whiter white', which doesn't actually *say* it gets clothes whiter than other detergents...it's just there as an innuendo. And innuendo isn't part of the rules and regulations.

On this basis, cigarette companies are allowed to advertise small cigars on television, bearing the same name as the cigarettes that are banned from the air, with the same pack designs as the packs that are banned from the air. Despite the fact that the reason why the tobacco barons dress up their products in this particular way is simply to get the brand name across to their cigarette customers. But, in the eyes of the I.T.C.A., the word 'cigar' is not the same as the word 'cigarette', so they may appear. This despite Clause 15 of the I.T.C.A. Code: 'Any advertiser who markets more than one product may not use advertising devoted to an acceptable product for purposes of publicising the brand names or other identification of an unacceptable product.'

The I.T.C.A. show their literalness both in commission and in omission. One case concerns a visual for a hand cream showing the product being rubbed into a dried leaf which is 'restored'. Even though it was clear from the script that this was a simile a member of the I.T.C.A. spent a morning in Hanover Square diligently applying the hand cream to leaves. And they objected to the copy line for a Post Office Telephone Commercial 'One word is worth a thousand pictures' because they felt it might upset the photographic people.

However, the doctrine of 'an advertisement is only saying what it's saying' applies *only* when an advertisement is apparently meant to be believed. If the advertisement is formulated in such a way that, in the eyes of the I.T.C.A. it is not meant to be believed, it may pass unchallenged.

One such category which the I.T.C.A., like the Advertising Association and even the Trade Descriptions Act, allow as *not* requiring any substantiation are the so called 'trade puffs'; 'The best tobacco you can buy'. 'The name on the world's finest blade'. 'The best sherry in the world', etc. Such claims are allowable without any sort of verification. Whether or not they have an impact on consumers is a matter to be discussed later. But the point is worth making at this stage that there is certainly *no* prima facie case for allowing such claims on the grounds that no one takes them seriously. A type of claim that companies have used repeatedly over the last thirty years is a claim – prima facie – that works. And as such it should be subject to just the same controls as other claims.

But the strange position under the so called 'knocking copy' regulations is that to claim you are 'the best in the world' by *substantiating* your superiority over rival brands is an unfair practice and not to be permitted. The sort of substantiation of claims that is now being demanded in America is starting to cover just these points. And the looseness of the English law will, in the end, be the chink through which consumerism slips.

Even if it were found that these trade puffs are of no benefit to the advertiser because the public do not take them seriously (as a study in Germany has suggested) they are still undesirable. They create a climate of exaggeration and disbelief that makes it harder for the more scrupulous advertiser to sell his wares. There are now four rival cigarettes claiming that they are in some way the best : Embassy, 'the best in smoking'; Rothman's King Size, 'the best tobacco money can buy'; Player's Special, 'the best virginia cigarette'; Piccadilly, 'from the makers of Britain's finest cigarettes'. This chorus of unsubstantiated superlatives only serves to further debase the coinage of advertising.

Just how common are these superlatives was clear when I decided to carry out my own check on the type of advertising claims used in Great Britain, to help assess how vulnerable they would be to a Naderite attack. Over a week's noting of television and press advertisements I found that over half contained a trade puff. I then decided to check out those trade puffs with the company concerned, to see how they could stand up to scrutiny. And at the same time check out a dozen of the more factual claims.

The table overleaf shows the results of my investigation. And though it was only a small pilot study, it left me feeling that the British advertising industry is far more vulnerable than they imagine to a Naderite attack.

67

Company	Claim	Reply time (days)	Substantiation confirmed?	Substantiation effort
Anadin	'Nothing acts faster than Anadin'	15	No	Slight
Bass Charrington	'The most welcoming pub in the world'	10	No	Slight
Colgate	Gardol and 'the ring of confidence'	123	Partially	Reasonable
Courvoisier	'The brandy of Napoleon'	5	Partially	Reasonable
Elida Gibbs	Signal: 'the mouthwash in the stripes'	5	No	Slight
Fairy Liquid	'Hands that do dishes can feel soft as your face'	33	No	Slight
Flour Advisory Bureau	'Six slices a day is the well balanced way'	6	Yes	Good
Heinz	'More tomato in Heinz spaghetti hoops'	4	Yes	Adequate
Heinz	'The happiest sounds come from babies fed with Heinz'	8	No	Reasonable
Iron Jelloids	'Puts back the iron you're missing'	3	No	None
Haig Dimple	'Rarest Scotch whisky' and 'best known bottle in the world'	13	No	Slight
Harvey's Bristol Cream	'The best sherry in the world'	5	No	Reasonable
Kelloggs Cornflakes	'The best to you each morning'	20	Partially	Slight
McKewan's Export Ale	'The best buy in beer'	11	No	Reasonable
Nabisco Shredded Wheat	'And I give them both the best with natural shredded wheat'	23	No	Reasonable
Omo	'The understains'	105	Partially	Reasonable
Player's Special Virginia	'The best virginia cigarette in the world'	19	No	Slight
Radiant	'The whiter white'	No reply received		
Rothman's King Size	'The best tobacco that money can buy'	7	No	Slight
Sanatogen Tonic wine	'Glowing goodness' for tiredness	28	No	Slight
Rank	'Litton's speaker sounds better than a live orchestra in your living room'	20	Partially	Good
Triumph cars	'Chosen by Concorde men'	14	No	Slight
Tynebrand pie fillings	'The fork test'	7	No	Good

The first interesting point that this shows is the very wide range of time these companies took to give an answer. Quickest was Beecham's with three days (but their answer really only amounted to no more than a polite V sign). Slowest were Omo and Colgate with almost a third of a year to reply to my question. And Radiant didn't even send me an answer – only an acknowledgement. If 14 days is a reasonable response period to this sort of question (as I believe it is) then only half the companies replied within a reasonable period of time. And for two of the companies it took three recorded delivery letters to squeeze any attempt at substantiation out of them.

The extent to which the companies were able to substantiate their claims is naturally a matter of subjective judgement. They would doubtless argue that they had either substantiated their claims or provided as much substantiation as the law or common sense required. My view of the extent to which their claim was substantiated by the evidence they supplied is given in column four. And column five is the amount of effort I felt, from the correspondence, that the company put into making their substantiation.

Assuming, for the moment, that my assessment is fair, this means that not one of the trade puffs was fully substantiated; it means that only two of the specific claims were fully substantiated; and it means a further five claims were partially – though not completely – substantiated. And, finally, it means that five companies were either unwilling or unable to provide full substantiation for their claims *even though these claims were not trade puffs* and should have been covered by the existing advertising regulations.

In three cases (Harvey's Bristol Cream, Tynebrand pie fillings, and Heinz baby food) I persisted with further questions after the company's first response. In all three cases they improved on the answers given in their original letters. But still none of these three companies, could, even on extra probing, provide full substantiation for their claim (in my eyes).

One of the most hilarious substantiations came from Bass Charrington, endeavouring to prove they had 'The most welcoming pubs in the world'. To my questions they replied 'The campaign is based on our belief that public houses which carry our new company livery, and which have been renovated and redecorated over the past couple of years offer the highest

69

overall standards.' So far so good. Then came the punch line:
'For your information, I would like to point out that the
redecorations, and hence the campaign, is currently confined to
the London I.T.V. area.' Possible revised claim: 'The most welcoming pubs in the Greater London I.T.V. area.'

Almost as entertaining was the substantiation supplied by
Courvoisier to explain why they called their cognac 'The Brandy
of Napoleon'. Apparently when Napoleon was about to flee
from France after meeting his Waterloo, two ships were made
ready for his escape, from the Bordeaux area. M. Emanuel
Courvoisier, as a tribute to his former Emperor, placed a consignment of his brandy aboard these boats to console the fleeing
ruler. Then the plan changed. Napoleon chose to surrender to
the British, and the two ships that had been prepared for his
escape were used by the British to convey Napoleon to his place
of confinement. British officers travelling with Napoleon as escorts
soon discovered the consignment of cognac and referred to it as
they drank it as 'the Brandy of Napoleon' (perhaps in the same
sense as one talks of 'la plume de ma tante' or 'those are Charles'
socks').

Since the term 'Napoleon Brandy' is the highest praise granted
to cognac, it is understandable that the shrewd men at Courvoisier should exploit this historical coincidence to increase
their sales. But no evidence was supplied to show that
Napoleon either asked for this particular brand of cognac to be
waiting for him, or that it was in any sense his favourite tipple
amongst cognacs, both of which facts are surely implied by
this phrase.

But this substantiation is certainly a lot more satisfactory
than that proffered by Rothman's to prove that their King
Size cigarettes contain 'The best tobacco that money can buy'.
This apparently is so because 'expert buyers in important world
growing areas are under instructions by the company to buy
the best tobacco available with our special blend in mind'. The
idea that Rothmans can afford to have the tobacco auctions
scoured, with no regard for cost, to buy tobacco destined for a
cigarette retailing at this price seems an unlikely act of charity
from a hard-nosed tobacco company.

Maybe Player's were being a little more honest in their reply to
a similar question about the claim that John Player's Special
is 'the best virginia cigarette in the world'. They frankly

admitted that their 'advertising slogan comes within the realm of the advertising puffery and such slogans are common to all consumer advertising'.

Of course, companies are entitled to a subjective opinion as to the merits of their product. One would have thought, however, that the large number of 'blind-tests' (where consumers don't know which brand's which) that Player's would have done before putting the brand on the market could have resolved this question.

Certainly a declaration like 'Our reputation is a guarantee that we would not make any claim that we did not believe to be true' supplied by Harvey's of Bristol is no substitute for a few hard facts. The Harvey's superlative, 'The best sherry in the world', has two things to support it : that Harvey's Bristol Cream is the best selling sherry in the world as well as the most expensive. For these two things to be true it must also, in the view of Harvey's, be the best (otherwise they would never manage to charge so much and sell such quantity). There are several snags with this defence (as the correspondence makes clear) not the least being a sherry tasting report in *The Times* of February 1972. This reported the tasting of 14 cream sherries which 'included all the big names' and therefore presumably Harvey's Bristol Cream. The tasting was by both amateurs and professionals, but Harvey's Bristol Cream was not placed in the top three by either group. Harvey's specifically refused to comment on this sherry tasting and a director of the company wrote to tell me they had decided to terminate the correspondence.

Haig's were no more convincing in defence of their claim that their Dimple Scotch was 'The rarest scotch whisky in the best-known bottle in the world'. Their advertising agents wrote to inform me that 'they [the claims] emanate from a company whose integrity and quality of products are beyond question and the superlative is used to convey a sincere belief'. Sincere it may be, but that is all. Single blend malts are clearly 'rarer' than a nationally advertised brand of whisky. And how an allegedly 'rare' whisky can have 'the best known bottle in the world' defies both common sense and veracity.

A slightly different defence from the Haig/Harvey's 'our word is our bond' came from Kellogg's and Anadin. Their defence rested on a hair splitting interpretation of their words. 'Nothing acts faster than Anadin' is defended by arguing that 'the slogan does not claim Anadin tablets act faster than any other pain killer; we do not say "Anadin is the fastest pain killer" or "nothing acts as fast as Anadin" : the message is just that you won't find a faster acting pain killer than Anadin and it is so simply expressed, we do not believe that anyone can be misled by it'. No evidence, even of the parity position for Anadin with other headache remedies, was provided. And some reports that I have heard (for example, from a major drug company suggesting that Alka Seltzer – even though not promoted as a headache relief – is in fact the fastest acting headache remedy) make me doubt whether Anadin would even be able to substantiate a parity claim. But even if they could, the weakness of the substantiation they have provided – and it comes from their marketing director – is to argue that a phrase means something other than normal English usage says it means. 'Nobody in class is cleverer than Charles' means to most people that Charles is the cleverest boy in class. And the same is surely true of the 'simply expressed' Anadin claim. Certainly, a snap check round my office indicated that this was how they understood the claim, and I've no doubt that Anadin – for all their casuistry – intended it.

Kellogg's also engage in special pleading to defend their ad. 'The best to you each morning' : 'We maintain that Kellogg's Cornflakes offer "the best to you each morning" because they lead all other *cornflakes* [my italics] in texture and flavour and because they're the only ones which are vitamin fortified'. The fact is they are the only brand of cornflakes, full stop. The Grocers' Buff List doesn't list any other brand of cornflakes on the market at all. There are certainly some retailers' own brands, but Kelloggs' real competition isn't these so much as *other cereals* and it is against them that this claim needs to be measured.

While Kellogg's used the fact that they *were* vitamin fortified, Nabisco, by contrast, boast that they *weren't*. Substantiating their claim that 'I give them both the best with natural Shredded Wheat' Nabisco spoke glowingly of the product's 'natural goodness' and critically of their rivals who were 'synthetic or boosted with additives'. Despite such enthusiams for their product, the nutrition table that Nabisco supplied showed that even with all its 'natural goodness' it was still short of thiamin, riboflavin and niacin.

Perhaps the most extraordinary way of attempting to substantiate a claim was Fairy Liquid's, where they simply denied that they were even making a claim. 'Fairy Liquid', they stated, 'is a very mild product, and we believe that we are entitled to draw attention to that fact. The phrase quoted above ("hands that do dishes can feel soft as your face with mild, green Fairy Liquid") is a vivid figurative way of doing this and *not a claim as such* [my italics], and our experience is that this is readily understood by most housewives.' Knowing Proctor and Gamble a little the fact is that their arsenal of research must be full of evidence that this phrase *is* seen as a claim, and an effective claim at that. I do not believe they would have spent millions of pounds over the last twelve years publicizing a phrase, however figurative, if it was not seen as a good solid claim for the product.

If these sorts of replies to a stiffish consumerist style letter from a member of the public is the best that these companies can do, they will make ripe plucking when the consumerist holocaust spreads its wings over here. Only the Flour Advisory Bureau provided the chapter and verse substantiation that would satisfy a militant consumerist. They sent the exact information requested in the letter to substantiate their claim 'six slices a day is the well balanced way' (whose truth I must admit, came as something of a surprise to me).

Spillers were almost as forthcoming for their Tyne Brand pie fillings but, as I think the evidence makes clear, they were less convincing. Their 'fork test' commercial showed the large chunky meat pieces in Tyne Brand actually being compared with the pulpy gruel offered by rival products for which 'you need a spoon'. I asked Spillers for substantiation for their product's vastly superior chunkiness (clearly implied by the commercial) and for details of its meat content.

The reply from their Commercial Manager (Domestic Foods) indicated that their stewed steak pie filling had 'in excess of 50% meat content', which was a lot more than the legal minimum of 35% for pie filling. And I was also offered the chance to see a demonstration of their product at their offices.

Before accepting this I wanted to find out which was the Brand X product that had to be eaten with a spoon. They replied: 'If you examine samples of leading brands (of stewed steak) such as Casserole or Crown "E"...you will not find the Brand X mixture particularly surprising or misleading.'

73

This I did, and examined chunks of meat taken from cans of the three brands. The chunk from the Casserole brand was the largest I found in any can and overall, though the Tyne Brand chunks were *slightly* chunkier, the other two brands weren't far behind and would have certainly passed the 'fork test'. Undoubtedly, neither of them were such a gruel that 'you need a spoon' to eat them.

Of course, when you do eat these products they're re-cooked, and the chunks I had examined weren't. So rather than just see cans of Tyne Brand at the Spiller offices, I asked an independent body, the Domestic Advisory Service of Metal Box, to make me up three steak and kidney pies using Tyne Brand, Casserole and Crown 'E'.

The results from this test confirmed my suspicions were justified. First, that the sample of Tyne Brand, as prepared by Metal Box, bore precious little resemblance to the one shown in the television commercial (prepared by Spillers' own kitchens). More important, though Tyne Brand *was* slightly more chunky than Crown 'E' or Casserole, neither of these needed to be eaten with a spoon. Indeed you were more in need of a spoon to eat the enormous amount of gravy that came with the Tyne Brand chunks. Both Casserole and Crown 'E' made solid, meaty pies quite unlike the thin gruel shown in the Tyne Brand commercial.

The final point emerged when I asked the makers of Crown 'E' and Casserole for their meat content figures: Crown 'E' was 75% meat and Casserole 95% meat. So Brand X was up to almost double the meat content of Tyne Brand itself.

Spiller's judiciously took the precaution of pointing out in their original letter that 'the commercial to which you refer makes no claim or inference regarding meat content'. But I believe that if you asked the average housewife *after* she'd seen the Tyne Brand commercial which of the two pies contained the most meat she'd say the Tyne Brand one. To check whether this was in fact so I arranged with a research company to discover whether this was the impression communicated by the commercial. But without an actual print of the commercial, this final research wasn't possible.

Altogether, in the circumstances I find it difficult to understand how the I.T.C.A. who approved this commercial after a thorough investigation of its claims could believe that it conformed with their own code: that it was 'fair, capable of substantiation, and *in no way misleading*' [my italics].

The same point could be made against the Heinz claim that I queried: 'The happiest sounds come from babies fed on Heinz'. 'I was rather surprised that you expect to be able to interpret it literally', wrote the lady from Heinz, after I had asked them for details of the comparisons they must doubtless have made of the noises babies made after eating various brands of baby food. I also queried in my letter the implications of one of their baby food advertisements which showed a woman straining vegetables through a colander under the headline: 'Do you pour more vitamins down the drain than you feed to your baby?' I felt that this ad. suggested that there would be more vitamins in a can of Heinz baby food than in home prepared baby food. But no, said the lady from Heinz, this was 'merely an eye-catching expression'.

Colgate, after a long delay, did provide more substantiation for the claim they make for Gardol. Gardol was 'not a mouth-wash but a detergent with anti-enzyme properties'. Most bad breath arose from 'the oral cavity' (mouth?) and brushing with an efficient dental cream (namely Colgate with Gardol) was 'necessary in order to remove the debris which forms the incubating medium for the flora responsible for creating mal-odour'. A dental consultant confirmed to me that these state-ments were accurate. What wasn't confirmed was the statement in the Colgate promotion that 'only Colgate can be relied on to do all this'. Colgate has already been singled out in America for making claims which, though true, are not unique to Col-gate. There seems no reason why the same sort of attack shouldn't be made against Colgate here.

A similar vulnerability seems to face Omo and their 'under-stains'. I queried the implication in their commercial that stains could be removed by biological Omo that couldn't be removed by soaking in an ordinary detergent (following the *Which* exposé of a similar commercial for Ariel). Against the *Which* test, Lever Brothers cited a test by the Good Housekeeping Institute. This test was certainly more favourable than *Which* to biological detergents. But it still found them only 'marginally more effect-ive', which wasn't the impression I got from watching the under-stains commercial.

Radiant never replied to my question about their 'whiter

white' claim (possibly because my secretary originally mistyped my letter and accused them of saying 'whiter than white' and so they decided I was some sort of nut).

And Triumph, who entirely failed to supply any evidence that 'Naturally, Concorde men choose the Triumph 2000', seemed baffled: 'We cannot fully understand the purpose of your enquiry'.

Having read through all these letters from companies defending their claims, Blake's telling lines came to mind:

> 'A truth that's told with bad intent
> Beats all the lies you can invent.'

As well as their lack of strictness, the other question to be put against the rules that govern British advertising is whether – as they exist – they are in the best interests of the consumer. Or whether they amount to a restrictive practice operated by the advertising controllers in the interests of the media owners' larger clients.

The centre of the problem concerns the way the regulations concerning comparative advertising are enforced. Clause 3 of the British Code of Advertising Practice states that 'advertisements should not unfairly attack or discredit other products or advertisements directly or by implication'. (This is about the first time the concept of implication is accepted by the admens' law makers.)

It may, of course, be a foolish practice for an advertiser to speak slightingly of his rivals in an advertisement. But that is his decision and his risk.

In actual practice this clause is used both by the C.A.P. Committee, the I.T.C.A., and the media owners' committee to protect the interests of established companies and make it harder for a new, younger company (or brand) to make headway in the market place. It wasn't a coincidence that the Creative Circle's sub-committee on the I.T.C.A. found that the bulk of complaints came from the medium or small agencies (with the medium or small companies as clients) rather than the large TV agencies (with the giant brands).

Take the case of Heinz Baked Beans. The interests of Heinz is probably to preserve the *status quo* where they have about three-quarters of the baked bean market. Their advertising strategy will be to encourage their existing users to eat more, and to fend off challenges by companies hungry for their market share. Suppose you are a smaller food processing company and come up with a formula that uses twice as many tomatoes in your tomato sauce. You may well decide to have an advertisement showing, say, two tomatoes going to make the Heinz tomato sauce and four tomatoes going to make your own. And you might even like to name Heinz to sharpen your point. That advertisement could not appear on television. And in this sense the comparative advertising rules tend to preserve the *status quo.* (Armour, in fact, were not allowed to run a commercial for their lower priced baked beans with the words 'a million housewives every day are spending too much on their baked beans'.)

Anybody in the advertising industry worth his salt must have been foiled at some stage or another by these particular regulations. But the reason why they will never be changed is that they are in the interests of the larger companies who have a disproportionate weight in the advertising establishment. It was indeed a wise man who observed that if the motor car was invented today, Clause 3 would not allow you to call it a 'horseless carriage' because that would be regarded as unfairly discrediting horses.

Restrictive practices apart, perhaps the most important test to be applied against any control system is not what the controls are as such, but what the consumers *feel* about the sort of advertising – in terms of truthfulness – that the controls allow to appear in print or on television.

The Gallup figures from America show that about one-third of the population believe that advertising presents a true picture of the product. The surprising thing is that the figure for Britain is almost exactly the same. If our control system was really working to exclude in any significant way, through its superior filtering system, the sorts of advertisements that are allowed in America, then one would surely expect a reasonable difference between these two figures. And if there isn't a remarkable difference between these two figures, unless there is another convincing explanation, it seems reasonable to assume that it is because *both* control systems allow through a *similar* proportion of misleading claims.

If this is so then it means that the other controls in the British environment, mainly statutory controls, are also far less effective than is generally believed. And, in fact, if one examines the statutory control system it appears as vulnerable to and as inciting of consumerist activity as its voluntary partner.

The Trade Descriptions Act has proved to be largely a paper tiger, though listening to the man who steered it through Parliament, Mr George Darling M.P., one would think this paltry and inadequate statute is a veritable Sir Launcelot saving consumers in distress. It was he who rose in the plush Café Royal in October 1971 to tell Ralph Nader that this British law gave the British consumer just the sort of protection that Mr Nader was demanding for the American consumer. If there was as much control over inaccurate statements by politicians as there is meant to be over inaccurate statements by advertisers (a sort of Political Descriptions Act) such a statement would have got the former government minister into as much trouble as a second-hand car dealer who winds back the milometer. For only a week after Mr Darling eulogized over his own legal creation, Croydon Quarter Sessions ruled that the Trade Descriptions Act does *not* provide for a trader who offends under it to have to pay any compensation to his victim. To obtain compensation the consumer has to launch an entirely separate, complicated and private legal action himself. As the judge in this case observed: 'We think the Trade Descriptions Act would be even more effective if magistrates could award compensation. Perhaps Parliament may think it right to give us this power.' And Parliament is now thinking of amending the Criminal Justices Bill to give magistrates precisely this power, which they do not have at the moment. Until this change is made, the Trade Descriptions Act is rather like the bogus guarantees that car manufacturers provide you with : they look all very well until you try to actually make a claim under one.

The area of bogus guarantees, in fact, provides a further example of a statutory position ripe for consumerist attack. In 1962, the Molony Committee argued that a change in the law on guarantees was necessary. It declared that the ones in common use, on everything from transistor radios to cars, had the effect of 'consistently to impose unfair terms on the consumer and to deny him what the law means him to have'. This arose because by accepting his so called 'guarantee' the consumer effectively signed away many of his statutory rights under the 1893 Sale of Goods Act. For several years after this major recommendation, nothing happened. Then the Law Commissioners drew up draft legislation. Then, two years later, a Government Bill is planned to make exclusion clauses, limiting a consumer's Common Law rights, null and void. It will probably not be until 1973, eleven years after Molony, that this becomes law. And even when reformed, it may not provide any readily understandable help to the consumer.

This is certainly the case with the well-intentioned canned meat labelling regulations. They provide strict minimum meat contents for certain sorts of canned meat. For example, stewed steak with gravy must be not less than 70% 'meat'. But unless a consumer is familiar with these regulations she is unlikely to know that stewed steak with onions in sauce contains almost *half* the minimum meat content of stewed steak with gravy. And that stewed steak pie filling contains even less (as Tyne Brand, above, showed). Or that a stewed steak 'ready meal' could contain as little as $12\frac{1}{2}$% 'meat'. And that the 'meat', by the way, includes things not normally eaten like gristle and muscle.

There are many other equally unsatisfactory – from the consumerist standpoint – creations of the law which one can expect to come under attack (not to mention the legal profession itself for its ponderous slowness and prohibitive expense in protecting our interests). One such legal creation which shows just how inadequately the consumer is represented here compared to America is the now defunct Consumer Council. On the principle of never speaking ill of the dead, this body has been collecting posthumous plaudits ever since it was axed by a Conservative Government.

The fact is that the Consumer Council was supremely ill conceived in terms of being able to do the things consumers are now mourning its absence for. First of all, it was not allowed to deal with individual complaints. It received about 5,000 a year of these, a tiny number compared to the 120,000 a year made to the Weights and Measures Inspectors and the 124,000 a year made to bodies like the Citizens' Advice Bureau. The small number of individual complaints wasn't so much due to people being aware that the Consumer Council wasn't the right body to complain to, but more that people were simply not aware of the Consumer Council itself. Largely because it wasn't able, with a tiny staff and budget, to do anything very significant.

Over its eight-year life it certainly helped to get three-star petrol on most forecourts, to abolish resale price maintenance, to

79

make life easier for caravan dwellers etc. Compare this, however with the sort of things that the Federal Trade Commission in America is doing to advertising and business, or what the Swedish Consumer Agency can do, and the Consumer Council comes a very poor third. It never had the full hearted endorsement of Parliament (i.e. funds) and it never had the full hearted endorsement of the people.

For reasons which will be looked at when we examine some more of the background forces behind consumerism, the British consumer of the late sixties wasn't in a mood to require (and support) the Consumer Council to do what in 1971 everybody said it could have done if it hadn't been axed.

The Teltag labelling scheme is a good case in point. This was a basically Swedish system of having factual performance labels on consumer durables. Like how long a kettle took to boil. Or what was a distortion level on a loudspeaker, etc. It took the Swedes twelve years to get it going, and a lot of money. The Consumer Council only had £20,000 a year for their Teltag scheme (compared with, say, the £63 million spent over five years to build up the Woolmark as the quality control label for woollen garments). No wonder then the Teltag scheme didn't make a great deal of impact.

One might even argue that the Consumer Council wasn't even correctly formulated to be the 'watchdog consumer' combining the roles of authoritative spokesman for shoppers and guardian of their interests, when so many of its members weren't 'consumers' but representatives of industry or government.

Had the Consumer Council been other than it was, had it acted like Nader's Centre for Responsive Law, and had it thus carved out a niche for itself in the power structure, it would have been unaxable. But the fact that its removal caused virtually no more than a moaning from the heights of Hampstead is the ultimate evidence of its failure. Nevertheless, its absence leaves a void. A void which the proposed Tory Minister of Consumer Affairs won't necessarily fill.

The third area, after the consumer laws and the statutory consumer bodies, where the British statutory system is found wanting from a consumerist standpoint are the consumer consultative committees of the nationalized industries. As market forces are obviously less operative in a nationalized industry than in private industry, such committees provide the only way of redress for the consumer. (After all, if you are dissatisfied with the phone service switching over to the bush telegraph is hardly a feasible proposition.)

The 1971 report of the House of Commons Select Committee on Nationalized Industries on 'Relations with the Public' shows the failures of consumers to exert any muscle as yet on the nationalized industries. In reporting their activities to Members of Parliament, all of these bodies from the central Transport Consultative Committee to the Domestic Coal Consumer Council sound a paean of praise to the tiny number of complaints they had received. But when M.P.s probed a little further the cosy picture was slightly shattered. First, as a Consumer Council study revealed, only 8% of the population know of the existence of any of these bodies. Second, in dealing with these complaints from the tiny number of the public who discover that these bodies exist, they do so through the limited facilities paid for by the Board which they are meant to be policing, generally with a heavyweight member of the Board sitting in on their deliberations. And never with any power or funds to publish any criticism unless they receive first the kind permission of the Board to be criticized.

In such a situation, there must be a large pile of dirty washing in one form or another only waiting for a little bit of ethical whistle blowing to get the news into the hands of militant consumerist groups. These groups will be filling another void, namely the absence of a militant consumerist group in a society that is rapidly reaching that critical mass of affluence where consumerism will develop as naturally as trade unionism did in the late nineteenth century.

But the form the Consumer Association has chosen to take does not provide a natural focus for this sort of feeling. Five years ago it is arguable that in Britain at least the Consumer Association's approach was appropriate. But now its sedate middle-class activity seems really rather out of touch. It has belatedly recognized this by setting up its own Consumer Campaign Committee. But it hasn't really established itself as a force, to be reckoned with by business (as opposed to being granted polite attention when it talks). The comment of a young girl who tried to get her money back from an Oxford Street store put the matter in perspective: 'When I said I'd been to the Consumer Association, they just laughed at me.' In America, if she'd spoken of the Centre for Responsive Law, a store would not have laughed at her.

In fact, the Consumer Association people rather abhor the vulgar gospel slinging style of the consumerists who are, thank heaven, separated from them by many miles of Atlantic Ocean. 'We need a British approach,' said Eirlys Roberts of *Which* on a Radio 3 programme, 'which is a different approach.'

Certainly the style of the dowager duchess of British consumerism, Dame Elizabeth Ackroyd, seems to resemble nothing so much as that of Victorian middle-class ladies who felt it their bounden duty to minister to less fortunate classes. And already rival organizations are springing in an attempt to put a rather sharper cutting edge on consumerism than the well meaning old ladies of Buckingham Street can manage. Given the numerous openings that appear in the field of advertising alone, you can be sure that there will be many, all eager to decorate themselves with Nader's laurels.

But such supply implies a demand. The evidence already presented in other chapters has shown that this demand is increasing with geometric rather than arithmetic progression. It's estimated, for example, that there are 4 million complaints a year by consumers about the shoes they purchase. Only 5,000 of these are dealt with by the shoe industry's consumer body. Some are obviously satisfactorily dealt with by the shoe shops themselves. But there must be a very large number of people with grievances about shoes, just waiting for something to focus their grievance onto.

The same was shown to be true about dishwashers (possessed by only 2% of the population) when a chance letter in *The Times* triggered off a barrage of letters from people fed up, in one way or another, with the service they were getting.

Bad servicing by garages has already led to the setting up of a government approved body to guard against malpractices, after the A.A. found the majority of 78,000 complaints they received were justified.

The same healthy conditions for the growth of consumerism are present in the travel trade. Even after the 1971 spate of unfinished hotels and cancelled cruises, a spot check by *The Times* in January 1972 (just two months before the holiday season began) showed that out of fourteen hotels not built when the glossy brochures went to press, only three had been completed.

But even if there wasn't a natural demand, an induced demand would probably emerge from what one might call 'exported Naderism'. For though militant consumerism developed in America, America isn't a separate planet. Spread by our exports to it and by the multi-national companies that trade both here and there, consumerism will grow internationally.

The effect on our exports shows up most clearly in motor cars, which have to meet America's safety standards. By 1975-6 this means that British cars sold to America will be much safer and much less polluting than British cars sold to Britons. Nader has already made this charge about the 1970 models, but in five years' time the difference in safety standards will be far greater. Whatever the private views of the British motor industry about the merits or value of these safety measures, they will find it increasingly less easy to defend this position of selling one sort of car at home and another abroad.

The other way consumerism can be exported is through multi-national companies feeling it necessary to bring their business practices in Europe into line with their practices in America. For example, how long can Lever Brothers go on selling enzyme detergents in Britain when they had to drop selling them for safety reasons in parts of America. Shell found that pressures to change their Platformate advertising in America led to pressures to change their advertising in Britain. And all the major baby food companies in Britain have followed the example of baby food manufacturers in America of dropping monosodium glutamate from their products even though there has not yet been any consumerist attack on it in this country.

The Japanese car manufacturers learnt a salutary lesson about how consumerism could be exported in June 1969. The compulsory public confessions by Toyota and Nissan of selling defective cars didn't originate in Japan. It originated with a story in the *New York Times* that thousands of the cars sold in the U.S.A. and Japan were being secretly recalled. The Japanese press then picked up this story, added chapter and verse to it by illustrating the actual accidents that occurred and could be blamed on these defective parts, and the rest followed.

Of course, the export of consumerism can also work merely by following the example of another country. Open dating, which began in America spread, by example, to France and Germany (where it is now compulsory on almost all perishable pre-packaged foods). By the time this book is published open dating and unit pricing will have probably crossed the Channel in force.

In Britain, however, there are still two limitations that could slow down (though not in my view halt) the growth of consumerism. The first of these is a question of the credibility of consumerist groups. It was the Molony Committee of 1962 who warned against the risks of having only one consumer testing organization. And since 1962 the only rival to *Which,* the *Shoppers' Guide,* has been judged a worse buy by the public and ceased publication. This isn't to say that *Which* can therefore abuse a monopoly position, but it does raise the ancient question of 'quis custos custodiet'? Assuming the Consumer Association remains for ever unexposed to largesse from manufacturers, there is still the question mark against their tests, as to how good they are.

Nader has made the point, and it is a fair one, that the alternative testing of products is provided by the people who make them. That if his Raiders slip up, there is no shortage of people to jump down their throats.

Two recent cases show the counter-attack system working and how – if effective – it could rob Nader and his Raiders of some of their armour of credibility. These are his attacks on Volkswagen and Volvo, both quality image cars.

According to Nader, Volkswagen is the most dangerous car on the road in America in significant numbers (by which he means over 500,000 vehicles). It is 'uniquely hazardous' because of its instability in side winds, a deficient suspension system, poor seat anchorages, doors that are liable to fly open in a crash, and so on and so forth. Volkswagen, whose technical credibility as a company was still intact, counter-attacked by citing a 1964 study by the Cornell Aeronautical Laboratory, which showed that – over thirty States – the distribution of Volkswagen accident severity was essentially the same for the Beetle as most other cars.

At first, it seemed as though this argument outgunned the Raiders. Then the British Road Research Laboratory published a report they had done on 1965 cars. It found that of the cars tested, a Mini, 1100, 1800, Renault 1100, Hillman Imp, and

Beetle, the Beetle was by far the most dangerous. That, because of its rigid chassis, it pulled up very sharply in an accident, causing passengers and drivers to hit the dashboard and steering column at roughly two-thirds of the vehicle speed before impact, even if they were belted in.

It was after this that the word spread (to be confirmed) that the American Government were planning to order Volkswagen to modify the 4 million Volkswagens which had been sold in the United States, at an estimated cost to Volkswagen of about $200 million. So though Nader's credibility was questioned in this incident, he seems to have emerged with it intact.

To date, however, the attack on Volvo hasn't fared quite so well. Volvo Inc. of America have, according to his Centre for Car Safety, been guilty of 'monumentally deceptive advertising'. This was advertising stating that nine out of ten Volvos registered eleven years ago were still on the road. The Naderite attack claimed that this implied very different things from the harsh realities of Volvo ownership, including difficulties in starting the engine and premature wearing of brakes.

Like Volkswagen, but unlike General Motors, Volvo still had their technical integrity available to rebut such charges (and so try to make the consumerists sound like spokesmen for the American motor industry anxious to knock imports). In fact, a British survey by *Motor* magazine on Volvo owners showed the joys of owning this car were quite in line with the promises of the advertisements. Eighty per cent said they would buy a Volvo next time they bought a car. And 98% said they would recommend the make to their friends. Certainly as close as a car can come to acquittal from such hyper-criticisms.

Even when consumerists do make charges that in retrospect are found to be wrong, their credibility is not normally impaired. Take the case of mercury in tuna fish. You will doubtless remember the scare when word went round that the mercury levels in tuna fish, because of man's pollution of the oceans by mercury products, had led to an alarming rise of mercury in tuna which for some reason attracted more of this mineral to its body than other fishes. This story was all over the newspapers, and it was used as one more stick to beat business with by the consumer lobbyists. Then some American naval scientists in 1971 bored into the permanent ice floes of Greenland and so measured the mercury content of the frozen sea water going back for several millennia. It's true they did find that there had been over these millions of years some increase in the level of mercury in the water, but this level of mercury in the water was certainly no reason for not eating tuna. The interesting point is that not one of the papers who had carried the 'mercury danger story' carried the 'no mercury danger story' with anything like the same weight. No news may be good news. But good news is certainly no news. *The Times* for instance, ran the story under the heading: 'Pollution: No Danger from Mercury' at the bottom of their Court page, appropriately buried beneath the obituaries.

So even when there is a prima facie case for the loss of credibility of consumerists as an information source on an issue, the media – perhaps sensing that their readers would not thank them for the premature destruction of their new gods – lets the opportunity slip. Mind you, even if they took it, and let us say Nader's credibility was shattered the result would only be to see him replaced by another of his ilk (if you accept the argument of the earlier chapters that positions him as an *effect* rather than a cause).

A more central attack on the consumerists is of a quite different nature. In essence it's a sophisticated rehash of the argument that if the market really wants something it will pay for it, and if it doesn't want something badly enough to pay for it who are you to say that they should buy it?

The formulation of the argument in more acceptable terms for liberal ears goes as follows: that after a certain point the marginal cost of increasing safety or reducing pollution begins to escalate very dramatically. After this point, it is argued, such measures 'will serve to aggrandize the consumerists without helping the consumer' (in the words of Dr Joe Juran, the quality control expert who voiced this view).

The $1,000 million the U.S. car industry has now spent each year as a result of safety and pollution laws, it's argued, have very definite costs for the consumers and rather remote benefits. And the higher price of the safer, less polluting vehicles may stop people from buying them so that they may drive around still longer in their older, unsafe, more polluting vehicle.

This is an argument that tries, in short, to challenge the *cost-effectiveness* of consumerism in direct cost benefit analysis terms.

Forgetting even the Naderist point that a safer dashboard

doesn't *necessarily* cost more than an unsafe dashboard, there is a still more persuasive rebuttal to those who question the cost effectiveness of consumerism. Why is a safety or pollution feature on a car an 'extra' that causes high prices when something that is more a contributory factor to high prices, styling, is regarded as 'standard'? Why is a sharp chromium-plated fin something that doesn't need to defend its cost effectiveness when a feature that could stop that sharp chromium-plated fin killing somebody has to?

If one compares the benefit to the driver of a bumper that protects the vehicle properly, against one that allows $300 worth of damage from a 7 m.p.h. collision, the cost effectiveness of the former over the latter is clear. And the reduction of over a thousand fatalities in American road accidents in 1970 (which is already a third of all the fatal road accidents in Britain) is surely worth quite a lot in cost-effectiveness terms.

But even if neither an undermining of its credibility or a questioning of its benefits is likely to dampen the spreading of consumerism in Britain or its further development in America, it will have its setbacks.

One central problem will be a wavering of government support (as was the case with the Consumer Council). In October 1971 the American Bill to get a Consumer Protection Agency was so watered down during a two day debate in the House of Representatives that its main sponsors actively voted against the Bill in its final form. And two months earlier, in New York State, the Consumer Protection Board lost the services of the vigorous Betty Furness because of the hostility of the State Legislature for anything she wished to do as well as the lethargy of Governor Rockefeller about the State Legislature's hostility.

Clearly, the stick of grass root consumer pressures and the carrot of vote catching reforms isn't enough always to beat the infrastructure of City Hall. The ratio of 2.8 government lobbyists in Washington to every member of government or administration may be apocryphal, but it reflects the name of the game. In Britain, there are many lobby groups who can be expected to oppose all or some of the reforms consumerists demand. Like the C.B.I., the National Union of Manufacturers, the Association of British Chambers of Commerce, and the Advertising Association. All of these have their governmental contacts to ensure their case is heard and, where possible, to defang legislation (as in the case of the minced up Trade Descriptions Act).

But in the contexts of the new consumer attitudes we will talk about, such rearguard action will be increasingly seen for what it is: emergency action by groups with vested interests in the inequalities of the *status quo* struggling to preserve their commercial sinecures.

If for no other reason than that the normal response of business consumer pressure is to behave like a cross between an ostrich and King Canute one can be sure that it will not be long before the British Ralph Nader opens his shop, and finds not a few customers already banging on the door.

5
The Businessmen Who Forgot They Were Consumers

'Only Shell petrol in all the world is spelt 'S-h-e-l-l'. 'Only Bayer aspirin comes in the Bayer aspirin packet'. These caustic suggestions, from the creative director of a Texas advertising agency, are a common response to the new rules of parting consumers from their wage packets.

A response which says that it is an undeserved strait jacket worthy of either a hammer and sickle society or one of Alice in Wonderland's absurdities. And certainly not appropriate for the U.S. where not only is what is good for General Motors good for America but where, to quote the head of J. Walter Thompson, 'good business is good for the world, for the true business of the world is business'; thus implying that the good sense of Americans will prevent them from biting the hand that so graciously feeds them. And that when those irritating ladies like Esther Petersen and Virginia Knaur are well and truly chased from the White House, all will be well.

It was in this spirit that in 1967 a former chairman of General Foods urged the American Business Council to fight 'the rising tide of consumerism'. Tides, of course, recede. And even at the end of 1971, after all the corporate harassment already described, Dr Joe Juran (no friend of militant consumerism) put on record that American businessmen 'think consumerism is going to walk by and not attack them'.

If business is still showing widespread resistance to consumerism, it is because it is sustained with the sort of argument advanced by the ex-publisher of the now defunct *Look* magazine,

89

Thomas Shepherd, in January 1971. He used the phrase 'disaster lobby' to describe the consumerists, calling them 'the most dangerous men and women in America today'. Not Black Panthers, not Weathermen, not the Southern Segregationalists, but it's the Naders, the Knauers, Ribicoffs and Mosses of this world that imperil 'the consumer freedom to live the way he wants and buy the thing he wants without some Big Brother in Washington telling him he can't'.

The attentive 44th annual meeting of the Soap and Detergent Association was further informed by Mr Shepherd that air pollution was less than ever; that water was less polluted; that mercury in tuna fish came only from nature and not from man, and that the youth rebellion was just 'a very small gaggle of young troublemakers who are sorely in need of education, a spanking and a bath'. It may be that some of Mr Shepherd's ferocity in attacking the foes of business was motivated by his need for businesses to support to save his ailing magazine. But, alas no white knight on a charger arrived and *Look* has now ceased to be published.

But in other ways, American business has shown their support for Mr Shepherd's views, if not for his publications. For example, this is what happened when E. B. Weiss, executive vice-president of Doyle, Dane, Bernbach wrote in 1968 to Fortune's Top 500 companies asking this important question: 'Would you be willing to furnish me with an outline of just one project recently developed by your organisation that represents a new step in implementing a broader policy of social responsibility'. Two hundred of the 500 didn't even reply. One hundred admitted they couldn't cite a recent project representing such a step. One hundred cited projects that weren't recent. Fifty cited bare minimum responsibility projects. And only 50 out of the 500 reported projects that could be said to represent any form of advanced concept of social responsibility. 'But', according to Weiss, 'not one of those programmes related in adequate scope to the fearful problem of our deteriorating physical environment'.

This narrow sense of corporate responsibility (which makes a company vulnerable to consumerist pressures) showed up again when the biggest of the Fortune Top 500, General Motors, was cross-examined by Federal Trade Commissioner Phillip Elman in 1969. H. Bridenstine of General Motors was asked 'What do you think of the limitations that you have in your warranty?' Bridenstine replied, 'Well, I think with the type of product we are talking about, Mr Chairman, the limitations are reasonable'. 'Reasonable?' parried Elman. 'That is correct. There must be an understanding' or an attempt to 'eliminate argument with consumers'. (Elman had earlier observed that what General Motors referred to as an 'occasional mistake' represented 160,000 complaints from buyers of General Motors' cars in 1968.)

'Does any General Motors' customer have a choice?' said Elman, fastening on the key issue. 'Is it a take or leave it basis?' After all the consumer must buy a car 'with the warranties they're given, and, contrary to what a lot of people believe, these warranties take away from the car buyer's rights. They give him less than he would have without his warranty... The consumer has nothing to say about this understanding'. But this was not true, insisted the man from General Motors: 'He doesn't have to buy the car'.

The attitude that because an American doesn't have to buy a car he has a choice over the guarantee on that car isn't peculiar to America. British Leyland even have an interpretation of their guarantee (which also reduces in effect, not adds to your statutory rights) that only allows 'adjustments' as opposed to 'repairs' under the guarantee up to the first 1,000 miles. For the next 11,000 miles, despite the wording of the guarantee, you need a lawyer to get your 'adjustments' carried out under the guarantee.

If you try and find the reasoning behind this sort of attitude, you discover a naïve double-think which persuades otherwise shrewd businessmen that in this sphere of their company's activities, at least, commonsense becomes nonsense. For example, one of the arguments used by Chrysler for extending the government deadline by which all cars should have bumpers capable of taking a 5 m.p.h. impact was that 'drivers of vehicles which have such exterior protection systems might be more careless in operating their vehicles and hit structures that they would now avoid'.

Perhaps the most telling example that shows the blinkered sort of obligation companies feel towards their consumers emerged when Ralph Nader asked 58 advertisers to substantiate to him, as a private citizen, their advertising claims. Fifty-five of these 58 were either unwilling or unable to do so. But the sort

91

of reasons they gave, and this was in December 1970, are illuminating.

From Bristol Meyers, those wonderful people who've brought you Exedrin: bafflement. 'We can recall no other inquiries like yours. In the past consumers seem not to have felt it necessary to obtain advertising clarification or substantiation from us.'

From Whitehall Laboratories who make Anadin, the reassurance that the 'product has been sold for many years to millions of satisfied users'.

From Beechams, who claim that 'a major dental clinic studies show that Macleans get teeth whiter', the brush off: 'no company can afford time and expense to detail its operations for every enquiring consumer'. The similar test I carried out on twenty-three British advertisers was only slightly more encouraging: at most, a third of the companies gave any indications that a consumerist-style letter would be taken seriously. In their hearts, most of the men and women who wrote back to me still probably regarded consumerism as a menace, something that gets in the way of their business.

It makes me wonder if Britain has come such a long way since the outburst by Sir Miles Thomas against *Which* in 1964: 'It undermines consumer confidence and is a very bad factor in the present economic system. Its opinions are blown up by the B.B.C. giving it quite spurious importance,' said Sir Miles. Which confirms the comment made seven years later by the Professor of Marketing at Bradford University that 'manufacturers think of their customers as purchasing units'.

The people who tell businessmen how to make these 'units' purchase are, of course, the advertising agents. And some of them have taken a similar attitude to their paymasters. That ageing creative whizz kid, Jerry Della Femina told the London Creative Circle in November 1971, that, just as Hitler had chosen to persecute the gypsies, so the American Government – in looking for something to persecute – had chosen advertising.

One could continue to relate the views of the not so silent majority of American advertisers and admen who have found their own Spiro Agnews. But even the more moderate admen greet the impact of consumerism with a good deal less than enthusiasm. Andrew Kershaw, president of Ogilvy and Mather New York, has argued that the tighter controls will lead to *less* informative advertising. As the tighter controls are a direct result of a lack of informative advertising this seems a paradoxical outcome. But, in Mr Kershaw's view, the tighter the controls the greater the business uncertainty about what they can say. And so the more the empty advertising, the sort of emotional stuff that says 'we're very good' and 'gee aren't we nice people' and 'look at this pretty package' and so on.

This development is certainly an arguable possibility. But one should also remember that the tighter controls that are being objected to are precisely the sort that would stop things like the Shell Platformate commercial (page 60) from getting on the air, a commercial that was made by Mr Kershaw's own advertising agency.

Rushing to the defence of what seems your best interest isn't an exclusively American phenomenon. When in July 1971 a Canadian marketing professor had the nerve to criticize the John Player Special slogan 'The best virginia cigarette in the world' as a 'lie', the managing director of Leo Burnett who had created the advertisement snapped 'there is nothing less useful than the ill informed personal judgements of an overseas academic on individual British advertisements'. A comment that appears even more inappropriate in view of the admission reported earlier by the solicitor for Players that his claim was to be regarded as no more than 'advertising puffery'.

There is certainly very little evidence that consumerism will be greeted by a red carpet when it arrives here. Despite a manifesto on the 'Social Contribution of Advertising' no more than token gestures of goodwill are forthcoming from the advertising establishment. Goodwill that's more designed to appease the critics than promote real change. At least, the attitude here isn't so different from America.

Here, as in America, the first response of business to consumerism tends to be to deny everything and, if that denial fails, to blame the wrongdoings on the small company. And if that also fails to turn on the critics and try and discredit them.

But what if all these efforts fail, and the mud still sticks? Then the predictable response is to engage some public relations style campaign to try and scrape the mud off. This is an exercise in changing the image rather than a reality, perhaps because after fifteen years of brand image advertising the businessmen find it difficult to tell the image from the reality (a sort of Stork and butter problem on a rather grander scale). Or if the reality is changed, it is certainly not enough to justify the image which is built on it. This is clearly the case over industrial pollution in America. The pressure here from consumerists has been that industry should replace the social capital it uses, like clean air, clean water and clean soil, when it makes its products. The public relations response is to spend money *not* on doing this but telling people that you're doing it. And to pat yourself on the back for being a front line fighter against the pollution you've been churning out for years.

As a result, you have a situation where the American glossies show advertisements telling how company X's selfless concern for its fellow men is the only thing that makes being in business worth while. How company Y is benefiting workers by the thousand by cleaning up the mess it made yesterday. How company Z shows how, in so many little but important ways, the products they produce help make your life worth living. All of which such wisdoms receive crisp encapsulation in phrases like 'Men helping man', 'Progress through chemistry', 'The discovery company', etc. Indeed a survey by *Business Week* showed that 30% of the annual company reports of 1971 involved discussion of corporate social responsibility.

The following estimates put these claims and that statistic into perspective. Senator Jackson has estimated that if business is to clear up the air and water pollution it makes it'll have to spend at a rate of $8 billion a year for the next five years. It's currently only spending at a fifth of this rate. And the missing four-fifths is a gap between image and reality.

These responses don't represent a substantial shift from the 'what can we get away with' morality. It is just that one can get away with less. The animals are getting craftier, so me must hunt them more cunningly. And it's not so much of a change of heart that occurs, as a new layer of make-up that's applied to the old face. If finally that cracks, you still have one card left to play. The 'it's not possible' syndrome.

'A degradable soft drink container sounds like a fine idea,' said Coca Cola, 'but it doesn't exist. And the chances are that one can't be made.' Non-polluting car engines are a fine idea too. But, according to the president of General Motors 'the technology does not exist – inside or outside the automobile industry – to meet the stringent emission levels in the specified time'. Ford have even run television commercials criticizing the

94

air bag – another fine idea that no one knows how to make safe enough for the public. Perhaps it's significant that Ford have changed their slogan from 'Ford has a better idea' to 'we listen better'.

The advertising industry, apart from being the purveyors of their clients' images, has also had to move from a straightforward 'denying everything' approach.

First they have tried to discredit the critics. In the words of the chairman of Pepsi Cola: 'I believe very honestly that advertising offers the highest silhouette, the most convenient aiming point for these people. But I think the ultimate target is free enterprise itself.' Or, like Dan Seymour of J. Walter Thompson talking to the International Advertising Association you could put the blame for the rising hostility towards business on the shoulders of 'a generation of faculty members' who have taught the young that no business is good business. And this, according to Mr Seymour, is a myth which has only been accepted because business hasn't fought back. Hence the need for a mighty counter-attack to reburnish the image of commerce. For the truth is that 'we (in business and advertising) are among the few people who can go home every night knowing that we have done something to make the world better'.

The accuracy of this viewpoint isn't as important as whether or not it's credible in an environment where consumers, as we shall see, are becoming more and more hostile to advertising and less and less enthusiastic about the product it brings. In any event, Time Inc. has given away $600,000 worth of free space to let advertising agencies polish up their professional image. No doubt that was intended to answer Mr Seymour's suggestion that 'perhaps it's time we did for ourselves what we did for Smokey the Bear'. But Smokey the Bear, advertising's most successful public service campaign, is alas a blind alley. The late Nicholas Sanstag was once provoked to observe: 'To explain to the advertising industry that public responsibility goes beyond Smokey the Bear is like trying to convince a ten-year-old that making love is more fun than a cone of chocolate ice-cream.'

To believe that a Smokey the Bear approach is the solution is to reveal not only a diminished sense of responsibility, but also an over-developed belief in the power of commercial persuasion. Maybe the advertising men feel that if they don't show their belief in advertising, who will? Certainly, to believe that, in the words of another distinguished alumnus of the industry, to 'tell a fair story of advertising's role in building 1,300,000 new jobs a year in the American economy' will help the problem is a major act of faith.

It's a faith that's shared in France, where a campaign on $1.7 million worth of media space ran in 1971 to demonstrate the need for advertising. Underneath a photograph of various unidentified products in plain unlabelled packs the copy says 'Choose! But what is it? What's it for? How much does it cost? Where can I buy it? Advertising tells you'. It is, of course, the label on the pack that tells you most of this, but the French approach does at least make a little more sense than the advertisement for the U.S. Freedom Foundation with the headline 'think of freedom as eleven kinds of chicken soup'.

The pity of all this virtuous mouthing is that, as we shall see later, it's not so much the principle of 'advertising in a free society' that's attracting the brickbats. As the practice of it in a media saturated one.

One more annoying advertisement to prove that advertisements aren't annoying is hardly a solution. For, as will become clearer when we look at the techniques of the advertising industry, it's these techniques that annoy. And there is no evidence to date of any serious attempt by the advertising industry on either side of the Atlantic to try to develop techniques that can raise sales without raising blood pressures. It is no more than a surface solution to tell the world all about the useful way that advertising people have applied their talents to solving the ills that beset our society if the next moment the ads. are back on the air and spoiling the evenings viewing.

Of course, it's good that a campaign by Cambell-Ewald tripled the number of applicants for police jobs in Detroit (unless, of course, you happened to be on the receiving end of a riot stick). Of course, it's good that 75 American P.R. and advertising agencies should band together to help a summer youth opportunity project. Of course, it's good that the Women's Advertising Club in Chicago runs a campaign designed to help Spanish people to shop wisely for food. But probably some of the energies behind such projects are fuelled by guilty consciences. (One reason, for example, more policemen are needed in Detroit is because of more drug taking. And one reason for the increase in drug taking, according to the Commissioner of the Food and Drug

96

Administration is the 'tremendous wave of advertising over the media, especially T.V., in which the consumer feels that in reaching for a pill...is a panacea for all ills'.)

Even forgetting this, the penance of good works is probably insufficient mollification to placate the consumer God. So the next P.R. offering is the promise to erect a strong watchdog to round up all the black sheep, 'the tiny minority who are responsible for the vast majority of malpractices'.

Judging by the very partial success of the voluntary control system in Britain (where, as we've mentioned, the same proportion of people regard advertising as less than truthful as in uncontrolled America) this isn't a complete solution, either. Nevertheless, to save itself from the unbridled tyranny of government, the American advertising industry is now prepared to place itself under the yoke of the National Advertising Review Board, chaired by the former American ambassador to the United Nations (for he must have heard plenty of unsubstantiated claims). It can publicize abuse, and call on the media to refuse advertisements that fail the tests. But if it turns out to be inadequate, full of sound and fury but signifying nothing, then the American advertising industry – like business – will find that it will be forcibly prodded towards a fuller response to consumerism.

Half way between pretending to do something and really doing something lies a twilight zone of conspicuously making an effort. Into this come the recent moves by Chrysler, Ford, and General Motors to have a 'man in Detroit' who could sort out the complaints that the Big Three's dealers haven't sorted out. For the Chicago area alone, General Motors has a staff of twenty specially trained girls to answer the phones, and aims to get an answer back to the complainant within twenty-four hours. Ford has its 'we listen better' monitoring system. One interesting analysis of the first 8,000 letters they received was that only 34% contained a complaint. When Ford tried a similar approach, but using a telephone bar at the Chicago Car Show where people could record their complaints, they got fourteen hours of solid obscenities on their tape.

A similar feed back technique has been tried by the Traveller's Insurance Company since they found out that 47% of people thought insurance companies wouldn't talk straight to people. You can now ring, toll free, their Traveller's Office of Consumer Information to get any sort of information you like about insurance without any selling. And Avis has run advertisements inviting the public to 'Yell if Avis does something wrong. You'll get it out of your system. And we'll get it out of ours', with an invitation to ring the Avis Hot Line again toll free. (Maybe the whole thing is something cooked up by old Ma Bell).

In one sense, of course, these are no more than what Nader might call 'Band Aid solutions'. Shouldn't car companies cut down on the things that cause complaints and not just hire pretty little voices to pour oil on troubled waters? Shouldn't insurance companies give better value for money, have less small print, and simplify claim procedures, rather than make token gestures of free telephone calls?

If the companies who engage in these gestures believe that this 'tokenism' will propitiate the consumer gods, they are mistaken. Because once a company starts to offer these sorts of things for the consumer at a modest level, sooner or later the consumer demands a response at a much higher level. And all these attempts – including the multifold claims of social responsibility – to show a response to consumer pressures merely create a greater consumer pressure for a further response.

Perhaps it's only when you give the impression in black and white that you don't pollute, that you're responsible towards the environment, that you're sensitive to consumers' needs, that consumers really demand all these things of you. It was, after all, only *after* the Potlach Timber Company ran an advertisement saying it spent a small fortune keeping the Clearwater River clear, but actually used in that advertisement a photograph of the river several miles *upstream* from the Potlach factory, that this timber company found itself under great environmental pressure. (In this sense, the exaggerations of the advertisers can be said to have done the consumerist and pollution cause a good turn.)

The spur that finally gets businessmen and advertisers to do something is usually fear. 'Let's face the facts', said the President of Norman Craig and Kummel, 'we are scared. Make no mistake, we are.' And so, in the words of the chairman of the Missouri Air Pollution Control Commission 'they moan and gripe, but in the end they comply'. And not just because of tougher laws. Because it's actually starting to get through to the big corporation boards that if you can't beat them, you'd better join them.

Some companies have already learnt that to ignore the things consumers are paying attention to can cost more money than the expense of paying attention to them. But they've learnt the hard way. In 1970 the giant Unilever combine's fourth quarter results in Britain were 'adversely affected' by the ban on cyclamates. In 1966, after Ralph Nader had finished with the Corvair, General Motors found that sales were reduced by 87% of the 1965 level.

Pressure from the shareholders has had an influence, too. For seeing companies torn apart in public has changed a lot of shareholders' views about what 'responsibility' means in 1972. A poll by the Opinion Research Corporation showed that 65% of American stockholders thought that business should play an active role in the war on poverty. This means, in the short term, smaller dividends.

But it's not only amongst their owners that executives are finding a change of heart. For at last their crude measuring sensors are starting to pick up some of the grumbles amongst their customers. General Foods now conducts more than 30,000 consumer interviews a year. The Hoover Company has tripled its market research budget in three years. And even Detroit really has started to listen better and begun to pick up the changed attitudes of consumers to material goods that will be the subject of a later chapter. 'There are a growing number of people', observed the marketing director of Chevrolet, almost regretfully, 'who look on a car as they would a well engineered lawnmower.'

And some businessmen are even beginning to recognize that their deafness to consumerism was a phenomenon that created an environment in which consumerism could flourish. And have started to accept the philosophy of some of the flower children which businessmen scorned and derided: 'American business-men must accept that humane and ethical values are going to have to be corporate products just as much as what we manufac-ture.' The speaker wasn't Charles Reich or J. K. Galbraith but the President of Hunt-Wesson Foods.

But be sure that the lion hasn't lain down with the lamb in a hurry. By and large the greatest response of a company to con-sumerism is only when it is carried screaming into the second half of the twentieth century. The Ford 'Sure' scheme (provid-ing guarantees of decent servicing) only developed after the scandal about the bad servicing of motor cars described in the previous chapter. Or take the case of the Union Carbide, who

99

kicked and struggled for almost ten years before they agreed to cut their emission of sulphur dioxide gas in West Virginia by 70%. This was only after a grass roots campaign by the people who had to breathe all this in (one stack down there used to spew out a third as much particulate matter as the whole of New York in a year).

And following this example, the Aleyska Pipeline Company, who wanted to build a 789-mile pipeline in Alaska, felt it necessary to present twenty-nine volumes of proposals of how they were going to minimize the mess they created and how they were going to clear up the unavoidable mess. Boulders which aid fish runs wouldn't be displaced. Construction timetables would avoid lambing and high salt lick seasons for sheep. Simulated pipelines would test the response of caribou and reindeer. It sounds more like an R.S.P.C.A. inspector's report than a document prepared by an oil mogul.

Another industry which only responded after coming under the consumerist lash was the cereal industry. And their response is interesting because they seem to have realized a little quicker than their colleagues making motor cars which way the wind was blowing.

At first, *Marketing Communications* reported in March 1971 : 'To a company the major ready-to-eat cereals marketing men told M/C that impact from the Choate contentions had been modest at most.' But according to *Advertising Age* 'In the wake of Mr Choate's attack on breakfast cereals, sales of the cereals that he had rated high in nutritional value had soared, while sales of the cereals at the bottom of his list have fallen.' Apparently sales of Choate's top five cereals had gone up by 85% compared to a similar period before the attack.

For the marketing men to admit that nutritional values *were* useful selling points would be to admit their failure to detect this prior to Mr Choate's attack. But in their new advertising they quickly started to put their money where the consumer's mouth now was. Kellogg's Cornflakes (38 out of 60 on the Choate analysis) showed a bowl of cereal with milk and fruit encased in captions as to the amounts of everything from niacin to riboflavin inside those golden flakes. And Rice Crispies (39 out of 60) informed its readers that rice is 'one of the world's most nourishing grains'. In fact of the 40 dry cereals which Choate described in July 1970 as being over advertised and under nutritious,

26 had been dramatically reformulated by November 1971.

A parallel example of a sensible response only after a hefty kick up the backside is that of Schweppes and their non-returnable bottles in Britain. Non-returnable bottles aren't exactly the pin-up products of the ecologists. In America, Coca Cola has switched back to returnables and Canada Dry has even set up centres to recycle not only their own glass, but any other glass the public brings to them. So what was the first response of Schweppes' chairman to a campaign by the Friends of the Earth trying to get Schweppes to follow these examples: 'It's a bit of nonsense. We're not proposing to do any more than we have done.' But after six weeks, after thousands of Schweppes bottles had been dumped on their doorsteps by the Friends of the Earth and their shareholders had been lobbied (and all this well covered on television and in the press), only then did Schweppes make a sensible response. They invited round the head of the Friends of the Earth and together it was agreed to ask the government to look into the environmental effects of packaging.

The question that arises from all this is why it takes the advertising and business community so long to reach positions where they're able to regard consumerism not as a new formulation of the red menace but – at the very least – an important new ingredient in the marketing mix. Why this charade of denial, discrediting of critics, blaming it on others, P.R. phoney response and then only as a last resort – when all else had failed – a full and sensible response.

Is consumerism really a threat to the profits of a company? In the nineteenth century that's what industry thought of trade unionism. But little by little out of the dialectical clash a new synthesis emerged. And, by and large, the most successful companies in the long term have been those companies that most re-orientated their thinking towards the workers.

This re-orientation will probably happen much quicker in the case of consumerism. Because while there are very few employers who also have a role as employees, all businessmen have a role in life as consumers. And as consumers they are changing in the sort of ways that the following chapter will describe. It is only the conditioned reflexes of how businessmen 'should' behave that is holding them back. And the evidence I have seen is that it is atrophying the younger managers less and less.

But even if business *didn't* have this dual role, it would still find that it was more profitable to put on the butter generously rather than skimp with margarine. A British study of 15 large companies and their responsibilities to shareholders, employees, and the community concluded that, in the long term, rather than a battle which leads to a conflict of interests there was a balance that led to an eventual coincidence of interests. (*Company boards: Their responsibilities to shareholders, employees and the community,* P. E. P. Shenfield.) And that socially responsible corporate behaviour and long-run profit maximization can be more or less equivalent *provided* that social institutions and the pressures of the market are sufficiently strong.

There is moreover quite a lot of supporting evidence to this point of view. Study in New York State showed that the lowest polluting companies were also the most profitable. They had the most modern plant, and weren't cushioned by a 'company town' infrastructure. So far from pollution being the smell of progress it may well be the stench of decay. And Whirlpool, who have stuck their neck out to respond to consumerism, finds that their reward is not only in heaven. In the last three years Whirlpool's rate of sales increase has tripled that of the industry average.

In Britain one finds that those companies that are best at dealing with consumer complaints and have the most 'generous' policy of accepting returned merchandise are also the ones which are the most profitable. Like Marks & Spencers, Mothercare, Selfridges, Tesco, Sainsburys. But the ones who are worst in this respect, like B.L.M.C. have less impressive profits.

Maybe the best example of how consumerism can actually provide companies with new marketing opportunities that make everybody happy comes from the food industry and concerns the issues of open dating and unit pricing. The life cycle of this issue has been quite normal. First of all newspapers exposed the practice of hiding the freshness of packaged food behind secret codes and so making consumers buy packaged foods whose shelf life has expired. This was met by manufacturers' response that it wasn't their fault, but the fault of the retailers. The retailers said that if consumers knew the relative freshness of the various packets of food on their shelves, the less fresh ones (though still perfectly fresh) would never sell. And open dating, like anything from less pollution in the air to safer cars, would – of course – push prices up. But the media replied that if open dating worked for fresh food, like vegetables and meat, which have nature's own version of date stamping (called mould) why shouldn't it work for packaged food? Why should the supermarket escape a discipline that the greengrocer and the butcher and the fishmonger had to submit to?

The argument was irresistible to supermarkets trying to win new customers. And only nine months after the original charges in Congress about secret dating in America which had sparked off such a furore, *Business Week* could report that 'food chains had discovered a hot new marketing tool'. And they were talking not about plastic daffodils or trading stamps but open dating. And by the end of 1971 unit pricing was available virtually in every urban area of America.

The same is happening already with unit pricing. Even individual companies are trying to use it as a way of showing consumers they're really on their side. Purex ran an advertisement in New York with the headline 'Why you should shop an ounce at a time' with the copy offering all purchasers of 'Sweetheart line washing-up liquid' a handy little pocket calculator to tell the housewife at a glance the cost per ounce of an item.

The evidence is that these new consumerist approaches to marketing really do pay. One food chain in America using both open dating and unit pricing is Pathmark. Their per store average of $7 million in annual sales volume is *double* that of the food industry. And one reason why was revealed by an executive of Jewel Supermarkets, another food chain using these same techniques: 'We have found that making the dates available eliminated the customers' feeling that they had to check the dates ... as with unit pricing, we are simply enhancing the reputation of the store.'

But what happens when a similar exposé of secret dating is made in England? The head of Lyons Groceries (one of the exposed companies) gets onto the television screen to trot out the standard – and unconvincing – arguments about it being impossible and that it is up to the shops to control their stock properly. It won't, however, come as a surprise to those who invest in shares to learn which was the first food store to go over to open dating: Marks & Spencers, a company with a return on capital that makes most British managers go green.

Some critics regard all these sorts of responses by companies with cynicism. Michael Harrington, author of the *Other America* observed that businessmen 'have acquired a conscience at the precise moment when ... there is money to be made in doing good'. But, in a capitalist society, is that such a bad reason? The real charge against business is not that its motives are commercial, but that they took so long to realize that 'doing good' and profitability were not natural enemies.

Why businessmen had to prolong the period of conflict with consumers, why indeed they had to engage in conflict at all, is a question that goes right to the heart of the impasse that business and advertising now faces. Guided by advertising men who have very often no more idea of the consumer than what they read in tabulated columns in their market research reports, the blind have entrusted themselves to the blind. And the revolutionary changes amongst consumers in the last ten years, changes that ensure that Mrs 1972 resembles her predecessor of ten years ago only in name, have been ignored, overlooked, or forgotten.

It is to this changing consumer that our attention now turns.

6

Birth of the New Consumer: the Child is Father of the Man

'Plus ça change, plus c'est la même chose.'

Propelled by such brave sentiments the advertising industry has leapt boldly into the second half of the twentieth century. As they say in the advertisements 'unbelievable, but true'.

Who would have thought that a profession who claimed to be equipped with the tools to see into the souls of men would not have foreseen the crumbling of the concept of authority and predicted the development of consumerism as a result? And that having failed this one, they would have also failed to predict that consumerism would be a real force in the market place and not just a matter of blue-stockings wanting money off instead of plastic roses? And, finally, who would have thought that once consumerism did turn out to be a man-eating shark and not just a shoal of intellectual angel fish, that they would also fail to equip their clients to market their products in this new situation?

But, as the previous chapter endeavoured to show, there was no intelligent response from the majority of businessmen or advertising agencies to consumerism until it became a threat to survival of their business (as opposed to a simple opportunity to make more profits). Then, having been forced to change, they tended to talk about 'consumerism' as though it was their own private invention.

The basic reason behind this wearying challenge and non-response is distressingly simple. Okay, they say, Mrs 1970 isn't Mrs 1950. But in your heart you know she's still white, willing, and able to buy your goodies. In short, the same as ever, just wearing a new wrapping. Okay, they say, Mrs 1970 has a different shell to Mrs 1950. But probe beneath that oh-so-shallow surface and you'll find a heart that beats with the same old rhythm. But there's a fly in the martini. The sociologists have noticed it. The economists have noticed it. Even the politicians have noted it. It's the wealth and information explosion of the last twenty years. And it's such a taken-for-granted phenomenon that one tends to forget the enormous implications packed within that rather humdrum sentence.

First, a few statistics. Advanced societies are now doubling their output of goods and services about every ten to fifteen years. Even in a so-called depressed economy like Britain, the G.N.P. grew between 1960 and 1970 by 87%. And by 127% in the U.S.A. So perhaps the most truthful political slogan for some time was Harold Macmillan's 'you've never had it so good'.

In the thirteen years from 1947 to 1960 the *real* income of the average employee both in Europe and the United States rose by almost as much as it had in the *entire* preceding half century. In dollars of 1970 purchasing power, in 1929 only one in six of American households earned over $7,500. By 1970 more than one household in two had this income.

This explosion of wealth, then, is one that differs not only in degree but in direction from previous sudden increases in wealth (like the Spanish discovery of gold in the New World). Previous increases of wealth had been characterized by much for the few. This one was characterized by more for the many. We are in fact talking about the first mass affluent society.

Never before have so many people lived so far above subsistence. Of course there is poverty. But the poor are now a minority, not a majority (and this is true even when Britain has a million people out of work). Of course there are old age pensioners, people with large families and small family allowances, unskilled immigrants and so on and so forth. But the plain fact is the average worker has a wealth today which only fifteen years ago was a well-to-do middle-class ideal.

Fifteen years ago the most widely owned domestic appliance was the vacuum cleaner. Five out of ten homes had one. Now eight out of ten homes have one.

Fifteen years ago only four out of ten homes had a television. Now over nine out of ten homes have one.

Then, only one home in six had a car. Now three homes in six have a car.

Then only one home in five had a washing machine. Now more than three out of five homes have a washing machine.

Then only one home in fourteen had a fridge. Now nine homes in fourteen have a fridge.

Then only one home in twenty had central heating, now over seven homes in twenty have central heating.

Then only one home in ten had a hairdryer, now five homes in ten have a hairdryer.

And in those fifteen years, while the total population has increased by 8% the number of people taking a holiday abroad has increased by 87%. And so on through all the component pieces of the affluent society. In fact, by the end of this fifteen-year period, after a time when most would say the economy had been stagnating more often than it had been growing, a *majority* of all the homes in the country have a car, a TV set, a vacuum cleaner, a fridge, an electric iron, a washing machine, a sewing machine, and an electric hair dryer.

How this increase of wealth has changed people's attitudes to wealth itself is a story for a later chapter. Suffice it to say at this point that companies have got so used to seeing their sales graphs rising that they have forgotten to look beyond the graph, to the full meaning of that ever-skyward-pointing thin red line.

Forgetting to look at what is staring you in the face, also shows itself if one looks at the other half of the equation of change, the information explosion. This has two dimensions: formal and informal. Looking at the formal level of information, otherwise known as education, what is true for wealth is also true for this. Ours is the first mass educated society. And this means both a higher proportion at school and a higher proportion going on to higher education.

In the 1920s there were 20,000 people in Britain in higher education. In 1970 there were almost half a million. In 1963, only one-third of the 21-29 age group had a higher education. But by 1971, half as many children again – or 55% – were staying on in school beyond the school leaving age to have a higher education.

The position in Britain is still well behind the position in America, if you make the generous assumption that one year in a British school equals one year in an American school. According to Katona (*Aspirations and Affluence*) almost every second American youngster, boy or girl, aged eighteen is in college. While in Europe only every tenth youngster of that age goes to school full time. Fifty years ago this tremendous gap didn't exist. Then in America only 2% of the college age population actually went to college. But the gap came about because America has treated education as its biggest growth industry (particularly after being pipped at the post by Sputnik).

By the middle of this decade it's been estimated that one-third of *all* American homes will contain a graduate. That means a thinking sophisticated being to confront the advertiser and his agency. But even in less educated Britain the average girl leaving school has spent 25% more time at school than her mother. As well as being educated by superior education techniques.

There is no simple measure of educational efficiency, of course, but school is obviously not what it was in *Tom Brown's School-days*: 'A grey tedium relieved by moments of brutality'. Pesta-lozzi, Froebel, Herbart, Freud, Adler, Dewey, Montessori and even Dr Arnold have seen to that.

From the marketing and advertising standpoint, all this means that every year the proportion of well-educated consumers in the market place is rising and the proportion of spending power at their disposal is rising too.

But as every schoolboy knows, his schoolteacher isn't his greatest teacher: it's television that really wears the mortar-board. According to Dr Gerald Looney of the University of Arizona the average American pre-kindergarten child spends 64% of his waking hours watching television. And in Europe, the French journalist Servan-Schreiber has calculated that a child sees about 2,000 hours of television *before* he goes to school. Then when he gets to school he pays almost as much atten-tion to the television set as to the teacher. The British Bureau of Television Advertising has worked out that the average viewer watches television for rather more than eighteen hours every week. For over 2½ hours every day.

With homework, and so on, you might think this would be lower for schoolchildren. But according to Gilbert Youth Research in America, the figures for high school students is on average 2 hours 13 minutes of television a day plus 1 hour 45 minutes of radio (plus 36 minutes of reading a newspaper).

By the time a child leaves school, aged sixteen, he has probably spent two thousand *more* hours in front of the square screen than in front of the teacher. And he'll go on watching (even though he won't see any more of the teacher). By the age of forty-five, going by the B.B.T.A. figures, he will have seen about 50,000 hours of television. (Which taken at one burst would mean over six years of solidly sitting in front of the television screen.)

What the new consumer sees on that screen in all that time does things to him that never happened to the pre-television consumer. Tiny tots of two and three learn things from 'Sesame Street' that they didn't learn previously till they went to kindergarten. It's part of a phenomenon that may eventually replace the school system as we know it today. In the words of Ivan B. Illich (in *De-Schooling Society*): 'A major illusion on which the school system rests is that most learning is the result of teaching. Teaching, it is true, may contribute to certain kinds of learning under certain circumstances. But most people acquired most of their knowledge outside school, and in school only in so far as school...has become their place of confinement during an increasing part of their lives.' Television is a new sort of knowledge outside school. Cup Finals, Moon landings, cowboys and indians, the News by satellite from Biafra ... all the clichés come true and the classroom has become the world.

Dr Richard Feinbloom of Harvard University has argued that parents are now 'turning their children over to the television set'. And the set in this sense becomes the father of the child.

Of course, not everything the child sees is quite as Mary Whitehouse would like it, scrubbed and disinfected in a clean plastic bag. By the age of fourteen, the American child will have seen about 18,000 people die on television. While British children will get off lightly with about 9,000 slayings before their very eyes. Happily for Mrs Whitehouse, it is not just baddies being bumped off by goodies that is carried over the air waves. For at the same time as – and maybe because of – the development of new technologies fo communication has come the greatest ever increase in knowledge to be communicated by these new technologies.

Alvin Toffler in *Future Shock* calculates that 'at the rate at which knowledge is growing, by the time a child born today graduates from college, the amount of knowledge in the world will be four times as great. And by the time that same child is fifty years old it will be thirty times as great, and 97% of everything known in the world will have been learnt since the time he was born'.

Marshall McLuhan has argued that it is not the content of the electronic media which is the most shattering thing about it, as the way that content is delivered: instantly, with a low-definition, high-involvement picture. By thus extending the viewer's senses, by letting her be part of the programme, by letting her be *present* ten thousand miles away at the battle front in Vietnam, or on the football pitch at Wembley, or on the lawn of the White House, or on the surface of the Moon, she is educated, aroused, stimulated – McLuhan uses the word 'massaged' – in a way that the pre-television consumer never was.

There is a circular effect at work here: the new media change their readers and viewers, some of whom are contributors to the new media themselves, who then further develop the media. The end result of this cycle of change is best seen in the case of the reporting of the Vietnam War. It is not just the existence of television bringing the war into American living rooms (even in glorious colour) that has made this conflict different from, say, the Second World War. Then, at a Press Conference in 1941, Roosevelt laid down the two rules of war reporting: that it should be accurate, that it shouldn't give succour to the enemy. Neither of these two conditions applied to the reporting of the war in Vietnam. Because of the demand of the electronic media, reporting is of the events of the day, often when it is not possible to put a particular event in overall strategic context. And reporting is unrestricted by censorship. Had the First World War been reported in the way that the Vietnam war is being reported, it is probable that the civil population would have rioted when they were made aware of the true scale of casualties.

Many would argue that this would have been a profoundly good thing. But the point more pertinent to this discussion is that it shows the interaction of the media changing people who then further change the media which in turn further change people on an enormous scale. The net result of all these inter-actions is that the consumer goes through a range of experiences and sensations that *sophisticate* him in a quite new way. And the more he or she watches the greater this process of sophistication. If we look at the different levels of television viewing through the population, some interesting implications of this arise. For example, young boys watch 35% more television than their fathers. So a father who in any way judges a child by how *he* thought and felt at the boy's age is making a bad mistake. Another bad mistake is to assume that the so-called 'A' class people are a great deal more sophisticated than the so-called 'C' class people. The fact is that this second group watches 31% more television than the first group. As you will see later, there are many 'A' class admen who still persist in talking to their 'C' class consumers as though television hadn't had its enormously sophisticating effect.

This media-developed sophistication is, of course, in a different dimension to I.Q. tests and 'O' Levels. It is not so much that it makes more people *understand* what the term 'Sterling Area' means (which only 9% of the lower-income group does). Even people in this group have their senses *exercised* in a way that makes them able (and eager) to cope with quite different sets of stimuli than their predecessors. According to experiments done by the U.S. Navy, for example, a child of four-and-a-half today (i.e. who hasn't yet been to school) has the *awareness* of a seven-year-old of twenty years ago.

So much for the statistics, all twenty-five of them, sprinkled through the 2,000 words of prose with which I have tried to indicate the extent of the changes that separate the past from the present; and, if we are on the continuum of change that Alvin Toffler's *Future Shock* describes, that also separates the present from the future.

Expressing the equation of change in a mathematical sense it is simply that $W \times I = ?$, where wealth represents the wealth explosion and I the information explosion. The unpredictability of the interaction I and W tend to make the consequences not only unexpected, but also so large that, for reasons which will become clearer when the cognitive dissonance theory is explained in a later chapter, many people in business and advertising find them unacceptable. It is this, perhaps, as well as sheer short-sighted bloodymindedness, which explains their non-response to the new consumer.

For what is inconceivable is by definition unacceptable. And though, if you take many of the consequences of $W \times I$ separately they appear harmless and of the nothing-but-good-can-come-out-of-it variety, yet when multiplied together these changes pull the rug from under many of the assumptions of marketing and advertising.

The first consequence of W x I which has both this effect and this reaction is its impact on what used to be called the 'generation gap'. If you talk to a businessman about the 'younger generation' the typical response is to say that they differ only in degree, and not in principle, from earlier younger generations. The 'I-was-young-once' syndrome. Or, anthropologically speaking, it's the co-figurative cultural model: the second of three types of culture that Margaret Mead so perceptively described in three lectures which she gave in Washington, later reprinted in *Culture and Commitment*.

Prior to the co-figurative culture, the post-figurative culture existed: 'The only essential and defining characteristics of a post-figurative culture is that a group of people consisting of at least three generations take the culture for granted, so that a child as he grows up accepts unquestioningly whatever is unquestioned by those around him.' And so, given the lack of questioning and the lack of consciousness that makes this unquestioning possible, 'the past of the adult is the future of each new generation'.

Two key points about this post-figurative culture. First, it depends on the grandparents' presence, physically, in the world in which a child is bred. This ensures that the parent applies the culturally correct upbringing to the new-born child. Second, it doesn't mean that the inter-generational relationships are necessarily smooth: 'In some societies, each generation is expected to rebel back, to flout the express wishes of the old men and to take over power from men older than themselves.'

This sort of 'generation gap' is really a ritualized conflict avoidance. However, with the emergence of Mead's co-figurative culture, these two points change. First, the grandparents are no longer physically part of the world in which the child is bred. So 'the child's expectation of his future is shortened by a generation and his links with the past are weakening'. Second, the nature of the inter-generational gap changes. The concept of a 'generation gap' is no longer a stage through which one ritually passes on the way to senility. It is the experience that comes from living in a technologically different world from that of the parents.

The expectation of this sort of generation gap doesn't, in Miss Mead's telling phrase, 'extend to a recognition that a change between generations may be of a new order. *Children in our own and many other cultures are being reared to an expectation of change within changelessness.*' [My italics]. The conflicts inherent in such a position, incompatible not only with the findings of the seer McLuhan but also with the evidence of anthropologists and historians that changes in technology change culture, are profound.

To those who accept the co-figurative norm (even if its only expression is the I-was-young-once syndrome) the revolt of youth means one thing. But to anthropologists like Mead it means the starting of her third cultural pattern: pre-figurative culture. The particular events that trigger off revolts amongst students in China, England, Pakistan, Japan, Holland, the United States, and New Guinea are not enough to explain the revolts themselves. Mead attributes them to two new things: the emergence of a world community, which is really the product of the information explosion. And the fact that this community has emerged during the lifetime of one generation (which is really Alvin Toffler's point about the speeded up rate of change).

The result is that the generation gap becomes a great divide that may be unbridgeable. For the parental generation, life has to be lived in an environment where the eternal verities, Rolls Royce or the British Empire, are crumbling left, right and centre. One is obliged to quote from Miss Mead once more to find the very words which describe their state of mind: 'Today, everyone born and bred before World War II is an immigrant in time – as its forebears were in space – struggling to grapple with the unfamiliar conditions of life in a new era.' The immigrant in space, *par excellence,* were those who emigrated to America. 'As the children of the pioneers had no access to the memories which could still move their parents to tears, the young today cannot share their parents' response to events which deeply moved them in the past.'

And in *this* so important sense, the generation gap of 1970 is very different from the one that split the oh-so-darling flappers from their Harris-tweeded parents in the 1930s. 'Today, nowhere in the world are there elders who know what their children know. . . in the past there were always some elders who knew more than any children in terms of experience of having grown up within a cultural system. Today there are none. In this sense, we must recognize that we have no descendants as our children have no forebears.' This final quotation from Margaret Mead should be engraved in the foyer of every advertising agency in the affluent society of the world. For in just a few words it shows up the futility of trying to get your message across the generation gap by yelling louder or frugging faster. And it implies a development of an *entirely* new sort of consumer.

The consequences of the end of the myth that elders are betters will be re-structuring the market place as well as life itself for many years to come. For when the ancestral wisdom goes into the rubbish bin it takes with it many of the component parts of the society that worshipped at the temple of its forefathers.

But before we see just what life is like on the other side of the generation gap it is worth looking at just one more dimension of it in slightly more detail. If the 'generation gap' is essentially a speed up rate of change, fuelled by W x I, then (unless the rate of change starts to flag, we could expect the generation gap to widen or – which is really the same thing – for the gap to emerge in less and less time. The sociologist Daniel Bell has developed this idea further. Defining a generation as a 'category employed to point to the consciousness of difference of experience and identity in different ages'; he goes on to say that this was once a concept which was held to rest on a term of thirty years (which it still does as far as the Oxford English Dictionary is concerned), then fifteen years, more recently seven years, and most recently six months. From this reasoning, there is now sixty times as much difference between 'the generations' (in the O.E.D. sense of the words) as previously.

A society without traditions is a totally new sort of phenomenon and the mass media fills the vacuum to become the new arbiter. Or, rather, by communicating globally any new development by the *avant garde,* it diffuses and outdates innovation at electronic speed. The result of this is that the *avant garde* – be they pop musicians or shirt designers – have to search more relentlessly for another innovation. Thus ensuring that the rate of change increases in direct proportion to the rate at which change itself increases.

Alvin Toffler uses the term 'future shock' to describe the

disease that is brought about by this accelerating rate of change on those who are unable to deal with it. Adaptation to it requires developing an approach of temporariness. For by living too firmly in the present one becomes embedded in the past.

In terms of physical distance most people have managed to make the mental adaptation. We have adapted to the fact that New York is closer to us in London than York itself was to the Victorians. What we have yet to recognize in its entirety is that next year is closer to us than next month was to the Victorians. We have yet to develop in our lives, let alone in our marketing, a full recognition of how a process of continual change leads to the development of what Toffler calls 'a system of temporary encounters' (think about what that means for brand loyalty). He quotes a young co-ed at Fort Lauderdale taking part in the annual migration to the Florida beaches for what amounts to an orgy in the sand giving as one reason *for* permissiveness as 'Frankly, you'll never see these people again'. This is just a non-academic way of saying what Dr Richard Farson, Dean of the California Institute of the Arts, said in an article in the *Saturday Review* : 'The only people who can live successfully in tomorrow's world are those who accept and enjoy temporary systems.'

A philosophy that it is better to build on sand rather than rock because rock anchors you too firmly is probably horrifying to anyone over forty. It is not even very appealing to the present writer (aged twenty-seven). But it makes quite a lot of sense to his twenty-four-year-old brother. And even more to a seventeen-year-old friend of his.

In principle, a fair proportion of businessmen on both sides of the Atlantic accept the fact that the under-thirty-fives are very different from their parents in outlook, habits and way of life. But this acceptance is nearly always based on the co-figurative model of Margaret Mead rather than the pre-figurative one.

Just ten years ago even a very close observer of the best educated part of the younger generation, Kenneth Keniston (Associate Professor of Psychology at the Yale Medical School) could conclude in the *American Scholar* that 'I see little likelihood of American students ever playing a radical role, much less a revolutionary role in our society'. But seven years after this statement was published 70% of students had worked in a political campaign.

Despite this sort of evidence, even in 1972 there are still many who dispute the principle of the generation gap being anything more than a sort of intellectual acne, curable by moderate doses of hygiene and commonsense. To return to Mr Thomas Shepherd, formerly of *Look* magazine : 'The big difference between 1970 and 1940 is that today's youngsters are being listened to seriously by adults. When we were children, the adults were too smart to pay attention to us.'

Peregrine Worsthorne the quintessence of the Old School upper-class journalism, revealed another aspect of the Shepherd syndrome when he was confronted on a B.B.C. television programme about the underground press by the Editor of the *International Times*. The most interesting point about this meeting of the generations was the very different way both of them approached the subject of print journalism. For Worsthorne, there was no logical argument behind either *International Times* or its writing. Trained and reared in a pre-television age he looked for formal, definite presentation by *International Times* as to *why* they existed and *what* they were trying to do. And as they had not provided one he concluded, with some gusto, that they were *intellectually* incompetent. By contrast, the Editor of the *International Times* saw his paper in very much post-television terms. It was loose, unfocused, unstructured, informal, deliberately and precisely *without* the logical purpose that for Mr Worsthorne was the *sine qua non* of intelligent existence. *International Times* was much more, in fact, a television programme in print, a phenomenon which Worsthorne, with the Gutenberg millstone round his neck, was literally quite unable to see. So they were in fact, in Disraeli's memorable phrase, 'Two nations between whom there is no sympathy and no understanding.'

A different sort of non-dialogue was reported by Dr Norman Vincent Peale the celebrated positive thinker. If you had gone to listen to him preaching at the Central Hall, Westminster in September 1971, you would have heard another example of a well-meaning old man failing to understand the young. He told the packed congregation the story of how a long-haired hippy had sat beside him on the plane trip from New York. The hippy, having said what a lousy world it was, was apparently impressed by Dr Peale's serenity and wanted to know how the reverend doctor achieved such peace of mind. 'I refused to tell him,' related Dr Peale, 'said that there was a generation gap and that made it difficult. In the end he demanded that I tell him. Just

as the plane was coming in, I gave in. "I've got peace of mind",
I said, "from Jesus". He didn't say a thing. He just got off the
seat and started to go. I thought I'd lost him. Then he turned
round and said: "Look Mister, thanks a lot. I might just buy
that sometime". Had I argued with him about theology or on
some other level', concluded Dr Peale, 'I would have lost him. I
talked about Jesus. That grabbed him.'

To generalize from one example of a 'Jesus Freak' and believe
that the Power of Positive Thinking is sufficient to make a
middle-aged nonconformist minister speak the same language as
a member of the groupy commune from Long Island is, to say
the least, overambitious. But Dr Peale is not alone in his opti-
mism. In a less godly form it is a feeling shared by many well
meaning businessmen. That nothing separates the young from
the old except separation itself.

That was certainly the message of a Gallup survey commissioned by *Look* magazine on the mood of America. Their finding
was that on virtually every issue the views of teenagers coincided
with those of adults. And on those issues where the kids did *not*
see eye to eye with their elders the youngsters tended to be more
conservative.

But a rather more detailed survey of Daniel Yankelovich for
Fortune magazine told a different story. They found *both* a
generation gap *and* an educational gap. That is, though there
was a clear gap in attitudes between parent and child, there
was an even more marked gap between parents of non-college
children and parents of college children. For example, only 25%
of college students thought it was 'worth fighting a war to defend
a nation's honour' compared to just 35% of the parents of
college students. But *twice as many* – 59% of non-college students
agreed with this and their parents were close to their children's
attitudes, with a score of 67%.

This extra division *between* parents of the same generation
suggests that different groups in society adapt to change better
(or at least quicker) than others. And that education is as much
a borderline between people as when they were born. Perhaps
one should extend Daniel Bell's definition of generation in terms
of 'a consciousness of differences of experience and identification' to include 'of education'. Certainly it would give Dr Peale
more hope to know that the long-haired hippy he sat beside was

a Phi Beta Kappa *cum laude* like himself (or whatever intellectual distinction he has).

But though there is a measure of consolation in this view there is also a measure of folly. For the likelihood is that the parents, living on the co-figurative model, tend to feel closer to the child than the child, living on the pre-figurative one, does to the parent. Those students whose attitude was dubbed 'forerunner' by these researchers, in that they judged them to be the shape of things to come, felt a greater sense of solidarity and identification with other students *than with their own parents.* The question wasn't put the other way round, but one would predict that – despite the attitude of their own student children – these parents would still profess to have more solidarity with their own children than with other parents.

Taking youth in general (college and non-college) Pan-Am's research into their attitudes found that the lure of the youth charter trip was not based solely on price. They also preferred the idea of sharing a plane with people of their own age, instead of middle-aged fat-cats from the Mid-West (or for that matter the Marble Collegiate Church, New York). Though parents, no doubt, would be less unhappy travelling on these flights.

There are other examples where one can see the pre-figurative cultural notion that the child is father of the man starting to operate. Teenage and parental values are starting to exist in the home on a basis of equal power and validity, thus echoing on an inter-personal level the structural redistribution of authority we spoke of in chapter one.

One very simple case is that the mother can no longer tell the daughter what to do in the cosmetic field: the daughter tells the mother. And when the daughter gets married, she tends to move away from an impersonal external authority imposing a sanctity on marriage and see it as a profession of mutual faith to be covered by the implicit caveat 'till boredom us do part'. In doing so she may well be ungluing her parents' marriage: be sure it is not the older generation that is setting the young a bad example, but vice versa.

It will probably not be possible for the twain ever to meet on exactly the same attitudes (for instance in the Yankelovich survey, 56% of forerunner students reckoned their parents were respectful persons in authority compared to 4% reckoning that they themselves were).

What is really happening is that the under-twenty-fives are presenting their elders with a set of non-negotiable demands. They are not demands which will wither if left unanswered. Nor can their questioners be relied on to mellow as wrinkles replace the exuberant freckles as did earlier rebels.

It is worth examining the philosophy of this group in a little more detail because a company's success or failure in understanding the young consumers in the seventies will determine its own success or failure as a business.

One way to reach an understanding of what makes the under twenty-fives tick is to take off your pin-stripe, and deck yourself out in slightly less constricting attire (in terms of your personality as much as your body), buy a copy of *Time Out* and wend your way round the underground (and I don't mean the tube). It was this approach that William D'Eath adopted in 1971 when, on behalf of the B.B.C., he carried out this mission to unknown lands to reveal to Balding Man what lay behind the long hair.

A more practical approach is to take out a subscription to one of the more entertaining underground newspapers, like *International Times* or *Rolling Stone*. Or if you want a more coherent analysis of what this group 'stands for' (which you will not receive from themselves) Charles Reich's *The Greening of America* will fortify the over-forties' understanding of those who had the good fortune to be born twenty years after them.

Reich's thesis concerns the reasons why and the ways in which a gap has grown between those who are willing to accept the conventional rule provided by the established social order and those who reject it all and seek instead a new basis for reorganizing the system to be more rewarding (in a non-fictional sense). Using the term 'consciousness' to mean 'a total configuration in any given individual which makes up his whole perception of reality, his whole world view', Reich postulates three grades: Consciousness I, Consciousness II, and Consciousness III.

The first of these is the psyche of smalltown America, the farmer, the small businessman believing in simple virtues and having simple vices: a competitive individualism that persuades him to love his neighbour only so long as he is beating him.

Industrialization, with the development of the market system where the individual is replaced from a central role by the organization, led to the development of the second sort of Consciousness. Consciousness II is the Protestant work-ethic, the liberal concept of the public state (typified by the New Deal, the philosophy of rationality). But it has taken the individualism of Consciousness I and adapted it to the demands of the machine to the point where 'work and living have become more and more pointless and empty. For most Americans work is mindless, exhausting, boring, servile and hateful while 'life' is confined to 'time off'. Consciousness II is a world in which nearly everybody over twenty-five lives.

Reich's requiem to it is both sensitive and sympathetic: 'Consciousness II is the victim of a cruel deception. It has been persuaded that the richness, the satisfaction, the joys of life are to be found in power, excess, status, acceptance, popularity, achievements, rewards, excellence and the rational competent mind. It wants nothing to do with dread, awe, wonder, mystery, accidents, failure, helplessness, magic. It has been deprived of the search for self that only these experiences make possible. And it has produced a society that is the image of its own alienation and impoverishment.'

The alternative society or counter-culture to a way of life that is nasty and brutish and long is Consciousness III. The central fact about Consciousness III, writes Reich, is 'its assertion of the power to choose a way of life'. This means a total, and unfettered, willingness to experiment with the possibilities of life (and even – as in the case of drugs – the possibilities of death): 'In the world that now exists a life of surfing *is* possible not as an escape from work, a recreation or a phase, but as a *life* if one chooses. The fact that this choice is actually available is a truth that the young generation knows and the older generation cannot know.' It is this which really separates Dr Peale from the long-haired hippy beside him on the transatlantic plane.

And those who reject the life that business brings are also going to reject the pay-packets with which it lures you. So it should be no surprise that of the Harvard Class of 1968 only 6% decided to go into business after graduation. The old choice for those who didn't like the society they found themselves in was sin or cynicism. But Consciousness III instead of just breaking the rules, actually challenges them.

Why Consciousness III should have developed among the

120

young is only clear if one considers whom the W x I equation would work on first. Youth in the past hasn't generally proved itself any more of a hotbed of innovation than any other age group. Christianity, for example, wasn't a Youth Movement. Neither was Communism in its original form. But the ever-watchful electronic eye of television has helped the under twenty-fives to see through pretence and hypocrisy with a corrosive ease that was not common in the past.

And, of course, the chief harbingers of hypocrisy and pretence, or at least the most visible and the most voluble ones, are the advertising men. Briefly, for it is something I shall return to later, the advertising men have helped the destruction of Consciousness II by scenting the life it offers with perfumes that don't belong to it. The products not only claimed too central a role in the life of the consumer; they attempted to justify that role by promising in return benefits, like sex, status and excitement, which they just weren't able to deliver.

At a factual level the wash simply isn't whiter, the razor blade isn't sharper, the food isn't tastier. And at an emotional level, even when the product performs as promised, all it has got is its performance. For the icing of sexual innuendo is found by the new consumer to be a thin and unsatisfying diet. Pan-Am showed a young couple in a dreamy island scene with the head-line 'The time is now. The girl is your wife'. But all that your money is buying is an airline ticket. Your appetite, however, is not satisfied and you're left somewhere between arousal and orgasm – which as Masters and Johnson will tell you isn't the best place to be.

'Advertising', observes Reich, 'is designed to create, and does create, dissatisfaction. But dissatisfaction is no mere toy, it is the stuff of revolution.' For revolution to work and be more than fairground antics, there needs to be some degree of popular support amongst the populace. And to what extent can one say that the Consciousness III syndrome is accepted by a significant part of either British or American society?

First of all, the section which has the strongest hold is without doubt the under twenty-fives. And the under twenty-fives are 46% of American society and 38% of British society. The majority of the under twenty-fives are students. Taking the American population as a whole, one person in four is a student.

And one student in six is in college. The normal assumption is that the attitudes of Consciousness III are only present amongst the college population and then only amongst a tiny minority of them. But this, in fact, is just one of those pieces of conventional wisdom that trip off the tongues of the Spiro Agnews of this world. As for the college population itself, the Yankelovich survey showed that 40% of them – that's 2½ million Americans – had *already* adopted a Consciousness III point of view. And though their non-college buddies may disagree with them as to when a nation's honour should be defended; how that nation should treat its young citizens is something they see much more eye to eye on. The strikes at the General Motors factory at Lordstown is a practical demonstration that you don't have to have majored in philosophy to reject the work-style that your father and grandfather so meekly accepted.

Lordstown is probably the most automated consumer goods factory in the world. It has robot welding machines called 'unimates', a computer which works out the automated production flow, it can produce 100 cars an hour, and each of the workers has to spend only 35 seconds on each assigned task – which is where the problem lies. For the workers at Lordstown, who are typical of the new breed that will be coming into factories in all affluent societies, are striking for more interesting and responsible work, work that doesn't treat them as a machine. These young workers are not motivated by the Puritan work ethic one tiny bit. This shows clearly in the form their protest action takes: not just refusing to work but actually engaging in Luddite-like sabotage on the cars they're meant to be making (in fact the Chevrolet Vega). Seats are slashed, paintwork is deliberately scratched, gear levers are bent out of shape, etc. And this total alienation from their work even goes so far as telling people not to buy the Vega because it's a 'lousy car'.

In case you think this reaction is just a result of G.M.'s bad handling of their personnel, listen to a recent report of the National Industries Conference Board: 'Today's younger, better educated worker is unenthused by dull, repetitive, and dirty work in factories. Today's worker puts his personal life ahead of his work. A good percentage of the workforce has seen nothing but affluence since earliest childhood. He is younger and far less hungry than his depression-scarred parents and is willing to skip

a day or two to convert a weekend into a four-day holiday.'
Charles Reich could hardly have said it better.

The Lordstone rebellion has an extra significance in that these
young workers were not only well-educated, they were also well
off: 'My take home pay is $140 a week and sometimes $260
a week and that makes G.M. a goldmine,' said one young worker
there.

To some critics of youth the fact that these prosperous ones
are the ones that are dropping out demonstrates 'modern youth's'
ingratitude and selfishness. And when this criticism is applied
specifically to the upper classes it is to suggest, always with an
undertone of venom, that this 'dropping out' is no more than a
fashionable activity akin to scuba diving off Nassau or making
the Grand Tour of Europe. What these criticisms overlook, and
it's something to be explored in more detail in a later chapter, is
that it's just these very people who *have* been born with a silver
spoon in their mouths, who have been fattened and cherished by
all that money can buy, whose career patterns – be they on the
factory floor or in the executive suite – stretch glowingly and
enticingly ahead, it is *these* who are the ones saying 'No'.

Previous 'drop-outs', going back as far as the Protestant funda-
mentalists of seventeenth-century England, were not those who
had everything and decided it wasn't for them. They were
generally those who had not got everything and *in that position*
decided to try to build their own Utopias. It is this that gives
the real significance to the development of Consciousness III in
America. For the fact that the typical drop-out is an Ivy League
WASP carries with it the suggestion that the more educated (in
every sense) the young generation becomes and the greater the
amount of wealth and abundance that is showered on it, the
higher will be the proportion who *reject* all this and decide
instead to explore the possibilities of life in a way that is quite
outside the framework of Consciousness II.

But it's not only on the other side of the generation gap that
a new consumer is emerging. The forty-year-old Mum may not
look as revolutionary as her freaked-out teenage son, but she
is part of a revolution whose short-term effects may be even
greater than the latter's remodelling of our society. Mrs 1972
may not have been reared by television but she has still seen
40,000 hours of it. She may not be as transformed as her son by

the wealth explosion but she is still fundamentally changed. And so she is starting to question her role in society in a deeper more serious way than bra-burning with Women's Lib. She is finding that she can no longer fit into her mother's shoes. But what can she put on instead?

The question that Mrs 1972 is herself facing is the one to which our attention now turns.

7

§ Birth of the New Consumer: the Housewives Who Discovered They Were Women

America is not called a matriarchy without good reason. Between two-fifths and four-fifths of all consumer purchases (depending on whose estimate you believe) are under their watchful eyes. And on this side of the Atlantic the hand that rocks the cradle is not without its power. For by controlling the household purse it decides the fate of many companies within the land. If these supermarket shoppers were to be infected by any of the new heresies; if they started in significant numbers to reject the traditional role that society asks them to perform, then those companies whose fortunes are geared to that role would need to change gear.

The evidence that precisely this sort of role rejection is occurring is not just dependent on the fevered antics of Women's Lib. One can no more rely on Kate Millet's sexual politics as being an expression of feeling amongst women than accept Karl Marx's *Das Kapital* as a fair reflection of the feelings of the British working class at the end of the nineteenth century.

Fortunately liberationist diatribes have stimulated a fair amount of serious research into housewifery in the second half of the twentieth century. Perhaps the most exhaustive (and sometimes the most exhausting) of these is Helena Lopata's twelve-year study of housewives in various Chicago suburbs, *Occupation Housewife*. Mrs Lopata detected three sorts of housewives in her studies. The first was the traditional-restricted housewife who was relatively uneducated, home-bound in a non-creative sense, often deprived of anyone to be close to, not very successful with her children and feeling – as a result of all this – rather inadequate.

The second type she calls the 'uncrystallized' wife. As a young child and schoolgirl, indeed right up to the time she married, the uncrystallized wife had what Mrs Lopata calls a 'multi-dimensional role', i.e. she was heavily involved in various different levels of activity like work, school, clubs, and family. Because she's been taught that these are things that cannot survive the arrival of marriage (and certainly not the arrival of children) she carries out her temporary multi-dimensional role without at the same time building up a multi-dimensional personality. Hence her collapse into the home-bound world at a later stage, but it's a collapse that carries with it profound resentment and hence tension. For once the children are past the nursery age she then has time and energy available. But – apart from the return to work – there is no accepted role into which they can be channelled.

Those housewives who manage to retain their multi-dimensional role *within* marriage and children form the third, and smallest, category of housewives identified by Mrs Lopata. This one is likely to 'define home-making as extending into the community, mothering as utilizing all societal facilities to expand the world beyond, wifehood as many-levelled involvement in the various social roles of the husband'.

The language of the sociologist isn't always the easiest to grasp, but I think the essential direction of Mrs Lopata's remarks are clear enough. The multi-dimensional role is an outward-looking role, using the home only as a *base* to do a wide variety of things, a variety which is not possible within the normal career vocational structure. Mrs Lopata's types of housewives are, of course, drawn from a society which, by European standards, is predominantly middle-class. It is arguable that British, or French, or German society is still predominantly working-class as the various studies on the slowness of the process of embourgeoisement make clear. And this implies that these middle-class models might not apply on this side of the Atlantic.

But if you look at Hannah Gavron's study of *The Captive Wife* it's clear that the essential characteristics of the three types of housewife is probably as true in working-class Europe as in middle-class America. Of course, there are differences. British working-class wives, for example, are much more dominated by the building they live in than middle-class wives. Equality within marriage means *independence* for middle-class wives and *equality* for working-class wives. But the differences between the classes in the matter of housewifery are more in the particular arena in which their similar sorts of problems are acted out. And the extent to which they have managed to find solutions to them. It may be, for example, that working-class wives are in the phase of shifting from a traditional role to the uncrystallized one, whereas for the middle-class wife the normal shift is from the uncrystallized role to the multi-dimensional one. But the important point, which this sort of difference should not be allowed to hide, is that the direction of change is the same, even though the pace of change may be different. And anyone who is planning to woo the gentler sex in the next ten years, and the advertising and marketing industry will be amongst the most prominent suitors, probably needs a fuller description of the ways in which the targets for their affection are changing.

What keeps a fair proportion of women clutching to their traditional role? Well first of all there is a whole web of cultural assumptions that leaves Mrs 1972 trapped like a fly on a sticky filament. These assumptions state two things. First that a woman's place is in the home, and second that this home is a place for routine, unimaginative, not mentally stimulating activities by a creature who understands neither her husband's career nor her children's future (as soon as they are old enough to escape from the apron strings).

This is not just an assumption of western culture. In Japan though the housewives' consumer groups are more active than in any advanced society, they do not challenge the traditional role for women. For them her place is still in the home. And probably if Social Research Inc. had asked Japanese housewives to complete the sentence 'My family most appreciate me when...' 90% would have given an answer that had to do with *cooking*, just like their American soul-partners.

These blue-rinsed ladies revealed in 1971, in a poll for Virginia Slim Cigarettes, that Baby hadn't come such a long way after all. It showed that most American women saw themselves as 'home bodies' and considered housekeeping and child-raising 'more rewarding than having a job'. Which confirmed a report published in the 1965 *Sociological Review* that 56% of housewives in Britain thought their task of providing food and looking after the home 'compared reasonably' with the interest and satisfaction of their husbands' jobs.

But both these studies, which do something to confirm the sales manager's belief that Women's Lib. is just a lot of nonsense confined to over-educated and under-sexed Amazons residing within six miles of Piccadilly Circus, even these contain the seeds of doubt.

In the British survey *almost a third* thought they got a worse deal than their husbands, and in the American survey *over 40%* said they would welcome a broader role in society. Both these figures point to tension even within the traditional role. What keeps it, for the most part, under control, is the tremendous effect of all the years of having been told that the woman's place is in the home. Who, after all, learns Domestic Science at school (when in the end 41% of the boys will be involved in cooking when they become husbands)? Who gets strange looks from her school mates and often her parents if she's interested in 'books' (isn't that just for plain fat girls who aren't popular?) and so on and so forth.

Paradoxically, Women's Liberationists like Betty Friedan, probably reinforce the dominance of the traditional role when they write as though work for money is the only worthy alternative to it. As one will see in a moment, work is certainly a popular escape route from being chained to the sink. But for the very reason that nearly all the militant ladies are also career women they can hardly help but write in a way which justifies *their* desertion of the hearth for the office. In short, by going out of the home to fulfil themselves these ladies are endorsing the cultural assumption that there is nothing really worthwhile a woman can do by staying at home.

Once a young girl has left school and started to act as her traditional role commands, she is then subjected to a bombardment of reinforcing propaganda to ensure that she doesn't stray from the path that others have chosen for her. Chief amongst them are the well-phrased words of the advertisers. It is probably naïve to blame businessmen for trying to profit from a situation which they had no direct hand in creating as, for example, is the fevered cry of Miss Friedan: 'Somehow, somewhere, someone must have figured out that women would buy more things if they were kept in the under-used nameless-yearning-to-get-rid-of state of being housewives.'

128

Miss Friedan is driven to this conclusion by the absurd reports of the motivation researchers of how to sell to women (whereas, in fact, all that was being sold was the motivation researchers themselves). She described a survey reporting in the mid-fifties that the day's woman 'finds in housework a medium of expression for her femininity and her individuality'. To support this, the job of advertising, apart from stamping out that growing evil influence – the graduate career woman – is to justify her menial task by building up her role as 'the protector of the family – the killer of millions of microbes and germs...emphasize her king-pin role in the family, help her be an expert rather than a menial worker ...'

The result of all this, gentle reader, would be that 'losing herself in her work – surrounded by all the implements, creams, powders, soaps – she forgets for a time how soon she will have to re-do the task ... she seizes the moment of completion of a task as a moment of pleasure as if she had just finished a masterpiece of art to stand as a monument to her credit for ever'.

Even for a woman stuck in the rut of her traditional role, feeling incompetent without having a satisfying concept of competence to move towards, this is highly provocative. She knows that shining the furniture with lemon-scented polish does no more than get the furniture clean. But worse than that, there is in the corner of her living room a small square screen which tells her, that all the cleaning, polishing, sweeping, mending that she does is trivial and peripheral compared to what goes on in the big wide world. And that square screen is, of course the television set.

It is bad enough that ageing poets and blind visionaries can write such absurdities (the filing cabinets of the biggest agencies are crammed with thousands more examples of such statements). The tragedy is that businessmen have taken their soothsayers seriously.

On some traditional housewives, the effect of this propaganda must have been to restrict them to their traditional role, but on others it may have helped to push them over the threshold towards the second of Mrs Lopata's ladies, the uncrystallized housewife. For the traditional housewife it is reality itself which provides the core of tension. But for the uncrystallized housewife it is the gap *between* reality and the ideal that is more disturbing. Why has this gap grown so large, and what – if anything – can this woman do about it?

In the traditional role, she perhaps didn't have contentment. She did at least find a sort of passive joy in acquiescing. A woman's lot had always been hard and it was her job to make the best of it. But the uncrystallized lady is not so easily quietened. *Time* magazine reported four out of five German hausfraus were fed up with housekeeping, despite the glossy encrustations forced on it by the advertising industry. Indeed, Mrs Lopata makes the shrewd point that the existing cultural and social structure has both created the ideal and *thwarted* the realization of it. For it provides a definite, uneventful life cycle where a woman reaches her full mental growth by the age of marriage and where thereafter she expresses herself through others (be they husband, children or relatives) rather than through herself. Unless she is an exceptional lady (and by definition the average lady is not exceptional) she finds it hard to stop her horizons shrinking, simply as a defence mechanism trying to narrow the gap between ideal and reality.

A young Women's Lib. member gave a concise expression of this disillusionment when she said 'a marriage certificate and a bulge turn you into a non-person' (*Nova*). The marriage and the bulge, in actual fact, have just as much impact on the husband's *leisure* activities as on the wife. The two tables opposite show the impact of first marriage, then children, on the different things men and women are able to do with their leisure time. It shows that both made just about an equal sacrifice. But leisure time is still a small proportion of total time. And there are two changes within the home itself which have meant that women are called upon to change their lives on marriage and the arrival of children far more than are men.

First, as Philippe Aries observed in *Centuries in Childhood,* the location of the home in relation to society has changed. Prior to the eighteenth century the home was indeed an open house, a centre of social life. It was only in the eighteenth century that homes became closed-off private places of family residence and not places of public meeting as well. It may be, as Marshall McLuhan has suggested, that it was the invention of the printed book which introduced the concept of reading to oneself and with it the concept of privacy in the home. Prior to this invention manuscript books meant reading aloud to others, a public activity. In this context is worth noting that television has had an influence

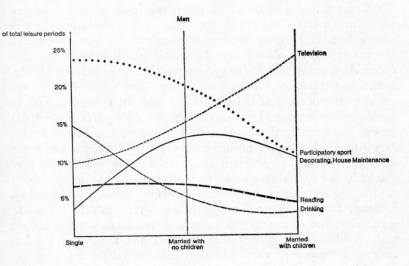

Men

of total leisure periods

25%
20%
15%
10%
5%

Television

Participatory sport
Decorating, House Maintenance

Reading
Drinking

Single   Married with no children   Married with children

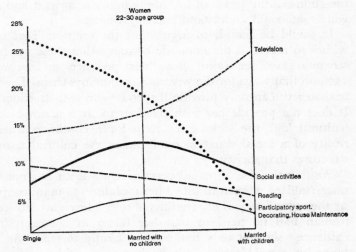

Women
22-30 age group

28%
25%
20%
15%
10%
5%

Television

Social activities

Reading

Participatory sport.
Decorating, House Maintenance

Single   Married with no children   Married with children

These two tables, derived from *Social Trend*, show that contrary to popular belief men (at least those in the 22 to 30 age group) make as much sacrifice in their leisure time as a result of marriage and their first child as their wives. If anything, the wife is better off—having a high proportion of her leisure time in social activities when she is married with one child than when she was single. But the man's main social activity, drinking, has gone down from 15% to 4% of his leisure time when he becomes a father.

131

on developing *group* activity (not private like a book or public like a manuscript) which is reflected in the rise of open plan rooms.

As well as the withdrawal of the home (and hence the housewife) from society, the other change in its function concerns not leisure but work. Prior to industrialization, the home was also the workplace for almost all adults, and it still is today in agricultural societies. But industry removed the workplace from the home and transferred it to the factory. The result is that ever since then woman has lost an empire without finding a role. It is this loss of a sense of usefulness which strikes particularly hard at our uncrystallized woman. For not only is she out of a job, but industry is for ever finding new ways to put her out of work at home. Tinned, frozen and dehydrated foods that can be prepared in twenty painless minutes, ready-to-wear clothes that need no making. Stockings that need no darning, shirts which need no ironing, floors that need no polishing, detergents that obviate scrubbing, not to mention a battery of polishers, whisks, mixers and blenders to complete the life of ease. And the Pill even takes away the unwanted extra children that added on ten years to the child-rearing phase of her life (where she at least had a role, which she could understand and appreciate).

It would be foolish to argue that the uncrystallized woman wishes to revert to the domestic bondage that these mechanical servants save her from. But their presence underscores the vacuum that waits for the woman that employs them. The industrial society can only provide the housewife with freedom from. It does not provide her with freedom to. It is a simple case of 'cultural lag', the sociologist's term for a condition where the reality of a social situation outdistances the cultural norm that structures that society.

Possibly the rise of sexual permissiveness is an attempt by the uncrystallized woman to prove her usefulness to man, confronted by the redundancy of her traditional role. The eighteenth-century woman had no need to tout her fanny as a reason for her existence – she not only had a large family to rear; she had a home to run (Mrs Beeton's book was a guide to household management not just cooking). As well as her husband's work to help with. But if you rob a woman of all her traditional roles, what is left to her but a non-reproductive use of her reproductive organs? In this, as in several of the partial responses to her problem, she may only be digging herself deeper into the rut.

Because the probable net result is that the last bastion of her role, the institution of marriage, begins to shake. In some ways this may not be a bad thing, but within the current assumptions that probably still leaves our uncrystallized lady no closer to crystallization. And it certainly leaves her with the worst deal; Desmond Morris in *The Naked Ape*, for example, reported that though by the age of forty 26% of married women will have engaged in extra-marital copulation, 50% of married men will have done so.

If sex isn't the best way an uncrystallized woman can fill the vacuum within herself, what is left to her? She can try to make her humble home rather more 'creative'. What else is it that makes the two of the most successful part-works in Britain the Cordon Bleu Cookery Course and the Golden Hands Needlework series? Why do over half the homes in the country have a sewing machine when ready-to-wear clothes come in amazing ranges, lots of sizes, and at reasonable prices? All these are examples of the uncrystallized woman trying to express herself through the existing system. But the main way, of course, is to go out to work.

The sad irony of expressing oneself as a housewife through leaving the house is lost upon those who clock in with their menfolk every day. And one third of all wives are now clocking in (compared to one tenth a decade ago). By 1979 there will be 50% more women working than there were in 1959 (even though the overall size of the work force will only have increased by 16%). And two-thirds of these women will be married, and their average age will be around forty. For having finished with bringing up children they are vigorously reacting against the prospect of being thrust onto the scrap heap.

Perhaps even more interesting than the high percentage of married women who work, is the percentage of married women who don't work but would like to. Viola Klein in *Britain's Married Women Workers* found that 46% of the housewives she interviewed who didn't work either full or part time, wished they did. Two years later (in 1966) Hannah Gavron found that the figure for non-working working-class wives who wished they did was 68% and for non-working middle-class wives was 75%.

What keeps many of these women at home against their wishes is the wishes of their husband and their worry about the effect of leaving home on the children. This is more a worry for Europeans than for Americans, twice as many of whom approve of a mother of children at school going out to work. Certainly, the evidence is that the woman who takes on a passive home-bound role 'because of the children' is misguided. The Swedish sociologist Teller concludes that 'the decisive factor is probably the quality of the contact between parents and the children rather than the quantity'. And he argues that there is a distinct risk in over-emphasizing the traditional role of a mother, on the grounds that this can lead ultimately to over-protected over-dependent children who have difficulties to adjusting to their adult role. One half of the uncrystallized woman knows this. But the other half is still vulnerable to the sort of remark made to a career woman: 'I suppose you won't mind when your baby doesn't recognize you' (quoted in the P.E.P. Publication, *Sex, Career and the Family*).

The sort of woman who makes this remark may refuse to separate herself from her child by sending herself to work. But, strangely enough, she is generally far less unhappy to send the child away to boarding school for an equal and some might argue more harmful separation. Separating a parent and child for educational reasons is accepted within the cultural norm but parental and child separation for work reasons is less accepted. And the argument about the effect on the child is really an alibi for a confused, unfocused feeling that is not fully able to express itself.

This confusion about her role shows through clearly if you probe and find out *why* a woman works. Very often she'll talk first about the financial advantages. But the evidence is that money is as much an alibi for working as children are an alibi for staying at home. Viola Klein found that about the *same proportion* of AB class as C class married women did full-time work. If money were really the main reason one would expect the figure for the C class housewives to be higher than the figure for the A class housewives (after all the latter has the household income of around double the former). And this point was confirmed by Katona's study from America showing that the higher her education the more a married woman plans to go on working *even though* the husband's higher than average income makes it increasingly unnecessary.

If it's not money that lures housewives from the hearth, it is also certainly not the sort of job they'll be going to. Only 13% in Viola Klein's survey mentioned 'enjoy work/doing a useful job' as their reason. Which is hardly surprising if you look at the jobs that are available for married women: they tend to be the least well-paid and the least attractive. Added to which is the fact that women generally get a raw deal in employment compared to the men (for instance half of all men workers are in a pension scheme compared to a quarter of all women workers).

In fact, by going out to work our uncrystallized housewife will be exposing herself to a set of cross-tensions as unsatisfying as if she stayed at home. As the jobs she'll accept indicate, she's desperate. She is caught like a nut in a nutcracker between a whole series of cultural norms, and whatever solution she adopts she will not find peace of mind. She feels that to go out to work is to some extent an indication that as a woman she's failing as a housewife. But if she stays at home she feels that she still can't find success for herself as a housewife.

Before one looks at the third group of housewives who have more successfully resolved this issue, it is perhaps worth pausing just to comment on one aspect of this conflict situation. To quantify matters; out of 18 million British housewives about 6 million work; 6 million don't work but wish they did (extrapolating Klein's sample on a national scale); and 6 million don't work and express no wish to. The uncrystallized women will be found primarily in the first two groups (i.e. representing up to two-thirds of housewives) and the last group will contain the traditional housewives (who are thus no more than a third of all married women).

But the picture of housewives presented by the advertising industry is rather different. It tends to present a housewife as though carrying out the traditional role was still the norm. Who would ever guess by looking at the television commercials that one woman in three worked?

And even when change is recognized, its real driving force remains unidentified. Few observe that the revolt is *from* the one sort of role *rather than* an eager adoption of another. So a cigarette tells women 'You've come a long way, Baby', making the assumption that modern woman is eagerly adopting a male career posture. That, after all, is the mythology of Women's Lib. But if we have approximately half the female population believing they might have come a long way but they really haven't got anywhere important then the message of the advertiser will not only be ineffective, it will be provocative.

The arrival in society of large numbers of multi-dimensional women (particularly young women entering the market place reared in a very different media environment to their parents) implies a further gap between the presentation of the dream and actual reality.

What the multi-dimensional woman is endeavouring to do is to sort out the confusion that results from a situation where the traditional role becomes clearly impossible and where there is no alternative role available instead. It is thus an exploratory and experimental role. It is also, for the moment, a minority role. When Mrs Lopata asked housewives to rank various of their roles (like daughter, housewife, wife) they all tended to rank the role of wife and the role of mother ahead of the role of woman. And even before the role of woman (with only the roles of grandmother and sister behind it) comes the role of housewife.

In so far as the multi-dimensional woman finds fulfilment in a radically different approach to the role of housewife, and that she's doing this for herself (as a woman) rather than doing it for others (as a wife or mother) the ranking of these two roles is a fair index of the spread of the multi-dimensional role. The multi-dimensional role, of course, is not what any of the militant bra-burners would regard as 'liberated'. For liberation in a multi-dimensional sense begins at home. Free contraception, abortion on demand and twenty-four-hour nurseries – the key plans of most Women's Lib. cells – may be worthwhile demands but they are demands in a different dimension. For unless she has a role to expand into, answering these demands only removes inconveniences in her life, and thus makes her more aware than ever of its true emptiness.

One of the earlier breeding grounds of multi-dimensional woman was the suburbs of America in the late fifties and early sixties. Young marrieds migrated away from the traditional controls on their behaviour, and started to look for like-minded neighbours to sort out the problems that left their uncrystallized sisters so baffled.

If one recalls Margaret Mead's co-figurative cultural model, Mrs Lopata's statistics of the reduced influence of the mother on this new suburban housewife is revealing. Whereas half the working housewives and two-fifths of urban housewives referred to their mothers as a source of knowledge after entrance into the home-making world, only one-quarter of suburban housewives saw their mothers as such a helpful influence. (Incidentally, the figures for working wives echo the point that the working woman is still stuck in the rut of the traditional world). 'Their grandmother had tradition,' observes Lopata of runaway marrieds, 'these revolutionaries only have each other'.

In a structural sense, the multi-dimensional role that these women created for themselves resembled both their lives before marriage and also the lives lived by upper-class women in European society. Many of the current ways of multi-dimensional middle-class society are adapted from the upper-class European cultural norm. Their dinner parties, their afternoons of sports, the evenings of conversational music where husbands and wives both have a role, contrasts with the sex-segrated leisure life in lower-class cultures. Men going out to the boozer and leaving the wives behind is a very common but simple example. (In this sense, for all its low-brow connotations, an evening spent with all the family watching television is a real descendant of the upper-class Victorian family sitting round the piano while the eldest daughter sang Schubert).

That Mrs 1972 is starting to move towards the sort of multi-dimensional role enjoyed by Lady 1772 shouldn't surprise us. The penetration levels of material goods in our society gives today's working man a standard of life that the professional middle classes of 1950 were yearning after. It is only a short step from this to argue that the life of leisure and cutural ease that was once for the few is now to be for the many (for what other reason have men been revolting and struggling all this time?).

What happened, however, is that we are approaching a situation where we have the resources to provide this life for the many but only the few have the necessary understanding of the difference between 'leisure' and 'boredom' to benefit from it.

The average businessman has no better understanding of the consequences of a shift from being home-bound to merely home-based in his customer. Here are just three examples of the sort of consequences one can reasonably expect from this shift.

The first of these is a changed position *vis-à-vis* the husband within the family unit. The multi-dimensional woman drops the traditional role where she was basically the one who prepared the bread paid for by the bread-winner. One of the implicit assumptions that held this belief in place was that in a money-based economy an occupation that doesn't earn money has neither value nor status. As housewifery is an occupation for which no pecuniary reward is made (until, ironically, divorce breaks up the household) it was kept in the traditional role in a defensive and cringing posture. The multi-dimensional woman has gone past this stage. Even taking Mrs Lopata's sample as a whole (consisting of all three types of housewives) two-thirds of the men assisted in making the purchases needed to run the house. (A family that pays together, stays together.) And this figure will increase as the traditional role, where women purchase all the household goods, withers away.

The consequence of this development means that housewifery instead of being the housewives' *raison-d'être* becomes no more than a chore which is to be jointly shared amongst all members of the family. And once housewifery has been put in its proper place, the sort of things which will interest the housewife will no longer come in little plastic boxes with plastic roses attached. So the advertising and marketing process, unless it changes tack, will be thrust into a peripheral position, offering the consumer things which are no longer of importance to her. This is a line of thought to be explored in more detail in the next chapter. But it does introduce a second practical consequence of the existence of the multi-dimensional woman: a change of relationship not only with the bread-winner but also the bread shop.

Shopping, for a traditional woman, was a very different exercise than it is either for the multi-dimensional or uncrystallized woman. Personal contacts with the shopkeeper, and elaborate examination of the merchandise were ways of both fulfilling the roles of, and showing expertise in, being a housewife. But in looking at the supermarket explosion, the changes among housewives that make the very concept of supermarket shopping acceptable is forgotten. Supermarkets turn the bulk of routine shopping into as rapid an exercise of household management as possible. Its attraction is less time shopping and not just a smaller shopping bill (because though item for item she saves, the open shelf structure of the supermarket encourages her to buy things she would otherwise not have thought of, so the *total bill* is probably larger). Incidentally, the growth of the supermarket would have been impossible without the growth of a feeling of competence by Mrs 1972. For in going to a traditional shop she could easily ask the shopkeeper for advice. But in going to a supermarket, she has to make the decision herself: something that would not have been possible until education and the media provided her with a feeling of self-confidence.

These two consequences of developments away from the traditional role as a housewife are clearly of some importance to marketing companies. But a phenomenon of even wider significance emerges when one considers how the multi-dimensional wife will regard the one-dimensional life of her husband. By 'one-dimensional' one is talking of the career-orientated Consciousness II man (to revert to Reich's phraseology). The findings of Drs R. and J. Pahl in *Managers and their Wives* is that the multi-dimensional wife could be the Trojan Horse that starts to move her husband away from the rat race and towards Consciousness III. While their battery-manager husbands are churning away ('They have internalized an ideology of self-coercion' say the Pahls) the wives are not under the same pressure to accept the logic that seems so natural and automatic to their husbands. The Pahls found, for a start, that the majority of wives didn't wish their children to follow in father's footsteps. The 'professional life' where there is time free for wife and children, and no need to rock around the clock in Ulcer Gulch, is what these mothers want for their children. If the husbands don't have this feeling, it is because they are so trapped by the rhythm of their lives that they are unable to ask themselves the question as to whether the long hours of toil are really worth it. But the Pahls' conclusion for those who earn their living by trying to persuade the rats to scramble up one more rung of their ladder clearly is a little chilling. 'Basically, we consider that what we may be detecting is the beginning of a middle-class reaction against competition.'

The Pahls' study was concentrated on the middle classes. But their conclusions show that the stirrings of Consciousness III are not restricted to those who wear flower headbands. It may well be that this group has acted as a catalyst, and that though the majority of housewives don't want to go all the way to living in a commune of free love, they regard the solution of the hippies as being no more than an extremist version of the point of view they are beginning to hold themselves.

The fact that there are different degrees and speeds of development by consumers in this direction should not allow one to miss the central point, that there *is* development and most of the development is in this one direction.

As consumers, the under-twenty-fives and the younger house-wives are not the children of their parents. 'As consumers' is, of course, a shorthand way of saying 'in their role of consuming the goods and services created by society'. And if the consumer changes, so will her consumption. It is this changed attitude to consumption that forms the next step in our study.

8

When the Standard of Living Stops Being the Standard of Life

Uncertainty + Greed = Growth. It may not be quite as natty as $e = mc^2$, but strip the affluent society of its jargon and this is the magic formula which gives it its energy. An apparently limitless appetite for more goods and services leads to an endlessly upward spiral of consumption. Where even a stop-go economy is more go than stop.

But though the spiral is ever upwards, there is always the spectre that the golden times will end. Economists have worked out all sorts of basic rhythms for the economy, sophisticating the seven fat year, seven lean year econometric model that sufficed for the Israelites.

Thus, despite the continual sunshine, there's always the prospect of a rainy day. So, as well as increasing consumption there's also a need for savings. Savings return to the economic system as investment and stoke once more the factory furnaces which will spew out yet more products for the ever open mouths.

This is more than a theory. This is how the economies of all advanced western societies have functioned since the war. The question which has to be faced by any businessman planning his marketing effort over the next decade is whether this equation of growth can still operate? Or will the new type of consumers that are emerging with new attitudes towards business call a halt to the golden years when like Topsy the G.N.P. just grew.

Part of the answer to this question lies in the key assumptions about the Theory of Limitless Growth. The first of these was well expressed by Robert G. Merton in *Social Theory and Social*

Structure : 'In the American Dream there is no final stopping point. At each income level, Americans want just about 25% more (but, of course, this 'just a bit more' continues to operate once it is obtained). The family, school, and work place . . . join to provide the discipline required if an individual is to retain intact a goal that remains illusively beyond reach.' But for this, prosperity would be its own grave digger. However, as long as satisfaction of existing wants stimulates the arrival of new ones rather than sates them, consumers will become hungrier through feeding.

Ensuring the continuance of this apparently unnatural situation is the job, according to the theory, of the marketing industry. 'Demand management' is the phrase used by Galbraith to describe this function: 'In the absence of massive and artful persuasion', he writes in the *New Industrial State,* 'increasing abundance might well have reduced the interest of people in aquiring more goods.' And so 'advertising and its related arts helps to develop the kind of man the logic of the industrial state requires – one that reliably spends his income and works reliably because he's always in need of more'. One reason why this is possible, according to Galbraith, is that the further a man is removed from the basic physical needs – like hunger and shelter – the more he's open to persuasion as to what he should buy. Status, for instance, means little to the starving African anxious for some dried milk. But it may mean a lot more to the film starlet buying a fabulous mink stole. Conspicuous consumption, in fact, is the result of all these pressures. And America as the most advanced – or degenerate – consumer society is the one where consumption is the most conspicuous. This probably isn't just because of the corrosive influence of popcorn. Conspicuous consumption, after all, has been practised by many societies to enable one member of that society to indicate to another their relative relationships. In some parts of Africa and India women still wear all their wealth as jewellery, and so enable strangers to assess their importance very quickly.

The role of products in establishing the relative position of people in society is far more necessary in a migrant, rootless society like America than in a static European society. Income in itself can't be a status symbol because earnings are secret. So people, in the Limitless Growth theory, inform each other of their income (and hence their importance) by their purchase of

142

goods and services.

It is possible to argue from this that the increased inter-class movements in European society, and the increased physical mobility of individuals, will make this sort of 'signalling' as important in Europe in the next decade as it is in America, and so make our consumption as conspicuous as theirs. This is the unqualified conclusion (albeit one based on quite different reasoning) made by the joint winners of the I.P.A. silver award of 1968 who wrote a study of *Advertising in the Twenty–First Century* (which, incidentally, doesn't use the word consumer once). 'Over the next fifty years', they say, 'the upward spiral of "Keeping up with the Joneses" is bound to increase in intensity as it has in the United States. When the position is reached where almost everyone has a car, washing machine, refrigerator, etc., the ownership of the latest model will become supreme.' And one reason for this, according to another exponent of the Limitless Growth theory, Ronald Brech of Unilever (*Britain 1984*), is that 'basically a man is uncertain of himself, and to bolster up his own esteem he must win the esteem of others'. And this, according to the model, conspicuous consumption provides.

Brech's model of the theory has two interesting variations. First it recognizes that 'temporary satiation' may develop. That people suddenly get fed up with keeping up with the Joneses and a 'maladjustment' occurs and they decide to stay where they are. But after a couple of years, the basic urges return and the economy starts growing. According to Brech 'temporary satiation' occurred in Britain in the latter half of the nineteenth century. One of the pressures that sets the economy moving again, on this analysis, is that the product graduates from satisfying mere material needs to satisfying psychological ones and by answering the needs of the psyche, the G.N.P. once more rolls healthily forwards.

These are the assumptions on which our economy is founded. And they are, as I shall argue, founded on sand. For they are part of a theory of economic growth that was quite unable to predict the consequences of its own success.

The first of the consequences that it failed to foresee was that the economic boom wouldn't only put cars in our hands. It would put exhaust fumes in our throats. It would send suds foaming out of our taps. And with our affluence it would give us so much effluent that even rivers could spontaneously ignite.

America, of course, the society that's first with everything leads the way in per capita output of pollution. But, because of the sheer size of the country, they can absorb more before the effect shows than can the more densely peopled countries like Britain, Germany, and Japan. For example, though the amount of lead discharged by petrol exhausts from American cars is thirty-two times greater than the amount discharged by British cars, as the American land mass is thirty-eight times the size of the British one, the lead levels in Britain per square mile are 18% higher than in America. It's for this sort of reason that the first country to have brought in low lead petrol by law was car-saturated West Germany, not open-spaced America.

Another motoring invention which one tends to regard as being an exclusively American phenomenon is photochemical smog, caused by the action of sunlight on exhaust fumes and sulphur-dioxide. But it is already developing on this side of the Atlantic. A team of scientists from the Atomic Energy Research Establishment at Harwell found in the depths of the English countryside a level of photochemical smog that was as much as the daily average for smog-choked Southern California.

Another great transport innovation of the affluent society is the aeroplane. Yet before one even reaches the age of the sonic boom with Concorde, it's clear that there's more to air travel than bustling hostesses pouring out the duty-free. Dr J. B. Large of the Institute of Sound and Vibration Research has shown that nearly 30% of the population of Britain suffers from what the scientists call 'aircraft noise nuisance'. The exact meaning of this neutral sounding phrase was put into context by the Professor of Theoretical Aeronautics at London University. He calculated that a Boeing 707 jet on take-off makes as much noise *as if every person in the world shouted simultaneously as loudly as they could*. It will come as no surprise then that the study by Bauer and Greyser (to which reference will be made in chapter nine) found 'noise' the most annoying everyday event faced by Americans.

The position has probably now been reached, on both sides of the Atlantic, that if the affluent society was offered to the beneficiaries of it with the type of 'full disclosure' that Naderites demand for advertising (no holding back on information about possible harmful side effects etc.) it must be wondered if it would find many customers.

The impact of the new environment on the new consumer has been manifold. At one level, the one concentrated on the professional Doomsdayers (another parasitic sub-economy produced in our society) is a distortion of humans themselves: 'You cannot defile the air and the environment', wrote Phillipa Pullar in the London *Times*, 'without defiling the people as well, without frustrating them, lowering their performance, their literacy, their humour, their means of communication.'

The reaction of humans to this desecration of themselves and their environment is revealing. Because if people *are* being raped, they're certainly not taking it lying down. Where once school-boys collected sticklebacks in jamjars and that was an end of the matter, the children of today's environment think differently. A change in the *level* of sticklebacks could be due to that big factory up river. The *Sunday Times* certainly found a massive interest by young children in their environment. A total of 10,000 children took part in an experiment arranged by this newspaper to discover the pollution level in British waterways. One of the conclusions which stood out, according to the director of the Monks Wood Experimental Station who analysed the replies was that 'children care about pollution'.

Amongst grown-ups, a TV programme on pollution arranged by the German Study Group for System Research, using a new participatory television programme, found that 70% of the three thousand viewers who took part would be prepared to pay 10% more in taxes to deal with pollution.

In America, in 1965 only 22% of city residents thought pollution a serious problem; in 1971 they had increased to 49% and 76% of these blamed industry for it (that doesn't just mean the power station with its belching stack. It means also the factory which churns out products with power from that belching stack).

This backlash, biting the hand that has fed it with chromium plated goodies, has one more side to it. It is the realization that affluent societies are using up more than their fair share of the world's resources, the so-called spaceship earth concept. With 57% of the world's population, America currently uses 40% of the world's minerals and spews out half the world's indus-trial pollution. If we really *are* knocking at the limits of the world's natural resources, then one man's growth becomes another man's starvation.

And so a mixture of the discomforts of affluence, plus a

guilty conscience about having too large a slice of the cake, is starting to change attitudes to economic growth in a way that the Theory of Limitless Growth never predicted.

First, contrary to the theory and for the first time in the history of capitalism, economic growth is no longer an end in itself. And not just because of the parasitic sub-economy argument or the counting-the-defecation arguments reviewed earlier. For now when vintage Cambridge dons like F. R. Leavis write to *The Times* deploring the fact that nothing matters that 'can't be weighed, statistically handled, and if necessary priced', *now* people listen. (The learned doctor's central argument, interestingly enough, was that the mere fact that the economic growth of the E.E.C. surpassed that of Britain was, by itself, no reason for joining the E.E.C.) Even President Nixon has started to climb aboard the band wagon (proof positive that it really is a band wagon). Commenting on the 50% forecast growth in America's G.N.P. by 1980 he queried (in the State of the Union message): 'Does this mean we will be 50% richer in a real sense, 50% better off, 50% happier?'

In fact, the march of economic progress was fired not so much by a vision of plenty as by a fear of poverty. The world at the end of the eighteenth century, where life was nasty, brutish and short, inspired men to build engines and develop new sciences to lift Victorian man from the mire of desolation and the scourge of disease. In such a situation growth *did* mean a better life. Hence the G.N.P. worship which declares that except ye have an expanding economy ye have nothing. Now, however, as J. K. Galbraith has observed: 'In a rational life style, some people could find contentment working modestly and then sitting by the street – and talking, thinking, drawing, painting, scribbling or making love a suitably discreet way. None of these requires an expanding economy.' And, so the argument goes, if this sounds like life in the despised manyanadoms of the Middle or Far East maybe, they know something that the puritan ethic doesn't.

Of course, all those who would like to see the end of the belching smoke stacks don't accept as fully as Galbraith the ultimate extension of their arguments. No doubt there are many on whom the full realization has not yet dawned that you can't not have your cake and still eat it, But whatever the inconsistencies, the essential *feeling* about the new consumer which separates him from his predecessors remains : that more no longer equals better.

'Industrial nations', declared Henry Ford II to the Harvard Business School in December 1969, 'have come far enough down the road to affluence to recognize that more goods do not necessarily mean more happiness. They recognize that more goods also mean more junk.' And this from the son of the man who really invented the affluent society back in 1914, when he introduced an eight-hour day in his factory and at the same time doubled wages. Thus giving the worker *leisure* (hitherto an upper-class luxury) and a new sort of consumer choice.

All these fifty or so years the mere act of production has been a virtue. Now the mere act of production starts to look like a vice. Perhaps it won't be long before Chancellors rise to their feet to boast that the G.N.P. went *down* 2% last year (to tumultuous applause). But if we are to fully grasp the full extent of the change of heart by consumers, the argument needs to be taken still further. For it is not just that we have got tummy ache from eating too many strawberries, or that we are conscience-stricken about being the only family in the road to live on a diet of strawberries. The comforts of affluence – strawberries every day – also have the effect of sating the appetite.

The Theory of Limitless Growth doesn't, of course, allow for the achievement of affluence to reduce the demand for further affluence. But consider the case given by Alvin Toffler in *Future Shock* of a fifteen-year-old boy. If, as in most advanced societies, the G.N.P. has doubled since he was a baby this means he is *literally* surrounded by twice as many things man-made at the age of fifteen than when he was a baby. This fifteen-year-old cannot be expected to share his parents' appetite for what is for him a simple part of his basic environment. Nor can one sensibly expect his parents to get the same pleasure from the satisfaction of material needs at the end of the fifteen-year period as at the beginning. The law of diminishing returns is likely to apply. When you already have one car, does the second car mean as much. And when you have two cars how much does a third car mean to you?

Katona and his partners (*Aspirations and Affluence*) found that in advanced societies only about half the population indicated that they had any outstanding 'unsatisfied wishes'. The other half of the population had all the wishes that they could conceive of already satisfied. And the unsatisfied ones weren't so much yearning for fridges and floor polishers either. The still-

F

to-be-granted satisfactions increasingly came from things which can't be packaged and put on a supermarket shelf (like peace and quiet).

It is now seven years since David Riesman wrote his essay *'Abundance for What?'* and the question has now travelled beyond the Groves of Academe. 'We appear to be in a trap,' wrote Riesman, 'in which we may become weary of the goods we have learnt to miss not having, without having learnt – other then inchoately – what we are missing when we do have them.' Hence the new litany of Consciousness III. But this particular aspect of Consciousness III affects many who don't wear flowers in their hair (or have acid in their veins), but who increasingly feel that consumption has no status and find that possession buys few pleasures. It is these people who start the move to a stage of development that few of the prophets of abundance foresaw. W. W. Rostow called it 'beyond high mass consumption' but even he only gave it three pages.

Here are some of the apparent characteristics of this stage of development that one may expect in a society where at least three-quarters of the population lives *well* above subsistence level.

First, the desire for things *for their own sake* declines. Second, the value of consumption *for its own sake* declines. This is the antithesis of the mythology of Thorsten Velben who believed that the more an individual consumed the more that person thought others would think of him. 'Beyond high mass consumption' it comes as no surprise that the newer (i.e. younger) members of society are increasingly turned off by today's consumer products. Total sales figures pumped up by inflation disguise reductions or slowing down in *per capita* consumption in several key areas. After all, if conspicuous consumption has no status, all you need is the basics without all the extras. Health foods are a basic. So are compact cars. So are craft goods. (They also represent a deliberate decision not to support the mass production economy – a point of such importance that it will be returned to in a few pages' time.)

The third characteristic of a 'beyond mass consumption' stage of economic growth is a trend to life simplification identified by Daniel Yankelovich. Where the consumer instead of being surrounded by choice feels that she is surrounded by muddle. When she feels she has become a tool of her tools, and so lost control of her own personal environment. To get away from this overwhelming swarm of goods and services she may simplify. This doesn't necessarily mean that the dishwasher is fed down the waste disposal unit. But it does represent a substantial difference from the consumer into whose house one more domestic appliance was for ever welcome.

Some measure of the extent to which consumers welcome additions to their material environment is the extent to which they welcome new products. And eight out of ten get the thumbs down. Of course, very often a major reason for these failures was the way the product was marketed or inadequacies in the product itself. And the sheer increase in the number of new products means that the majority can't succeed, or the consumer would never stop buying. But the scale of this rejection of the products of the marketing industry must surely give its executives a twinge of the ulcers. Can they really be turning out something for which there is a demand when there is an 80% rejection rate? Is industry in fact merely turning out the sorts of product that were right in the days of glossy materialism? On the next page you can see a list of new products introduced in America in November 1971, a month simply taken at random from the pages of *Advertising Age*. You can thus see the sorts of 'new products' that are being rejected.

A different slant on the same phenomenon occurs when workers cease to be satisfied with offers of more pay (more pay, in this context, being the equivalent of new products).

In an article in the *New York Times* Sylvia Fox wrote that New York City policemen had rejected an excellent wage settlement because they wanted something more. In the words of one police official: 'They're turning their backs on material things and going after other things – ego things.' If this sounds strange in strike-torn Britain with a million unemployed, consider how often workers appear to act *against* their best interests. But if you look at a strike as a collective ego trip, it makes a lot more sense.

New attitudes to work are, in fact, the other side of the coin to new attitudes to consumption. At first sight this may seem rather unlikely. Because for all the predictions in the past of the new leisure society, the average weekly hours worked in Britain in 1966 were only forty-five minutes a week less than in 1948. As the official week was reduced either the overtime increased (from an average of two hours per week then to six hours per

149

New products launched in America, November, 1971.

"Slight variations, or 'me too' changes in some toiletries and cosmetics products, are not included".

Aeroseal Corp.—Hot Melt self-heating de-icer spray.
Airwick Industries—testing ABT (Airwick bathroom tablets) in Atlanta.
American Cyanamid Co.—testing Breck Dri-Odorant aerosol extra-strength deodorant.
American Tobacco Co.—Pall Mall filter kings national. Testing Mermaid and Lucky Ten brands.
Armour & Co.—testing Toaster Things, six varieties of frozen toaster products in four markets, including Columbus and Boston.
Beecham Inc.—re-staging Macleans toothpaste by going national with Macleans freshmint.
Borden Co.—testing chocolate covered candies in Texas markets. Eight varieties.
Brazil Coffee Corp.—introducing Brazilia ground coffee, New York, Boston.
Brown & Williamson Tobacco Co.—testing Lyme line-menthol 85 mm. filter cigaret, Fort Wayne.
Chipurnoi Importers—to introduce Chips, Italian-made hard licorice candy.
Clairol Inc.—testing Final Net hair control spray, Indianapolis. Sunday supplements. To introduce permanent hair coloring. True Brunette. Market'ng the Skin Machine, automatic face cleaner, and Air Brush styling dryer. Plans to introduce the Steam Comb.
Clorox Co.—Clorox disinfectant cleaner testing in undisclosed markets.
Coopervision Inc.—Marketing a new self-contained home entertainment rear projector.
Dow Chemical Co.—reformulated Dow oven cleaner with a lemon scent.
Fleischmann Distilling Corp.—nears national distribution with Zhivago vodka.
General Food Corp.—introducing cheese-flavoured Gainesburgers in eastern states. Semi-moist dog food available in blue and cheddar cheese flavors. Jell-O division introducing semi-sweet chocolate chip and walnut cookie combination. Newspapers. Grey. Birds Eye division adds to International Recipe line with Hawaiian and Parisian-style items. Spot TV, magazines, newspapers. Adding Chinese Italian-style vegetables to International Recipe line, eastern markets.
Gillette Co.—toiletries division, Foamy Face Saver, aerosol lubricating shaving lather. Personal Care division tests You're a Woman anti-perspirant and feminine hygiene deodorant, Denver.
Gisman Enterprises—Jiffy Spreader, device to spread butter, margarine, catsup and mustard on bread, introduced in Florida, Indiana, Michigan.
Hunt-Wesson—testing Pizzands, refrigerated French roll with pizza-like topping. Also Reddi-Bacon, refrigerated, foil-wrapped bacon that cooks in a toaster, Phoenix.
Habitant Soup Co.—introducing three soups in New England and upstate New York.
Jeno's Inc.—rolling national with Break 'n Bake pizza, cheese and sausage varieties.
Jesus Watch Co.—marketing multi-coloured watch depicting a smiling Jesus.
S. C. Johnson & Son—introducing Regard cleaner/preserver for wood panelling.
Kitchens of Sara Lee—Sara Lee Snack Loaves in three flavors introduced nationally.
Kraftco Corp.—Kraft Foods division, introducing five chocolate-covered candies in 15 major markets. Marketing five natural cheeses under the Casino label, Los Angeles.
Libby, McNeill & Libby—going national with Libbyland Adventure frozen dinners for children. Expanding tests of Le Kitchen line of frozen fish entrees.
Liggett & Myers—Austin Nichols & Co. subsidiary, 86.8 proof version of Wild Turkey 101 proof bourbon. Adam cigarets for men.
Lipton Pet Foods—testing Tender Dinners for cats.
Loew's Corp.—Lorillard division, testing Maverick, "the taste cigaret," Houston, San Francisco, Atlanta. Expands distribution of Stag tipped cigars to Chicago from Indiana.
Mennon Co.—introducing Protein 21 conditioner nationally after Jan. 1. Introducing Trouble men's cologne nationally.
Philips Morris Inc.—testing Malboro Lights 14 mg. low-tar cigaret.
Noxell Corp.—testing Free Choice men's hair conditioner.
Ovaltine Food Products—testing Ovaltine in individual packets, Boston, Chicago.
Pale Corp.—introducing Colibri Electro-Flame butane fuel lighters.
Procter & Gamble—testing Epic freeze process coffee, Louisville, Lexington, Ky.
Quaker Oats Co.—going national with Aunt Jemima frozen French toast. Introducing chocolate-flavor oatmeal.
Ralston Purina Co.—going national with Piccadilly Circles ("the English muffin with the meal on top"). Tender Vittles cat food makes gains.
R. J. Reynolds Tobacco Co.—Camel Talls continues test in Kansas City, Atlanta.
Robinson Lloyds Ltd.—Strawberry Duck fruit-flavored wine, Apple Dapple apple wine, Cold Bird red grape wine, metropolitan markets.
Schick Electric—testing Lady Schick Warm & Creamy heated cleansing and moisturizing cream dispenser.
Special-T Hosiery Co.—Lady Bubbles hosiery line.
Sterling Drug—Lehn & Fink division, Mop & Glo floor cleaner-wax going national.
Terinex Ltd.—testing Look roasting wrap, New England markets.
Warner-Lambert Co.—American Chicle division, testing Trident brand sugarless candy mints.
Schick Safety Razor division introduces Easy Rider protective razor. TV.
Westinghouse Corp.—introducing "cooltop" cooking range next year.

week now). Or the worker took up a second job. About one-sixth of American and British workers now have a second job.

The politicians have naturally forecast that work will soon be a thing of the past (if only you'll vote for them). Against the politicians' view, the chief executive of E.M.I., one of Britain's main leisure companies, told an industry conference that by 1978 the average working day was likely to be only thirty minutes shorter than in 1970. And, going by a study published by the Survey Research Centre, 49% of Americans under thirty-five want to work more and only 7% want to work less.

Can one really take all these statistics at their face value? Or are consumers simply mouthing the platitudes of a Protestant ethic in which they decreasingly believe?

As attitudes to work affect attitudes to consumption so greatly it seems sensible to follow this question in a little more detail. First, what is it that sends millions of people to clock in every day? Karl Marx's view was simple: 'Work is *external* to the worker ...it is not part of his nature...consequently, he does not fulfil, himself in his work but denies himself, has a feeling of misery rather than well-being, does not develop freely his mental and physical energies, but is physically exhausted and mentally debased. The worker, therefore, feels himself at home only during his leisure time, when he is at work he feels homesick. His work is not voluntary, but *forced labour*. It is not the satisfaction of a need, but only a *means* for satisfying other ends.'

In this analysis affluence becomes the opium of the people. And in the study of car workers in Luton by Goldthorpe, 70% of the assemblers referred to the level of pay as a reason for staying in their present job. And in the case of 31% it was the only reason offered. In a production line economy the satisfaction of the job, which a craft economy provides, is missing. Even in Japan, the world's most go-go economy, almost half of the workers have a negative attitude of one sort or another to their job.

Apart from the money (or more precisely the desire for what the money can buy) keeping their noses to the grindstone, workers work simply for the lack of an alternative way of satisfactorily spending the day. It was this in fact that was given by 80% of industrial workers in a study quoted in Riesman's essay 'Leisure and Work in a Post Industrial Society'.

Both the consumption urge and the lack of alternatives are

likely to be very different for the new consumer as the Lordstown rebellion showed. And Katona found that almost one-third of American households were aware of better jobs yet, despite the competitive spirit meant to be driving them on, they did not act on this information by moving. No wonder that on Labour Day 1971 the American President felt it necessary to call for a return to the 'work ethic'. However, the 'leisure ethic' won't be blown away by such puffs of oratory. Leisure, according to Weber's analysis of the Protestant ethic is necessary for a man in order to work better. But for Aristotle, and increasingly the new consumer, work is only necessary to have leisure (rather than consumption).

All this, of course, is on the assumption that the good times will continue. For a generation not living in the shadow of the 1930s, the arrival of a rainy day seems remote indeed. And anyhow is it so bad not to be able to have a job? Americans, particularly, are confident that the good times will go on and the continuing progress won't fizzle into a depression or slump. To be numerate, one American in three feels better off than four years ago and *also* anticipates being better off four years hence. This compares with one Briton in four and only one German in eight (Katona). The greater the degree of uncertainty about the future one would expect the higher proportion of disposable income that is saved and not spent. And in the ten years up to 1965, British and Americans save on average about 6% of their disposable income and Germans about 13%. (And the insecure Japanese saved 16%.) Then from 1970 the American saving rate increased by a quarter, to 8%, as America in a mini-depression (what most countries in the world would call a boom) felt a bit less sure about the future. This 'uncertainty' is of course measured by the criteria of personal well-being in a material sense, aggregated on a national level as the G.N.P.

As G.N.P. worship and a minimal consumption society with a welfare-state style safety net keeping you above the bread line gathers momentum, the impact of 'uncertainty' causing people to go out to work, and work harder, will be less. In the short term, the saving rate may well rise (as people decide not to buy things they don't really want). But a non-consuming consumer will increasingly see less point in working to save for future non-consumption. Saving *rates* may stay at about 6% but the actual *amount* saved could, within a decade or two, show a substantial decrease.

There are those who give a nod to some of the broad trends about this new philosophy of consumption, but say that for the foreseeable future these people will remain a tiny minority, of sociological rather than business interest. But Arnold Mitchell of the Stamford Research Institute California has estimated that the number of Americans holding this viewpoint (he uses the word 'unfolders' to describe it) will rise to about one-fifth or one-sixth of the American population. 35 million 'unfolded' Americans is an awesome prospect. And it may well prove to be a serious underestimate.

For those in the marketing business, equally interesting is the fact that the working classes are steadily refusing to become middle-class. They're not adopting the consumer ethic in the way everybody expected them to. This phenomenon has less impact, perhaps, on American society where roughly 60% of the population are graded as middle-class. But in Britain – depending on how you classify people – that proportion of the population is working-class. And, contrary to the expectations of many eminent sociologists, the process of embourgeoisment is not occurring. It was the work of Goldthorpe and his fellow researchers looking at Luton manual workers which finally laid that ghost to rest: 'It appears to us', they concluded, 'that the idea of appreciable numbers of manual workers and their wives "turning middle-class" in a way that has been frequently suggested is shown by our research to be highly questionable.'

Affluence simply didn't result in an integration of the manual worker into the middle classes. For instance, manual workers who had been enriched by affluence still kept the same sort of social structure in their lives as before affluence. That is, they still treated their home as a place reserved for kin and very close friends. Socializing was done *outside* the home (e.g. in the pub). This compares with the characteristics of the middle-class, white-collar workers who invited much less close friends into their homes. Clearly then, the manual workers may acquire the apparatus of the mass consumption society but they don't necessarily acquire its attitudes. Included amongst which, of course, is a desire for consumption for the sake of being conspicuous.

This reluctance of the higher-income European manual workers to acquire the middle-class symbols of consumption was also noted by Katona. He and his fellow researchers felt it 'testified to the persistence of a ceiling to their goals and horizons'. Others might argue that it testified to their commonsense in not worshipping the new golden calves. There is certainly a different philosophy of consumption operating in Britain, America and Germany.

Of the three, America has developed furthest beyond high mass consumption and so has further to bounce back. Britain hasn't had as much growth, and hence less of an explosion of consumption and so the British appetites are probably less sated. On the other hand, there is the theory of Professor Galbraith that Britain may be deliberately sluggish in the G.N.P. race due to the collective, albeit intuitive, realization that 'Enjoyment does not come from working more and more and yet more to consume more and yet more'. This would argue that though we are not as yet saturated with consumption as the Americans our reaction against it may be equal to the Americans'. And the Pahls' study foresaw an 'acceptance in Britain of a less affluent and less materialistic way of life'.

Germany is a vivid contrast to all this. The Germans are driven not by the desire half of the equation that began this chapter but by the uncertainty element. Katona found that whereas only 26% of Americans in 1968 expected a major recession in the next twenty years, over twice that proportion of Germans are expecting one. So where Americans are happy to buy on credit, two-thirds of the Germans express unqualified opposition to it (*Schuld,* the German word for 'credit' is also the word for 'guilt'). German advertising has to spend twice as much per £ of consumer expenditure as advertising in Britain, such is the reluctance of the herrenvolk to part with their marks.

This is a different reason for a low consumption society and it is, of course, in no way the same as Consumption III's rejection of the consumer ethic. But it is significant none the less : The Germans have failed so far to adapt to a doubling of goods and services every ten years in the way that the mass consumer model of society demands. The endless appetite for goods and services is not there, and there is instead a worry that something will happen to imperil the satisfying of a far more modest hunger.

To argue that there is increasingly a limited not a limitless demand for material goods in advanced societies is, of course, to tell only half the story. What is equally important is that where there *is* demand for a product, be it a motor car or a packet of frozen peas, the new ideology of consumption predicts that it will be bought for very different reasons from those that prevailed some ten years ago. Ten years ago the prime motive for purchase was the actual pleasure of having the object, the *possession* experience. Now the trend is away from what it is to what it does, to *usage* or the pleasures you get from using it.

Possession is now no longer nine-tenths of the satisfaction. With abundance of products, few producers can provide the emotional 'possession' satisfaction that held sway in the early days of glossy materialism (for example, manufacturers of swimming pools still have some 'possession' appeal to make). 84% of European homes now have a fridge, so it, and virtually all other electrical household appliances, have lost their value as status symbols (only miniature colour television sets seem to have this position at the moment). All that most of these objects are good for now is the freezing of ice cubes, the cooking of toast, and the bringing of entertainment in the evenings. To paraphrase Corbusier, they have become machines for living with.

One or two voices in the marketing wilderness have foreseen this change. In June 1970 the head of marketing for Lees Carpets observed: 'Home furnishing customers of the 1970s will be less interested in possessing objects than in using and enjoying them.' But most advertisers, as one will have cause to observe later, are still presenting their products to the consumer as though the consumer was still in a 'possession' phase. Just how offbeam this makes the advertising message will become clearer if we look at some of the marketing consequences of this trend from possession to usage.

First, possession is measured by subjective criteria, usage by objective ones. Possession demands prestige, usage demands performance. This is even affecting the world of fashion, perhaps one of the most subjective-dominated product categories. What is happening is that it is becoming fashionable to have 'usage' clothes. At an obvious level, clothes become more comfortable at the expense of style. Stiff collars are undoubtedly smarter than soft collars, drip-dry dresses don't crease as smartly as starched. 'Performance' clothes will also tend to be fewer in number and more durable than 'prestige' clothes. And it has been estimated that the value at constant prices of the wardrobe of the average

Harvard student is a third of what it used to be five years ago. On this side of the Atlantic, too, J. K. Galbraith when he visited Cambridge, observed that you could clothe the entire freshman class in Trinity College for about £50. Even the colours, brown, greens and of course blue tend towards the functional drabness. Blue jeans are the universal item of apparel. Even the up-market Austin Reed menswear chain in Britain is opening a Jeans Shop.

Perhaps the ultimate evidence of objective criteria invading this most subjective of all markets is the second-hand clothes industry. Quite apart from a few trendy London shops selling second-hand cowboy jeans from America, there's a surge in the second-hand clothes market. The people who attend jumble sales are not just impoverished slum dwellers looking for cheap shirts. These sales are used by vast numbers of under-twenty-fives as a way of acquiring their clothes. Gone for these people is the 'joy' of a new coat. Instead they are looking for a simple functional item of apparel that – often inefficiently – hides their nakedness.

The same trend has shown itself in the world of films. The difference between *The Graduate* and *The Sound of Music* is the difference between subjective glamour and objective reality. Film stars no longer have to have square chins, perfect teeth and blue eyes. And in fact if they do this is deemed to take them too far away from their audiences. It is the difference between Cary Grant and Jean Paul Belmondo. Of course, there are still 'fantasy' films but the difference is that the average viewer now tends to take a more objective look at his own need for fantasy. To treat a James Bond film as a joke, albeit a very entertaining one, is to take fantasy objectively. Indeed, the fact that Sean Connery is still acceptable as 007 is of substantial significance. In *Dr No* he was playing a part in the subjective hero mould. But in *Diamonds are for Ever* we see a different sort of hero sending up his early roles. The P.R. man who spread the word that Sean Connery wore a toupée understood the subjective/objective shift precisely. The fact that everyone knows about his toupée makes Bond's screen antics delightful when they would otherwise be ridiculous. The toupée is a larger than life element to remind us that we are watching fantasy. But we know that when the picture fades our prancing hero once more becomes a balding forty-year-old with sagging stomach muscles.

Looking away from films to the food industry, the possession to usage shift shows itself again. 'Possession' in food marketing is that whole range of things like those big smiles that greet every spoonful, the cementing together of families by Jello, in short, all the *non-food* aspects of food selling. 'Usage' is the nutritional side, the vitamins in the cornflakes or – for certain sorts of foods – the convenience aspect.

In the mid-sixties, nutrition was not a good way to sell food. General Mills tried it with Subtract and Carnation tried it with Instant Breakfast. It seemed then that too much emphasis on nutrition turned off the consumer. Then by 1970 *Advertising Age* was reporting: 'The food industry is on a nutrient fortification kick that seems to be building into an important marketing effort.'

The use of the other usage aspect of food marketing, convenience, is also on the rise. In the European market convenience foods often made much slower headway in the sixties than the companies marketing them had hoped they would. Instant mashed potato, the go-go product of the end of the decade was a flop in the middle. The motivational psychologist declared that you shouldn't sell convenience foods on convenience alone because this created guilt feelings for the housewife. Hence the rash of products to which one had to add an egg, and so make a vital contribution to lift the burden of guilt.

What in fact happened was that convenience foods had been launched on a usage platform during a possession phase. At that time, it *was* necessary to add possession reassurance. But then, as the consumer shifted into a usage phase, convenience foods could be sold for convenience reasons. Smash mashed potato openly derided the inconvenience of the fresh product ('It's good, but it'll never catch on'). And instant coffee began to wean Frenchmen away from their fresh filtered brew.

A final example of how the possession to usage shift triggered a trend from subjective to objective product assessment comes from the consumer durable field. With half the population having almost a complete set of consumer durables, it means that the great proportion of purchases are for replacement of an old or worn out model. Already, for instance, 40% of Italy's domestic refrigerator sales are replacement ones. The important point is that the criteria of product choice for a replacement fridge are very different from a first time purchase. A study done by

General Electric of America spells this out. People purchasing fridges for the first time, maybe moving into their first home, took the time to stop and compare. They are building their home so not only do they want to feel they're getting the best at the price, but the fridge – as part of their new home – also has some emotional significance. When this new fridge, after seven or so years, breaks down or needs repairing rather different criteria of purchase are at work. First, the housewive's need is more immediate. She won't have time to shop around. She'll probably be more influenced by a point of sale than advertising (which she won't have looked at until her fridge breaks down because she wasn't in the market for a new fridge). And, which is where we come to usage, because the old refrigerator *broke down* she will be specially concerned about quality, performance and after sales service.

Another study found that users of a product who were replacing a similar or identical product *with which they were satisfied* generally spent little time or effort in considering their next purchase. They knew which to look for and where to look for it and they didn't need to concern themselves with a whole mass of features and subjective attractions that weren't relevant to their particular need.

An equally important second consequence of replacement purchase is that they have little – if any – of the joys of purchase that accompanied the first purchase. There are already large categories of products the purchase of which is basically an unpleasant event because it means that something has gone wrong, worn out, or run out. Light bulbs are a simple example, tyres are an even better one. They may even include items like suits whose purchase the motivation researchers said was full of psychological joy. But for all but a tiny proportion of the population a new suit is something you buy when your old one is worn out.

The joy-through-purchase experience is thus becoming more and more infrequent. And advertisers who treat their products as though the purchase of it was as pleasurable as a night out with Sophia Loren are a very long way off the mark.

One of the attributes of a product that was thought to enhance the pleasure of possessing it was its image. By modifying the image of the brand one could – so the adherents of this doctrine believed – manipulate reality. Indeed the image became reality.

158

There will be a full discussion of this theory in the chapter on how advertising works. But in so far as the brand image is a *subjective* phenomenon, any brand loyalty that this creates is likely to wane as the shift to usage waxes.

Loyalty in a my-country-right-or-wrong style is going out of fashion for countries and also for brands. In the German detergent market, for instance, the big three – Henkel, Proctor and Unilever – have been consistently losing ground to small independent manufacturers who make their products at a much lower price. Proctors have even seen their share slump by half – to well below 10%. Even the shops where you buy your brands receive less brand loyalty. As long ago as 1960 an Alfred Bird survey showed that the exclusive use of one grocer by housewives had declined from 52% in 1953 to 25% in 1960.

There are two other factors which have helped this shift away from subjective loyalty. First, the growth of brand *consciousness,* a function of the information explosion. There may in fact be fewer brands of soup on the market than in 1920 but people are conscious, through the media, of more brands of soup. As brand consciousness increases, brand loyalty is likely to weaken. For brand loyalty partly depends upon your mentally *suppressing* your knowledge of the existence of other brands.

The second factor to weaken brand loyalty is the reduced trust in the company that makes that brand. The decline of trust for companies described in chapter one is surely likely to have as its consequence in the market place the decline in trust for that company's brands. Of course, the reassurance of having a familiar face on your larder shelf will still prompt purchase of the well-known brand names. Even areas which have been saturated by loyalty-inducing image advertising like cosmetics, brand loyalty is already looking a little like a left-over from the early sixties. An I.P.C. survey amongst fifteen to twenty-four-year-old consumers found that the majority 'had no usual brand' of cosmetics. And that one woman in six used half a dozen or more different types of eye shadow. While one woman in ten had *six* different types of lipstick.

A J. Walter Thompson study of household purchasing patterns give this as an example that is 'by no means untypical' of multiple-brand choice. Each different letter represents the purchase of a different brand of tea. And this is the sequence – BOOcGBOCOBGBGABBGBBcBGBCBBGGBBB. A total of five

159

different brands, with even the most frequently purchased one having less than half of all purchases.

From petrol to peas, the well-known brand names are increasingly finding that the attracting power of their name measured by its ability to persuade the consumer to pay more for it than a less well-known brand name is declining. Witness the heavy inroads made by the own-brand products into the grocery market.

If brand loyalty is one of the casualties of the possession to usage shift, built-in obsolescence is the other. Built-in obsolescence worked in the fifties and sixties by giving the consumer the opportunity of a new 'possession' experience every two to three years. Very often the actual *performance* of the product had no significant difference between models. The changes tended to be in the *possession* area.

But the new usage customer will not forgive a product if it self-destructs after three years. Having got over the initial excitement of having their clothes washed and dried, their food mixed and cooked, their toast toasted and dishes washed at the flick of a switch, they simply demand that their machines do these tasks reliably day in day out.

Even non-working durables like furniture are feeling the anti-obsolescence backlash. For instance, the President of the Stanleytown furniture company told *Business Week* that more and more young couples are buying one or two high quality pieces of furniture and making do until their budget allows them to add to them. They are thus turning their backs on the old idea of buying a low price three piece suite, which is worn out after five years, and then having the fun of refurnishing their home.

One of the pressures against built-in obsolescence for working consumer durables is, of course, the shortage of people to service them. The trend to do-it-yourself is one result of this (the expense and palaver of getting a plumber is making doing it yourself sensible for even the most ham-fisted). But building products where it is the exception instead of the rule for them to fall apart after five years would be another.

If planned obsolescence is becoming obsolete, it is possible that it could be replaced by durable goods economy. Not only would products be expected to last longer, they would be expected to be assembled by the consumer, to be repaired by the consumer, and re-used in some way by the consumer when their original use was over. Furniture that you assemble yourself is already with us. So is an electric toaster that you can help to repair yourself. The rest will shortly follow.

A logical part of any durable goods economy would be the use of a product without ownership of that product: the ultimate consequence of the possession to usage shift.

One aspect of this phenomenon (which was shrewdly observed in a series of articles by E. B. Weiss in *Advertising Age*) is the growth of rental. With rental, by definition, you can have none of the joys of ownership, only the satisfaction of use. Car rental already makes up a fair slice of all car sales. Office furniture (partly because of tax concessions) is increasingly rented, but why not home furniture as well? In Britain, partly because of special hire purchase controls, more televisions are rented than purchased. One reason for which is that though renting costs are more it avoids the pains of ownership involved in servicing (see above).

If in the fifties and sixties the consumer would often own things he didn't use, now he increasingly uses things he doesn't own. The growth of the service industries further exemplifies this. For service industries are essentially usage : they provide service, something you use rather than something you possess. And it is this section of the economy of advanced societies that is expanding by far and away the fastest. Service industries already employ two out of every three American workers (compared to one out of two in 1950). And as well as traditional service industries like banks there are now service companies that baby-sit, wake you up in the morning, drive you to work. Even find you a new wife. And in business, companies are springing up that will plan your convention, design your products and supply you with a temporary managing director.

One extra attraction of a service is that it is effectively tailor-made to the person being serviced, while a possession tends to be mass-produced.

Individualism, in fact, is the other main aspect of the new consumers' attitudes towards material goods. 'What does this do for *me*?' is a relevant question rather than the old 'What does this do?' Mass-production of the old Henry Ford sort ('Have any car you like as long as it's black') becomes a quaint museum piece from the early days of affluence. Equally *passé* is the pre-packaged consumer who had to adjust herself to fit the product and not the other way round.

The new consumer, by contrast, is highly individualistic. Ten years ago it was an endorsement for a product that the next-door neighbour used it. Now, if the next-door neighbour uses it you probably won't want to touch it. Satisfaction is now obtained by being different from your peer group, which is now no more than a reference point for comparison. It is no longer, and this is an important point, a reference point for imitation.

Wealth, of course, finances the exercise of this sort of individuality. A poor woman may well go on using the same old cake recipe just because she can't run the risk of failure. But increased wealth makes this sort of individualistic risk-taking possible: if her cake recipe goes wrong it doesn't mean her children go hungry. She can simply just try another recipe tomorrow. And in doing this she will probably be using her consumption style as an expression of her personality. Each year St Tropez provides an interesting example of this phenomenon. There is a basic uniform which all residents in the town wear to show that they belong to St Trop and aren't just passing members of a package tour. In 1970 this was a pre-faded cotton jeans outfit. In 1971 it was an out-of-work-U.S.-army-unit style outfit that held the field. But despite this basic pattern, no St Trop regular wore the same outfit as anyone else. Each outfit was in some way unique. (The move to separates in the fashion world is a move to increasing the number of options in someone's wardrobe without actually increasing the number of clothes.)

For large turn-over products, instead of straightforward mass production, *differentiated* production is developing. This is a way of making a mass-produced product fit an individual's own personality. For example, the chairman of Genesco is promising custom-made suits for the masses with three-day delivery. And B.E.A.'s Sovereign holidays began business in 1970 to move people away from ordinary package holidays to a tailor-made vacation.

Tiffany's branch in Chicago has also felt this change. In 1970 they did 'unusual custom work' on one out of ten engagement rings they sold. And this in a shop where five years ago they only sold one sort of diamond engagement ring and that on a take it or leave it basis.

Why, apart from satisfying the personal quirks of their customers – should General Foods now offer the public sixteen different permutations of frozen peas? Yes, frozen peas.

With all this happening in the commercial field, it can hardly be a coincidence that the new religion of our day – astrology – is a religion that is customized for every worshipper. Instead of a religion like Christianity where you have to adjust to its beliefs, here is one where the beliefs literally adjust to you, and no one – but no one – has the same *credo*.

The central core of the individualistic trend is away from the importance of the product to the importance of the individual (so making it consistent with the possession to usage shift that stripped a product of part of its appeal). In the possession phase, the product was a *substitute* for personality. You *were* your car; it dominated you and did things to you. But in the usage phase, individualism ensures that the product becomes an *extension* of your personality; the car *is* you. You dominate it and you do things to it.

These customized consumers don't fit into any of the old pigeonholes that used to divide up the market place. Alvin Toffler uses the phrase 'micro cosmos' to describe the network of inter-connecting mini-worlds that form themselves out of the new individualistic consumers. But they *are* mini-markets not mass markets. And it is indeed a paradox that just as we have created a mass media, the mass market disappears.

Take the youth market. Mathematically, a teenage girl is somewhere between twelve and nineteen. To regard that age group as one market group is foolish. All you get, in the phrase of E. B. Weiss is 'demographic goulash'.

The obvious result of this is that no brand today can sell effectively to the whole market, but only to certain parts of the market. And a new industry has grown up to work out ways to segment the market, with things like gap analysis, contextual mapping, and cluster analysis. For example in 1962, the wrist-watch field could be broadly divided into (a) Those who want to pay the lowest price for any watch that works reasonably well. (b) People who want good craftsmanship and cosy style (c) People who want emotional qualities as well as timeless qualities from their wrist-watch. By 1971, new divisions had arrived. Like a group of people who treated a watch as jewellery and regarded its time-keeping ability as almost incidental. As well as a group of people who wanted special non-time-keeping features on their watches like deep sea pressure gauges when they never do more than jump in the lake or swimming pool.

The result of developments like this in every market has been a brand explosion (or – as in the case of cars – an option explosion). A Neilsen report in 1967 revealed that in one supermarket chain alone there was a 76% increase in brands of diet food; a 71% in brands of soup; a 61% increase in brands of dog food; and so on and so forth through all the lines they held.

In all these discussions of the shift to functionalism and individualism in products, one particular three-letter word has been hardly present when you might have expected it to appear rather more frequently. The word is c–a–r.

The car has, of course, a major role in bringing about a reduced importance for material goods and in changing the shape of that modified demand. And the saga of how the centre-piece of the affluent society has been knocked off its pedestal form the next part of our discussion. Anthropologists have reported how in several primitive tribes a new god is at first welcomed, worshipped and adored. And then after a time his magic seems to weaken and he is slain. Civilized man has done the same for his four-wheeled god. Once worshipped, it has now been slain, partly to propitiate the high priests of the environment.

What new idol will replace it is one of the big questions hungry young marketing men are trying to answer.

9
The Sex Symbol That Lost its Sex

The Kandy Coloured Tangerine Flake Streamlined Baby isn't just a radically chic book by Tom Wolfe. It was the apogee of a form of worship that beats anything since Aaron discovered the Golden Calf. How a piece of rubber and metal weighing a ton and upwards and costing hundreds of pounds could enter the realm of high fashion is a puzzle for historians and sociologists of the future to sort out. They will probably be as amazed as we are to think of our ancestors falling down before lumps of rock at Stonehenge.

The fact remains that onwards from the 1950s the motor car was as much a fashion item as the little black dress or even a new shade of lipstick, commodities designed to be far less useful than this replacement for the horse. The annual model change, with all its associated rituals, was as much a high fashion event as the Paris shows. And as the basic structure of four wheels, an engine and seats is a bit limiting, the car manufacturers developed the concept of 'over design' to allow them the same flexibility with metal as Balenciaga had with crepe.

Over designing simply means building into a mechanism more features than it requires in order to function. The American bureau of labour statistics reveals exactly what this means in dollars and cents. For the 1969 model change, General Motors, Ford, and American Motors spent 1.5 billion dollars. But the bureau's statistics show a net *reduction* in performance improvements of three dollars per car. This means that *more* than 1.5 billion was literally spent on putting some new make-up onto the old face.

This happened not so much from a desire to defraud the consumer, but as a direct result of the possession phase which the consumer was in. The new car did almost as much for the owner when it was sitting outside his front door as when he was being carried round by it. And it didn't just carry him around either. All the neighbours flocked round for a drive.

In 1960 General Motors corporate car campaign reflected the spirit of the whole thing with exquisite precision. Beneath a lovingly painted picture of a huge estate car surrounded by happy smiling children with parents proudly looking on – and done by an artist who'd managed to combine the styles of Norman Rockwell and Dame Laura Knight – was the legend that expressed the complete philosophy of selling cars at the particular moment in time: 'There's nothing like a new car to enrich your family life.' 'Enrich' is a possession word, full of hidden undertones. And a car manufacturer who tried to sell cars in any other way did so at his peril.

In 1955, for instance, Ford's advertising carried the 'Life Guard Design' slogan. It was a campaign to introduce safety door locks, safety steering wheels and rear view mirrors, which did not cause head wounds (this was before Nader's attack on General Motors). After a year, the conclusion of the car industry was that 'Ford sell safety and General Motors sell cars'. So deep was the impact of this on Ford that, thirteen years later, I discovered that Ford of Great Britain weren't interested in doing a safety campaign for their cars, because they felt, after the 1955 débâcle, that it wouldn't persuade the public to buy their cars.

In fact, by this time consumer attitude towards the motor car was shifting well into the usage phase, albeit personalized usage. This shift, in fact, had been predicted by David Riesman writing in 1957: 'It seems to us that as America becomes more accustomed to luxury, the motor car will lose some of its glamour and that eventually the cars which restore to us a sense of reality and functionalism may at least find a modest market.'

The first stirring that this was so came from the massive rejection of the Edsel. After that in Detroit they spoke of the hard sell, the soft sell, and the Edsel.

An even clearer indication that consumers were falling out of love with their cars was the extraordinary success of the Volkswagen in America. Here was a modernized version of a vehicle intended by Hitler to be the people's car in pre-war Germany, carving great chunks out of the car market in the toughest market in the world.

The success of Volkswagen, in fact, is a good illustration of the apparent paradox that buying a *usage* car can still be an *irrational* choice. In terms of value for money, seating, performance, – almost any aspect of the car apart from reliability and durability – the Volkswagen was really a weak car. To buy it very often probably wasn't the most cost effective use of your funds. Yet it was bought by people who believed they were making a cost effective decision, and who persuaded themselves they were making an objective, rational choice. This shows that in moving from possession to usage, the new consumer hasn't left his irrationality behind. He has merely applied it within a new frame of reference, a usage frame of reference instead of a possessional one. It was the brilliant advertising of Doyle, Dane, Bernbach who managed to pull this particular slight of hand.

Volkswagen was aided and abetted in this by the development of the second car market in America. Between 1960 and 1970 the number of cars owned by one-car families had increased by less than 2 million. The two-car families have added over 9 million vehicles to the total car population. One American home in three now has more than one car, compared to one in ten British homes (cars per million people we've got just about the same density as America had *before the war*). The Volkswagen presented itself as a second car that ran rings round a fat and sloppy first car. If the tide hadn't been turning against those over-powered chromium-plated monsters, with their baroque decor, the Volkswagen attack would not have worked so well. How well it did work is history. (The kind of history that even Henry Ford might not regard as bunk.) In 1950 350 Volkswagens were sold in America. By 1970 only one American car, the Chevrolet Impala, outsold the Volkswagen Beetle. All other models were outsold by this sparse, functional, chromeless puddle-jumper.

En passant, it may be worth noting that it wasn't only Volkswagen who were presenting their cars on a usage platform at that time. David Ogilvy's most famous headline for Rolls Royce was 100% usage (however possessiony the car itself might have been). 'At sixty miles an hour the loudest noise in this new Rolls Royce comes from the electric clock.'

But even in 1970, after the usage imported cars had been giving them the run-around for several years, Detroit was still pushing its own vehicles on the old possession platform 'Introducing automobiles to light your fire' said Buick. 'Pontiac announces the beginning of tomorrow', said the Firebird Company, with their car burnished and glistening on the glimmering water's edge. Pontiac's G.T.O. advertisement went even further. Showing the new G.T.O. (dubbed 'The Humbler') barrelling round the edge of a mountainside, it proclaimed: 'Move over mountain. This is the way it's going to be.' And Cadillac with their 'masterful approach to the seventies' was boasting about its 'newly contoured rear light assembly'. But perhaps the best expression of the Detroit philosophy was an advertisement for American Motors: 'People are demanding more "hot" in their hot cars ... More "big" in their big cars, more "new" in their new cars.'

But even with these possession oriented ads. the tacit recognition was there that the consumer had developed different attitudes to the car. The fashion accessories now had to be presented as quasi-functional items: 'Gauges that gauge, spoilers that spoil and scoops that scoop', said Pontiac, to prove that its ephemera was really 'usage' equipment. 'A high lift cam and four barrel carburettor which breathes through real air scoops to add performance', intoned Buick anxious to make the same point. Even Ford of Britain's Capri feels unable to simply plaster its side with dross: so the chrome panel at the back has to be dressed up as an Aeroflow ventilation outlet.

There may well always be a market for this sort of possession car, albeit with its alleged usage trims. But to turn out this type of car is no longer a sure fire formula for striking gold. The Capri sales in Britain were substantially lower than Ford had hoped. And one of the biggest selling UK cars is still the upturned bath-tub on wheels, the 1100/1300 series from British Leyland. And the tremendous growth of Fiat, with their boxey but brilliantly engineered cars show that the shape of things to come isn't very beautiful at all.

What has happened is that the car has not turned out to be quite the winged chariot the advertisers swore it was. 'We were promised a machine that freed us, gave us wings,' said Professor Charles Mason of the University of Southern Carolina, 'instead, it turned on us, trapping us in traffic jams, polluting our air, breaking apart in accidents, and in need of constant repair.'

And so the car has been relegated to a utilitarian role. Ten years ago under a third of all American cars were smaller than standard size. Today approaching two-thirds are. Of course, if the main thing you want from a car is transportation, why own the car? Why not use one when you need it and don't use it when you don't. Hence the growth of car rental and car leasing.

Looking at the new relationship of man to his transporter, you could say that the love affair with the car was over. Or that it had matured into marriage (depending upon whether or not you happen to have shares in a car company). One of Ford's vice presidents, Donald Petersen, compared the changed attitudes to that of a man towards his middle-aged wife: 'You're still in love, but you expect more. You expect her to cook.' At a more candid moment Mr Petersen expressed what is perhaps a truer reflection of the new relationship: 'More and more people view the automobile as an unfortunate necessity. As soon as you are viewed more as a necessity, people are less tolerant of your shortcomings.'

And studies by the Survey Research Centre (some of whose funds come from the car industry) showed the same sort of trend. They indicated that the car was increasingly becoming a means for serving important ends rather than being the highly prized possession it once was. The important ends could be simply clothes shopping or driving for a weekend to stay in a log cabin. But as a way of revealing a man's position in society (which was the basis of car marketing in the fifties and sixties) it is a non-runner. It is no longer possible in fact, to deduce an individual's status from knowing what transport he uses. A man driving a new Ford Cortina could be a professional man or a highly paid manual worker. And the parking lots of America's richest suburbs are full of small battered old cars.

It took Detroit some time to exactly fathom out just what was happening to consumers. And their tardiness in bringing out cars which satisfied the usage criteria (by being more reliable and by not falling apart so fast) is one of the most myopic marketing episodes of this decade. It wasn't until four million Volkswagens had been sold in America that Detroit brought out a serious rival. And to show the full recognition of the error of their old ways, they even started to run ads. for overtly possession cars presenting them as usage vehicles. A preposterousness that reached its peak with a headline for a Cadillac advertisement: 'Surprising Cadillac, as practical as it's beautiful.' And the 1972 model ads. (prompted by a few crisp words from General Motors' President: 'I think advertising has forgotten who and what the customer is.') started to tell a very different story from the newer, bigger, hotter story of the previous years.

American Motors kicked off with 'If anything goes wrong with our new '72s and it's our fault, we'll fix it free. Anything'. And Chevrolet lamely observed: 'Many people today have changed their attitude about new cars, so we have changed . . . and only made a few meaningful improvements.'

But perhaps the best example of the U-turn done by Detroit in car marketing is to look at one particular car advertisement for the Chevrolet Vega and compare it with the earlier General Motors one, 'There's nothing like a new car to enrich your family life'. Over a picture of a drawing of the Vega with five number plates on it, 1972, 1973, 1974, 1975, the headline says: 'If you like the 1971 you'll like the 1975.' This advertisement unequivocally states that the Chevrolet Vega will *not* be obsolete in four years. Any advertising agency that presented this sort of advertisement in Detroit just two years ago would probably have been fired. But this advertisement and the car it's for are the white hopes of the American car industry, facing the onslaught of the imports. (It may be of interest that in a study of the readership of new car advertisements by Starch, the highest read advertisement was for the Ford Pinto (their answer to G.M.'s Vega) which showed an old model Ford to point out that Pinto would not have an annual styling change: 'When you get back to basics you get back to Ford').

Even Britain has seen a similar sort of change in its car marketing. The advertising for the Rover 2000, which began by presenting it as a status car, is now firmly selling it as a non-obsolescent way of life: 'If all other cars had to be as safe as a Rover 2000, would there be any other cars on the road?'

In its new neutered role, the car no longer generates the loving attention it did when the shape of a bumper meant as much as a curve on Marilyn Monroe. Obsessive spit and polishing is a thing of the past. And cars, quite simply, are getting dirtier. 'Whatever happened to the booming car care market?'

asked the *Sunday Times* at the end of 1971. By then, despite the fact that motorists were spending about half as much again on buying their car as they had done in 1960, they were spending no more on general titivation.

But though their looks are being less well attended to, how well the car looks after the new owner is not. Remembering how the 1955 Ford safety campaign flopped, look at the results of a survey by *Drive* magazine to find out, apart from cost, which factors consumers considered most important in buying a new car. For one in three *safety* was first choice. And styling was only first choice for one in fourteen. Clearly the new safety standards for cars have widespread consumer support (and it is a measure of earlier consumer indifference as much as business neglect that they didn't come sooner).

The same *Drive* survey showed that almost three-quarters of motorists would welcome stricter government standards for car safety *even* if that would add £30 onto the new car they bought. And a study by the Insurance Bureau of Canada showed that the same proportion there would be willing to pay more for safer cars.

It's not hard to point out some inconsistencies within this new consumer's attitude towards his car. After all, if he is that concerned about safety why does he persistently refuse to put on a safety belt? And if he is that concerned about the side-effects of a car's impact on the environment, why does he own a car at all?

The small car apparently offers the most accepted compromise between the need for mobility and a revulsion for despoiling the environment or oneself (despite some evidence that the small car is neither less polluting nor any safer than the big car).

This at least shows the way subjective and objective mix in the usage phase. If you can stand the syllables, 'subjective objectivity' is a reasonable way of expressing the phenomenon. The Beetle, for instance, is in impartial, objective terms not the most sensible buy for large numbers of people who buy it (in terms of safety, road holding, and comfort). Yet subjectively, it appears a more objective choice for these people.

This new frame of reference also shows itself if you look at the way individualism manifests itself in motor cars. There are basically two ways in which a car company can allow the purchaser of that car to demonstrate his individualism. Either the car can remain neutral and functional like most Fiats and

Renault 4s, and so provide a pale background for the owner's own personality. Or the car can have a vast choice of options and permutations enabling the owner to customize his car to suit his personality. Hence the Mustangs and the Capris of this world. But in either case, despite the subjectivity of these emotions and feelings towards the car the car still remains subservient to the individual; man is master of his machine and not the other way round.

Such broad statements need the caveat that the changed attitude towards the car shows up in different advanced societies to different degrees. Sweden has probably the largest following of the usage concept in cars, but the possession phase never really developed there, even in the hey-day of American materialism. The greatest *change* of attitude is probably still in America. And in Europe, where many can still recall the not so distant past where they didn't own a car, it is still a more valued possession than in America.

In Germany, the car is still an object of worship. Unlike Britain, Saturday car washing is still an earnest ritual. And the absence of clapped-out old models is astonishing. Maybe the fact that in West Germany home ownership is rare compared to Britain means that a car has to satisfy the 'possession' yearnings that an Englishman answers by treating his home as his castle. But it can only be a matter of time before the Germans begin to develop the same sort of aloof almost hostile relationship to their winged chariots as the Americans and British are now developing (and the fact that the Germans have been first to introduce low lead petrol by law is an indication of things to come).

The public expression of a new view towards the motor car isn't just restricted to new types of motor cars presented in new sorts of ways. Government legislation, as the expression of the will of the people, may be expected eventually to reflect the Demos' new views. A car, after all, is not just a vehicle. It is the expression of a particular point of view about transportation. In this sense, Ford and General Motors haven't just been selling cars. They've also tried to affect public taste so that the demand for transportation is expressed as a demand for private cars not public buses. And it is probable that in rejecting General Motors' concept of a car, they will start to move against the General Motors' concept of transportation. Limits on the free use of the car in the city would be the consequence of this. And legislation generally restricting private transport at the expense of public can be expected.

Those who forecast that the car will go the way of the dinosaur are probably being too ambitious. But it has certainly experienced a profound reversal of its position in society in the space of under a decade. One could argue that this is a healthy development. That sexuality is the proper function of that which the good Lord gave to assuage these passions. But this volume is not intended as a treatise to make that sort of moral judgement.

However, in the role of observer, one point seems clear. That if the centre piece of our affluent society has had to respond to such a degree to changes of attitude by the new consumer, then we have at least a definite and important new trend. A trend which in the long term would have an effect on everything anyone tries to sell, be they mouse-traps or motor cars.

IO

Reading Between the Lies

If the consumer is starting to grow out of his toys, there's a fair chance that he might also be starting to grow out of his toy-shop. It may seem, indeed, utterly elementary that once significant numbers of the consumers began to change their attitude to material goods that they would also change their attitude to the things that brought them those material goods, namely advertising and marketing. Elementary, perhaps. But judging by the official research produced for the advertising establishment on either side of the Atlantic, it would be wrong.

According to the Institute of Practitioners in Advertising 1969 survey, 79% of the population approve either a little or a lot of advertising. That's almost eight out of ten. And this figure is only slightly less than the approval figure of 1961.

On the other side of the Atlantic, the position is apparently equally rosy. The 1969 Gallup study showed that two-thirds of Americans were favourable towards the statement that 'advertising is good for keeping you informed about the things you buy'. And 75%, according to a study done by Bauer and Grayser, had either a mixed or a favourable attitude towards advertising.

This same study also gave an analysis of people's reactions to the advertisements they paid attention to. Everyone in this exhaustive experiment was given a little counter which they were asked to press every time they noted an advertisement. And every time they felt that the advertisement they noted was either annoying, enjoyable, informative or offensive they were asked to

174

fill out a card saying so. Of all the cards counted under 4% were dubbed annoying in the sample. And this 4% of annoying ads. represented less than a quarter of all the advertisements to which the consumer paid sufficient attention to fill out a card.

A survey in 1969 by the Independent Television Authority on people's attitudes to television commercials reported similar glowing conclusions among the viewers, despite the fact that they were being bombarded by up to 80 commercials a day. Almost half of those interviewed said they found all advertisements enjoyable. A finding endorsed, in the I.T.A.'s view, by the fact that they only received sixty letters of complaint in 1971, and a quarter of these were about one specific television commercial (that for Omo and its understains).

To the reader, this apparent acceptance of the bombardment of persuasion may appear baffling. Have all our senses been so dulled that we stare with blind contentment at the advertisements, registering but the slightest twinge of displeasure as we all know in our hearts that advertising is essential for the Free Enterprise System? To anyone who's ever been in a room full of people where the television commercials have been on the air, this conclusion must seem insupportable. Indeed, looking at all these studies one would never be able to predict the consumer revolution as this book has so far described it. Looking at this data one would conclude that the consumer was in no important respect different from the consumer of 1950. That the wealth and information explosions had never existed. And that all that separated this decade from the last one was the passage of ten years.

But what is this conclusion-shaking data based on? It is simple *quantitative* data: you ask people a straight question with a limited number of options for answers. It's the sort of survey which is beloved by the numerates who believe that when scraping off these surface opinions they are in fact 'measuring' something. Whether they are right is a matter to come back to in a later chapter that looks at the whole mysterious way in which advertising works.

Probably a better guide to what people think deep down is provided by *qualitative* data. This doesn't involve asking direct questions with limited options for answers. It means not so much taking measurements as *soundings*. Qualitative data are often provided by group discussions where up to a dozen people sit round to discuss, under the supervision of a psychologist, some broad general issue which gradually focuses itself, through group participation, onto the topic you want discussed. It's true such data doesn't fit onto slide rules so easily. But it does provide a far more sensitive measurement of what people really feel.

With this in mind six group discussions with cross-sections of consumers in the Greater London Area were organized to see if their in-depth feelings tallied with the results of the other data. The result was something of a shock. The degree of hostility to advertisements that appeared was quite out of line with the contented smiles the other surveys had led one to expect. A few quotations from the tapes will give the flavour of the discussion.

'I thought they were trying to treat you as a very young child.'

'They try to make their products seem better than they are.'

'It absolutely irritates me, it's so corny.'

'I must say I resent buying magazines full of advertisements. . . I'm the one who's really paying for them.'

'At first the commercials are just silly, but when you see them time after time they really annoy you.'

'As soon as the commercials come on the air I leave the room.'

'You know that all the people giving testimonials have been paid.'

'What really makes me boil is when they use children in television commercials.'

The phrase that was repeated again and again was 'it's only advertising'. Clearly, for these consumers advertising had entirely ceased to be a useful source of information in making product choices. Something that isn't useful, but to which you're continually and forcibly exposed.

The other point which emerged clearly was the difference in attitude towards advertisements and advertising. The clean bill of health that the other studies gave was in fact for *advertising*. And these in-depth discussions also agreed that advertising in principle was, if not a 'good thing', at least as central a part of life as the motor car.

When the discussion changed from the principle to the practice, from advertising to *advertisements* a very different view predominated (as the examples make clear). The attitude of the consumer to advertising is, in short, very similar to the attitude of a crusty Tory to Harold Wilson. In principle, he believes in parliamentary government and the existence of a forceful opposition. But in practice he's likely to wish to have Mr Wilson's guts for garters.

Is it possible to reconcile the earlier data with these more pessimistic conclusions (which commonsense would have predicted anyhow)?

For a start, it's worth pointing out – if a trifle churlish – that all the figures I quoted earlier were from studies commissioned by bodies with a vested interest in giving advertising a clean bill of health. One of the I.P.A.'s jobs is to keep a shine on advertising's public image. The Bauer and Greyser study was sponsored by the American Association of Advertising Agencies, so it would have been a surprise if their overall conclusions had been vastly different from the expectations of their sponsors. And the I.T.A. have the job of making sure only appropriate advertisements get onto the television screen, so their standpoint cannot be unbiased.

This is not to say that the researchers who carried out these studies actually fudged their findings. But if you find, as did the I.T.A., that 44% enjoy television commercials, do you express it in this form (implying all is well) or do you say a minority of television viewers actually enjoy television commercials, an equally accurate version from the evidence? Or take the Bauer and Greyser figure that 'only' 25% of advertisements to which consumers paid attention were found annoying. On one premise that would be interpreted as meaning that people have basically a favourable attitude to advertising. On the other hand, once you find – as the group discussions showed – that consumers seem to have a far less favourable attitude then an alternative interpretation of this same statistic makes more sense. And the 25% annoyance level starts to look *high*, not low.

It is reasonable, after all, to expect the brain's filtering mechanism to admit only that information which, on an unconscious level, appeared useful to it. Assuming that the brain was an efficient filtering apparatus one would expect the vast majority of advertisements to which a consumer paid attention to be one that he or she expected to find useful or enjoyable. On this basis, every percentage point of disapproval for an advertisement by a consumer represents a degree of disappointment in finding that the message she admitted to her consciousness was not of any use to her.

Bauer and Greyser found that one out of four advertisements

to which a consumer paid sufficient attention to not only press a hand trigger but also fill out a card, came into this category. To have one advertisement in four disappoint the consumer in this way must be a source of great irritation. More especially so, if one believes, as commonsense suggests, that one percentage point of disapproval probably carries more weight than one percentage point of approval. In the same way that discomfort is a stronger sensation than comfort. In actual fact, if one looks at other parts of the voluminous Bauer and Greyser survey, figures arise from the morass of statistics that cast grave doubt on the overall favourable impression that emerges from reading the book.

They have, for example, a table of 'top of the mind sources of annoyance'. This was established by putting this question: 'Everyone has some things that annoy them like health, money and other people. Aside from that kind of personal problem what four or five things annoy you most?' Excluding the personal sources of annoyance like the inconsideration of your neighbour hanging up his washing just before your friends are coming in for tea, the main percentage of spontaneous mentions of annoyance were as follows:

Noise	13%
Things relating to advertising	9%
Government and government policies	6%
Traffic	4%
Weather	4%
Breaking down of machinery	4%
Politics and politicians	3%
Housework	1%

The fact that one American in ten finds advertising a source of everyday annoyance is serious enough for the advertising community. What is even more revealing than the absolute measurement is the ranking of advertising. It received as many *spontaneous* mentions as a source of annoyance as the whole apparatus of government, government policies, politics, and politicians. And it's *nine* times more annoying for most Americans than the everyday drudgery of housework.

This table was published over four years ago in America, but I've not yet seen it referred to in any of the American or European advertising trade papers. And it certainly wasn't referred to in the summary done for the I.P.A. by Dr John Treasure of J. Walter Thompson of the Bauer and Greyser study. Such is the power of selective perception (see page 219).

This Bauer and Greyser statistic is even more significant because they also found that advertising wasn't very 'salient' to people's lives. Three times as many people, for instance, mentioned the federal government as something they talked about most as mentioned advertising. Yet despite this peripheral position in people's consciousness, advertising is one of the main sources of public annoyance.

As a matter of fact, even though the I.P.A., guided by Dr Treasure, reported that the Bauer and Greyser survey said that 'when asked, the vast majority of people are in favour of advertising', this figure is in fact the combined favourable *and* mixed attitudes. If you just take the favourable *without* the mixed attitudes you find, according to Bauer and Greyser, that only a *minority* (41%) of Americans approve of advertising.

In the same vein of re-examining the published 'evidence', one figure from the I.T.A. study which whitewashed television advertising is interesting. The 42% of the sample of 1,100 people who said they found commercials 'enjoyable' were also asked to name any commercials that they had enjoyed. Out of these 4,000 different commercials transmitted in 1970, these 462 people could only name 50 advertisements between them. Granted that advertisements slip easily from the memory, but it still seems an extraordinarily low number of commercials to be mentioned by an audience alleged to 'enjoy' the transmissions of those 4,000 sales spiels.

A final comment on the ambiguous nature of the consumer's approval of television commercials recorded in the I.T.A.'s survey: one advertising trade paper (*Campaign*) headed their story on it 'Few think TV ads. mislead.' whereas the other trade paper (*Adweekly*) headed their story 'Half I.T.V. viewers distrust commercials'.

On those rare occasions when the advertising establishment in a moment of weakness is persuaded to concede the existence of some hostility towards advertising, they always add a proviso. They argue that this hostility is purely an educated middle-class quirk – 'a small percentage of narrow ascetic or clannish people' to quote Mr John Hobson, Chairman of the Advertising Association – and that amongst the bulk of the market place there is

179

still a benign tolerance for the advertising practitioner, whose excesses are allegedly taken with no more than a pinch of good humoured cynicism.

This belief is similar in pedigree to the idea that consumerism is a strictly middle-class kink. And in a formal sense it may be true. Few working-class wives have a coherently worked out position to justify their feeling of hostility towards a majority of advertisements. But you don't need to be able to justify a feeling in order to have it. And the evidence of all the in-depth discussions was that the hostility towards advertising spread right across the class scale. The fact that working-class papers like the *People, The News of the World, The Sun* and The *Mirror* run Nader-style exposés of advertising and its related arts surely confirm this. Anyone who believes that a docile proletariat exists happily lapping up the jingles has never walked down Coronation Street.

The development of hostility amongst the workers is worrying enough for the hidden persuaders. What is as alarming is that the business community is also growing hostile towards advertising. Businessmen wear two hats: they're both consumers and advertisers. And if this group is starting to bite the hand that allegedly feeds them, the ulcers of Madison Avenue have good reason to twinge. A study in the *Harvard Business Review,* carried out by the indefatigable Steven Greyser, found that 'Businessmen today take a somewhat more critical stance than they did nine years ago'. He found, for example, that a majority of the 2,700 businessmen thought that – compared to nine years ago – there was a greater proportion of advertisements which insulted the public's intelligence, which insulted their own intelligence, and which were irritating.

The most extraordinary aspect of this reaction against advertising is not that it should exist, but that the advertising industry should believe that it doesn't. Or if it does, then only in forms and in areas that are so tiny or so limited as to be of no practical significance. Very few admen sitting down to write an advertisement believe that they are addressing an overwhelmingly hostile audience. It is rather as though a Conservative politician were to address a meeting of staunch Labour Party supporters with the same speech and in the same way as he would address a rally of Tory Party faithfuls.

That enormous companies entrust equally enormous sums of

money and their reputation to people with this degree of fore-sight may surprise the reader. But we shall save our explanations of this for the following chapters, where the curious theory of how advertising works will be explored. But first a more pressing question demands an answer: if it is accepted that the majority of the population are far more hostile to advertising than the advertising industry has led itself to believe, can the industry still be blamed for this hostility? Hasn't sufficient already been said in this book, about a revolt against authority, about a more educated and sophisticated consumer, to show that this hostility is simply the backwash inevitably produced as our great society sails further and yet further forward?

It is a plausible argument, not the least because it is partly true, that the structural changes within affluent societies in the last twenty years *have* created conditions within which hostility towards advertising, as the torch bearer of a way of life increasingly under attack, was likely. But that is not to say that such hostility was *inevitable*. It was not inevitable that advertising should generate nine times more hostility than the drudgery of housework (which is also resented by the modern woman). It was not inevitable that advertising should generate as much hostility as the whole apparatus of government, government policies, politics and politicians (also resented as the concept of authority begins to crumble). What has happened is that, in ways which the rest of this chapter will endeavour to explain, the advertising industry has wilfully lit fires which are now threatening to roast it alive.

The first of these generators of hostility is admittedly something not easily within the control of the ad man himself: the sheer volume of advertising. Apart from selflessly cutting back his own budget there may be little an individual advertiser can do. That the whole industry is so helpless to restrict the volume of its own outpourings is not quite so obvious.

In fairness, it should be said that the growth of advertising is just another dimension of the information explosion spoken of in previous chapters. Malcolm Muggeridge has coined the phrase 'newsak' to describe the information pollution that harries him while he seeks peace and quiet in his car or in his bathroom. The total volume of this is reported by Alvin Toffler to be ten to twenty thousand words of print material and twenty thousand words of radio and television material 'ingested' per day. Taking television advertising alone, the American philosopher S. I. Hayakawa has calculated that by the age of eighteen the modern American child has watched 350,000 commercials.

And though the editorial side of this information input is huge, it is at least something which the consumer has chosen to look at. She turns on the television to watch Coronation Street or Bonanza. She opens the paper to read the news. But the battery of advertising messages has no such invitation. Very few people actually open a paper or turn on the television to see the advertisements.

Estimates of the number of these uninvited intrusions into the consumer's day vary from about 500 (based on a calculation done by a marketing director of General Foods) to 305 a day for for women and 285 a day for men (based on a recent study by BBDO New York). Even at this lowest figure it still represents an orgy of abrasive sound and sight all designed to induce the consumer to do something he or she might not otherwise do (which, again, is not a characteristic of the editorial information she receives). And all the time this din is getting louder. In Britain in 1952, for example, £126 million was the total expenditure on advertising. By 1969, at 1952 space rates, this had grown by *two and a half times* to £315 million (or £535 million in actual money). The growth of 'invisible' classified advertising accounts for some of the increase. But this 'invisible' advertising still had no higher proportion of all advertising in 1969 than 1952.

If you are in any doubt as to the commonsense consequence of this increase in weight of advertising look at the chart in Bauer and Greyser on page 298 of their overwhelmingly comprehensive treatise. This shows that advertisements for the six most heavily advertised product groups were thought to be *twice* as annoying and almost *half* as informative as the advertisements for the remaining (and less advertised) product groups. On this basis, the more you spend the more hostility you risk creating.

Of course, it is not just the weight of advertising that is irritating, the *content* has quite a lot to answer for as well. The deluge of persuasion might be *just* acceptable if like the vicar who knocked on your door, it was polite, respectful and truthful. But on the grounds of truthfulness alone advertising is found seriously wanting.

The *Reader's Digest* Survey of Europe showed that only 37% of people were either partially or generally favourable to the statement that 'in general, advertising presents a true picture of the product advertised'. In Britain and America, *two-thirds* of the population disagreed with this statement. And disbelief in advertising is growing. The biggest single shift measured by Steven Greyser in his *Harvard Business Review* study comparing businessmen's attitudes to advertising in 1962 and 1971 was in this area. He found that the proportion of businessmen who believed advertising presented a true picture of the product had slumped by 24%. By 1971 the proportion of businessmen who believed that advertising told the truth was even *lower* than the proportion of the general public who did. And businessmen, as the clients of the advertising agencies, are the ones who ought to know.

Returning to this side of the Atlantic, where those layers of regulations are meant to weed out terminological inexactitudes, a study by the International Publishing Corporation found that 42% of young consumers thought all advertisements were misleading. And about the same number told the I.T.A.'s researchers that television commercials weren't to be trusted. So if you put all the various statistics together you have about half the population believing that despite the rules and regulations advertising isn't truthful.

And, again, the *more* you advertise the *less* truthful your advertising appears to be. Bauer and Greyser found that amongst five of the seven top spending advertising categories 'informational failure' (a polite way of saying that the advertisement was judged by the consumer to be untruthful in some way or another) was often *double* the average of the lower spending product categories.

This is probably a measure of the degree to which big advertisers with their me-too products have continually succumbed to the temptation to stretch credulity further and further in order to add to their sales points. But all that has happened, as the following chapter will show, is that their advertisements are taken with approximately larger pinches of salt by the consumer. According to the ever quotable Professor Galbraith the consumer has now developed a mechanism for dealing with these untruths. He writes in the *New Industrial State*: 'Because modern man is exposed to a large degree of unreliable information, he establishes a system of discounts which he applies to the various sources (of information) almost without question. This discount becomes almost total for all forms of advertising.' It's a rather chilling thought for anyone whose livelihood depends on his ability to make consumers respond to the advertising messages he creates. But there was evidence enough in chapter four as to why this 'system of discounts' should be so severe on the admen.

Brian Young, Director General of the I.T.A., doubtless wouldn't agree with this. For he told a gathering of London admen that 'if there is a problem, it is not a question of deception. It's a question of disbelief'. In other words, though advertising has been telling the truth, the complete truth and nothing but the truth, a cruel and cynical public persists in disbelieving it.

A behavioural psychologist could tell him that this disbelief is no more than a conditioned reflex as a result of continual disappointments after taking advertisements at their word. And if one looks at a $1 million American government study. *The Effect's of Television Advertising on Children* you start to see how distrust for advertising develops even before a child can fully understand the advertisement itself. Kindergarten children, according to this study, had 'virtually no understanding of the purpose of the commercials'. Yet what did a kindergarten child answer to the question 'Do you think commercials always tell the truth?': 'Nooooo!'

By the age of *seven* children had a 'clear recognition that advertisements were intended to sell' and 'semi-recognition of the advertisers' motives'. For example : Question, 'what are advertisements for?': Answer, 'to make you buy (products)'. Question, 'why do they want you to buy?' Answer, 'so they can get more money and support the factories they have'. All from a seven-year-old.

This 'cue to manipulative intent' to use the psychologist's jargon, has somehow been learned by the child. Maybe by watching his parents' reaction to television commercials he has already grown this membrane of scepticism. But from then on the mere act of selling to him will put his psychological bristles up and trigger off the Galbraithian system of discounts.

But it's not just something he's learnt from his parents or teachers. 'Second graders', says the study, 'indicated concrete distrust of commercials *often based on experience of advertised products*' (my italics). 'Fourth graders exhibited mistrust of specific commercials and tricky elements of commercials and sixth graders (twelve-year-olds) exhibited global mistrust'. 'Global mistrust' from a boy whose voice hasn't even broke.

And the number one reason behind this generally contemptuous attitude of American children? A further study showed that products 'not like the ads. say they are' was the reason given.

Any grown-up who's never seen a commercial for toy racing cars that makes it seem as though they're selling formula two dragsters (like the Johnnie Lightning script quoted earlier) or watched a dancing doll commercial that suggests you're really buying a syncopated robot that frugs like a sixteen-year-old can understand the disillusion of a child. No wonder then that the *Financial Times* reported from the Brighton Toy Fair that retailers were now disenchanted with hard sell television advertising. Even though the manufacturers had jacked up their expenditure on television by 20%, it didn't work as effectively as the previous year. After reading this U.S. government report, the reason for this failure in Britain is surely clear: the children had learnt to disbelieve the exaggeration of the advertisements and weren't going to be taken in a second year running.

Up to this point, the assumption has been made that the consumer *requires* an advertisement to be truthful and if it isn't he places a black mark against it. But is this correct? Or do consumers grant poetic licence to the practitioners of commercial verse?

In one sense, the discussion is an old one: 'Doth any man doubt', asked Sir Francis Bacon in his essay on Truth, 'that if there were taken out of men's minds vain opinions, flattering hopes, false valuations, imaginations as one would, and the like, but it would leave the minds of a number of men poor shrunken things, full of melancholy and indisposition and unpleasing to themselves?'

Four centuries later came Harvard's distinguished Professor Theodore Levitt to press the same case for advertising. 'I shall argue', he wrote in the *Harvard Business Review*, 'that embellishment and distortion are among advertising's legitimate and socially desirable purposes.' For advertising, like art, achieved its effect by being larger than life. Moreover, echoing Master Bacon, 'without distortions, embellishment and elaboration life would be drab, dull, anguished and at its existential worst'.

Whether the exaggerations and distortions of advertising do in fact act like a ray of sunshine in the grey little lives all of us lead is something the reader must judge for himself. Certainly, a claim that is obviously not meant to be taken too seriously and is perhaps treated humorously ('Happiness is a cigar called Hamlet' or 'The disadvantages of smoking Benson and Hedges 100s') may come into the category of accepted embellishment. But do the whiter than white soap operas have the same charm?

The trouble with any argument that advertising is entitled to the same illusions as literature is that it forgets that literature declares quite openly that it is an illusion. Advertising generally does not, it hides this fact for nakedly commercial reasons. Keats' 'Ode to a Grecian Urn' may be embellishing the truth but it is intended to uplift your soul. But an ode to a new cake mix is intended only to uplift the sales graph.

Those who declare that the two situations are the same must answer for part of the credibility gap that now separates advertising from its audience. Is it any wonder that many consumers now believe advertising is simply lying raised to the heights of respectability when the admen are given this sort of encouragement to gild their lilies?

A cartoon in one of the American advertising papers shows the path to which a less than scrupulous regard for truth leads. A round table meeting of advertising executives was drawn with one of them saying 'seventy hospitals tested our product and found it completely ineffectual. But we can still advertise it as "hospital tested" '. This of course is a joke. But it betrays the core of cynicism about the value of verity that is alarming. Few who have worked even for a short time in an agency can have failed to be infected (and the present writer does not claim immunity) by the open acceptance of the stretching of truth which is the *practical* consequences of Theodore Levitt's philosophy.

Disbelief in advertising has led, naturally enough, to disbelief in the mouth that apparently utters these not so magic words: the advertiser. A study by the Supermarket Institute of America found that only car salesmen were thought to be lower in credibility than advertising executives. And government officials were regarded as being *forty* times more credible than advertising executives. The position, in a phrase, is that the advertisers are now regarded as compulsive liars. People whose job of selling their products makes them almost incapable of telling the truth.

In Victorian times it probably was possible for the untruth of advertising to be tolerable in the same way that someone always telling tall stories is tolerable (and sometimes amusing). You know that you're listening to a fib and so you don't take it too seriously. But how would you feel if this compulsive liar started to burst into your living room every night and pester you with fibs and half-truths? Would you still smile as you did when Beechams told you their pills were worth the (preposterous) sum of 'a guinea a box'? It is this barging in without even bothering to knock, the intrusiveness of the new advertising media – television – that has eroded still further the consumer's tolerance of his persuaders.

Reverting once more to our faithful friends Bauer and Greyser one finds that, when asked why they found certain advertisements annoying, consumers mention 'intrusiveness' *even more often than 'informational failure'*. In other words, the sheer act of having something rammed down your throat is as unpleasant as its nasty taste. The 'intrusive' media is, of course, television though 'involving' not 'intrusive' is the word Marshall McLuhan would use to describe the electronic medium.

Perhaps the point is that television, which should be a very low-pressure, open ended medium, has been used by advertisers as a high-pressure huckster. In McLuhan's terminology, they have treated a cool medium as though it was hot. The fact that most television commercial jingles are nearly always used as radio commercials as well shows how the advertiser treats television as though it was no more than 'radio with pictures'. You only need to look at the special television stars like Perry Como, Jack Paar, or even David Frost and compare their *style* with the style of the advertisements that slice up their shows. What has happened is that advertising has used the undoubted power of the television medium to *force* attention when perhaps it should have used it to *invite* involvement and participation.

In print advertising, advertisers can get away with this practice without being quite so irritating, because it is easier not to look at the advertisement. Being still and silent it carries less poke. And, even more important, there is alternative viewing matter while you are being exposed to the advertisement. This is not true of a television commercial. On television your programme is interrupted by an advertisement in a way that your newspaper is not. The consumer still has a whole battery of defence mechanisms to keep out the televison intrusion. But it is the fact that he has to work so hard not to pay attention to something he doesn't want to look at that is the source of irritation.

A study for the I.P.A. gives the scale of this compulsory exposure to advertisments for products in which the consumer isn't even interested (however brilliant the advertisement). In the first six months of 1969 the heaviest male viewers of I.T.V. saw over 200 commercials, 125 margarine commercials and 120 toilet soap commercials. The heaviest female viewers had the pleasure of seeing 125 draught beer commercials and 100 razor blade commercials. It is for this sort of reason that television advertising was shown in the same study to be ten times more annoying and ten times more silly than press advertising. With the result that five times as many people said they'd be happy to see television advertising done away with compared to press advertising.

The truth is that the very reversal is happening in many countries. Twenty years ago in Britain, for example, 0% of all advertising was spent on television. Since the introduction of commercial television in 1955 the proportion has steadily risen until today more than £1 in £4 spent by advertisers is spent on television. For the really big advertisers the proportion was even higher: 57 of the top 100 British advertisers spent more than half of their budget on television.

But even if the total level of television advertising wasn't rising, the way it was spent could still make the *amount* of this intrusive form of advertising appear to increase. In America, for example, the shift from 60-second to 30-second commercials helped to cause a 50% increase in the number of commercials transmitted on the network from 1964 to 1968. They shot up from 1,950 a month to 3,022 a month. Despite this growth even American television at the heaviest peak of advertising has no more than 27% of television time devoted to advertising (which is one of the highest figures in the world). The average magazine or newspaper carries, proportionately, a great deal more advertising than this. Few advertising managers feel satisfied unless they have sold 40% of the total space in the paper to advertisers. Clearly then, the same amount of money spent in the press would generate far less hostility than that amount spent on television. And the table opposite makes the point that, in Europe at least, the more minutes of television advertising which are allowed the greater the hostility towards advertising.

Country	Minutes of television advertising allowed per day	Percentage favourable to advertising (*Reader's Digest* Survey)
Holland	10	79%
France	13	72%
Switzerland	15	61%
Germany	20	51%
Austria	20	64%
Italy	27	61%
Spain	60	42%

In some of these countries there are extra restraints which would reduce still further the irritating impact of television commercials. In Italy, for instance, a television commercial can't be repeated more than five times: it has to be changed. So saving the viewer from the endlessly repetitive bombardment common in other countries.

There is one final aspect of the intrusiveness of television advertising which merits some consideration. The move to television in countries like Britain and America has shifted the brunt of advertising down the class scale. Print media, by virtue of the fact that they require some effort are read most by the best educated. Television, because it requires less effort, is watched most by the least educated. Workers in Britain, for instance, watch 31% more television than business executives.

Moreover, given the extraordinarily irritating nature of television advertising, one has here a further explanation of why consumer power has been provoked into existence in the working class as well as the middle class. For, contrary to a view popular in certain advertising agencies, the working classes are not simply the middle classes with less money and less brains. Their structure of life is profoundly different. And one of the key differences concerns the role of the home. The home for the affluent white-collar worker already regarding himself as middle-class, is a place to which even distant friends are invited. It is not a holy of holies reserved only for kin and very close friends which it is for the blue-collar worker (as Goldthorpe and his colleagues discovered in Luton).

It is into this very private sanctuary that the advertisers send their television commercials every night. To a middle-class home, which is not such a closed environment, these uninvited incursions into the living room are bad enough. But for the working-class man, his privacy has been shattered in a quite different sort of way. And, when the advertiser opens his mouth to actually deliver his sales spiel he generally does it in a way that alienates his audience still further. The blame for this lies with the various philosophies of advertising that lie behind the sales messages. And if one looks at these it becomes clear that the way advertisers have chosen to speak to their public has had the effect of rubbing salt into the already open wound. Of the five main philosophies of advertising, four must be regarded as profound irritants to the consumer.

If we take a thirty-five-year-old housewife of today we can trace over her lifespan a variety of theories of communication that have been practised on her, whose net affect has probably been to make her not so much think more of the product as to think less of the advertising. At the time this thirty-five-year-old was born Claude Hopkins was waging dreadful war on the jokey style of advertising that had held sway between the wars. The 'Alas my poor brother' for Bovril and the 'Guinness for strength' campaign.

Hopkins who wrote 'Washed in live steam' to make Schlitz the best selling beer in America (earning himself a salary at today's price of £250,000 a year) had no time for such pleasantries. 'The average person', he wrote, 'is constantly choosing between ways to spend his money. Appeal for money in a lightsome way and you'll never get it. Nobody can cite a permanent success built of frivolity. People do not buy from clowns.' This joyless doctrine, which eventually led to the view that if consumers actually liked your advertisement there was probably something wrong with it, runs like a thin thread of gloom through many of the subsequent theories of advertising.

Immediately after the war a man called Rosser Reeves put on the mantle of Hopkins. By then it was clear that the natural state of products in a mass production society was similarity. Some people write as though this was a recent phenomenon. But ever since Henry Ford got his Tin Lizzies rolling, it's been normal for the actual differences between competing products to be small. Of course, each product tended to be different in some way. But the difference was strictly marginal.

It was out of these marginal differences between brands that Rosser Reeves believed the admen should construct his own Unique Selling Proposition. The 'uniqueness' of the proposition was just as likely to result from making a unique claim about an otherwise homogenous product as it was from having a unique product itself. But having got your U.S.P., you then hammered those few magic words into the consumer's skull in the same way that a carpenter bangs a nail into a plank. And with very often the same results: the recipient got a severe headache.

Some of the better known U.S.P.s include Colgate's, 'Helps stop bad breath, fights tooth decay' (which had been running at least as long as Agatha Christie's *Mousetrap*); Treet's, 'Melts in your mouth, not in your hand'; and Fairy Liquid's, 'Hands that do dishes can feel soft as your face'.

In fairness to the U.S.P., it should be said that in the post-war economy, where consumer goods were in short supply and where the media environment was less saturated, this approach made some sort of sense. And judged by the measurements put against it by the agency who invented it (something to be discussed at a later stage) it certainly worked. But by the late fifties, as both wealth and education levels rose, some practitioners of the art began to feel that making major claims out of marginal product differences was no longer sensible : 'Let us remember', pontificated David Ogilvy, 'that it is always the total personality of the brand, rather than any trivial product differences which decides its ultimate position in the market.' In short, forget the quality, feel the myth. This was the theory of the brand image. Ogilvy became amazingly successful by his ability to put his client's products on a pedestal and worship them in magnificent English prose. Like Hathaway shirts, Schweppes tonic water and Rolls Royce cars.

But though this sort of advertising (which by the way was an addition to, and not a replacement of, the Hopkins/Reeves school) *did* create less hostility in the sense that it was less prone to bashing sales points into consumer's skulls, it created another sort of irritation instead. For the image of the product that could satisfy the whole dimension of the consumer's personality was (as the last three chapters have argued) far from the truth. And consumers knew it.

The other sort of irritation that resulted from Ogilvy related to the language he recommended admen to use. For though he was the man who said : 'The consumer is no moron, she is your wife', he was also the man who suggested a basic vocabulary for the would-be successful advertiser of twenty-five key words.

Like *new, free, important, sensational* etc. etc. Without any qualification as to how apposite they might be to the product concerned. Perhaps it's revealing that in none of his best advertisements did Ogilvy fall back on the formula he so keenly recommended to others.

After the publicity Ogilvy gave to brand imagery it soon ran out of control with motivation researchers rushing in to find that everything was full of hidden meaning. Even eating your breakfast cereal meant a lot more than simply filling your stomach. In the words of the high priest of motivation research, Ernest Ditcher: 'Breakfast, or breaking the fast has an interesting psychological role. The greater the fighting attitude people have towards the struggle of the day, the more they seem to be insistent on consuming a good breakfast. This is one of the reasons why mushy soft cereals are rejected.'

When it didn't stray over the lunatic fringe, most of this so-called motivation research was just sound common sense. But in the hands of an American professor of journalism called Vance Packard it became something else. Admen were 'hidden persuaders' and consumers were mere lumps of clay to be moulded and shaped to the ends of big business.

Whether or not this is how advertising works is something to be discussed later. But the important point to be made now is that all this persuaded many advertisers and their agencies that they possessed semi-magical powers. And that image-rich, motivation-inspired advertising ruled the world. And so this was the period when glossy materialism received its greatest promotion. The fact that many consumers were already falling out of love with it was something that most of the admen overlooked.

The lone voice in the wilderness was that of a man called Bill Bernbach who in 1948 had helped to start an agency called Doyle, Dane, Bernbach. Rather than hero worshipping the product, he treated it as an anti-hero. Like the consumer he took a slightly irreverent view of the product. He admitted that not every product was perfect (remember the advertisement showing a picture of a shining Volkswagen with the word 'lemon' underneath?). He recognized that for the consumer biggest didn't always mean best (remember Avis' 'we're number two' campaign?).

The tragedy of Bill Bernbach is that he wasn't as vigorous as Ogilvy or Reeves in selling his philosophy. For example, the other two wrote books to explain their beliefs, but Bernbach made no such missionary efforts for his particular cause. The result was that his view of advertising, which *could* have defused a lot of the hostility that has since built up, remained a minority cult. The new clean-limbed graphics of the Bernbach school were certainly widely adopted. But for the most part they were just new clothes for the old thoughts of Reeves and Ogilvy.

In Britain today, not more than 3% of the £600 million spent on advertising is spent in a way that takes full account of Bill Bernbach's beliefs. Hopkins, Reeves, and Ogilvy still rule the commercial air waves.

One of the most extraordinary facets of the development of these techniques is that they stopped around 1960. Since 1960 there's been virtually no new thinking of the advertising basics. The industry is still shuffling the pack of the pre-1960 ideas and coasting along on the dynamism of times very different from our own. This fashionable, highly paid, fast talking profession seems to have run out of ideas (as opposed to glib headlines). And they are now, by and large, selling to Mrs 1972 in *basically* the same way as they sold to Mrs 1952. If you strip their handiwork of the slick graphic and look at the central core, it isn't a *lot* different from the ads of yesteryear.

The only exception to this intellectual sterility has come from someone who's in no way part of Madison Avenue hurly-burly – Marshall McLuhan. McLuhan's particular style of writing is to throw out a barrage of ideas and ask the reader to sift the good from the bad: 'probes', he calls them. Some of McLuhan's 'probes' about advertising are just what one might expect from an ex-Wordsworth scholar who wanders lonely as a cloud to be suddenly confronted by a field of plastic daffodils (free with Daz). For example, he describes puns as one of the highest forms of advertising because they act as a decoy for the brain's rational defence mechanisms. While occupied unravelling the pun, the subjective imagery of the advertisement rushes with electronic speed into the consumer's cranium to manipulate her as the advertiser wishes. Which is a highbrow endorsement of an advertising practice that more often than not should be regarded as commercial self-abuse.

The sad point about McLuhan's impact on television advertising was that he did have some important things to say. Particularly about the impact of non-verbal, unfocused advertising messages on people. And the right and wrong ways to use

193

television as an advertising medium. But as the line of his argument ran directly counter to the practices of the admen it tended not to be identified.

So there we have it: Rosser Reeves, David Ogilvy, Ernest Dichter, Bill Bernbach, Marshall McLuhan: the stuffing that the hidden persuaders are made of.

If we go back to the American study of television advertising and children, an interesting parallel emerges between the assorted techniques of the admen and the cognitive development of a child. The authors of this part of the study, Blatt, Spencer and Ward, put together the work of educational psychologists on a child's cognitive development and deduced from that the sort of advertising appeals that would be most appropriate at each level. The first level of a child's development, at the age of five, is where he is impulsive, self-protective and submissive. 'At this level viewers respond principally to basic needs and fears and tend to be most receptive to commercials which demand, threaten or use hard sell.' And 'advertisements aimed at this level can be blunt, direct and concrete'. Cast your mind back to the Rosser Reeves/Hopkins school of advertising and you see that it will work like clockwork on a five-year-old.

Level two, according to this study, is characterized by 'intentional self interest'. 'Viewers at this level are most susceptible to appeals to "hedonistic" personal desires, "mastery" and "power". Themes which appeal to self-image...and sexual identity.'

So by the age of six to seven, the child has grown out of a susceptibility to Rosser Reeves and has become susceptible to what amounts to brand image advertising à la Dichter and Ogilvy. And the power of this sort of appeal lasts through level three (the eight-year-olds) when conformity is the order of the day. 'Viewers at this level are most susceptible to "other directed" appeals – comparisons with others, themes based on an individual's need for social approval, popularity and status.' This, in short, is brand image advertising that recognizes the influence of others in addition to the influence of self (of level two).

But by the time level four (aged ten) is reached the child is no longer under the influence of these sorts of spells. Now 'conscientiousness' is part of a child's mental development. So the viewer responds to appeals to duty, functional utility and rational role requirements.

Level four appeals, says this study, tend to be objective and

194

factual – which, of course, is almost a blueprint for Bill Bernbach. But by the age of twelve, a child has started to grow out of even this higher level. For the final level identified is what is called 'social utilitarian integrative and self-actualizing'. 'Viewers at this level respond preferentially to aesthetic, altruistic moral social concern appeals: buy this and you'll improve society while attaining your own highest potential.' This is the level that advertisers have not yet reached, but a child reaches by the age of twelve.

And it is this phenomenon which is the final irritation and that has, after twenty years, goaded consumers into a new sort of fury: the way that the advertiser continually and persistently insults their intelligence. First, by promoting trivia as though it was God's gift to humanity. And second, by talking to consumers as though they were the inhabitants of a school for backward children.

Taking the first point first, it isn't for a very worthy cause that 'Coronation Street' is sliced in half twice a week. It's for the deodorants, the drinks, the soaps, the toothpastes, the patent medicines, the detergents, the breakfast cereals. These are the pipsqueaks that make such a fuss about themselves. And it's not as though there is such a tremendous difference between them. The typical mass market product advertised on television duplicates the functions of its rivals so closely that, if the copywriter weren't paid to do so he would often be extremely reluctant to recommend one over the other to a friend. But you can't pull the 'new improved' wool over Mrs 1972's eyes. She knows in her heart that most brand advertising is trying to persuade the consumer that she is not buying a commodity product when in fact she is.

If the advertising was selling something important (like health insurance for example) hollering and shouting might be tolerable. But to simply dispose of what may be regarded as the flotsam and jetsam of the industrial state, the bombardment of persuasion is just too much. It isn't just the screams that upset the consumer. It's the way the advertiser always seems to be talking about things that are meaningless to the consumer. And talking about them in a way which gives the product a ludicrously over-important role in somebody's life. The detergent (it was Daz) that will make the neighbours think more of you when they see your nice white washing on the line. Or in America the detergent 'that will help these girls to get married' (a detergent? How does that grab you marriage bureaux?) The bedtime drink (it was Horlicks) that can turn a Weary Willy into a superman by the quaffing of flavoured malted milk every night. And always the suggestion that by swallowing some sort of simple chemical you can solve the sort of problems that would have baffled Freud. That this product or that product can either solve the problems of the modern woman or, at least, complete the enchantment she's meant to feel in her traditional role.

But the fact is these roll-on fairy godmothers exist only in the figment of the advertisers' fevered minds. Face creams don't subtract years from the face. A cigarette isn't the peak of a relationship that two people can reach (even when it is mentholated). No detergent, even when it's called Fab, can magic a crumpled thirty-five-year-old housewife into looking like 'a bride every time'. Nor is serving Atora beef suet the most a woman can do to show she still feels like she did on her wedding day ('Show him you love him with Atora').

Believe it or not there are people who turn out this sort of advertisement every day and who seriously feel that in doing so they're adding to the sum total of happiness in the world. As a copywriter at McCann Erickson explained : 'If you have "all day freshness" and a "ring of confidence" and you stopped making those "simple mistakes in every day English" you must be a better person for it.'

Must you? Forgetting the morality, the new customer as we have described her just doesn't think like that. The less she worships the 1950 concept of materialism, the more she declares its gods are false gods. And to suggest a mere twenty-five-penny product can perform any of these quasi-spiritual functions for her is to betray a lack of respect and understanding for Mrs 1972. She doesn't believe that the sum total of happiness is clean clothes, clean breath and (nowadays) a clean vagina. Fulfilment for her is not just a matter of showing her husband and their 2.4 children how much she loves them by the brand of soup she chooses for them.

This yawning gap between the values of the advertiser and the values of the consumer shows up sharpest in the so-called slice-of-life commercials. It's a slice that nobody lives. Not the advertiser. And certainly not the consumer. Even the businessman who pays for the advertisements 'don't think that people in advertisements are pretty much like the way people really are' (according to the *Harvard Business Review* study). After all, how many times has your next door neighbour rushed in to talk to you about a new lavatory cleaner? It may hurt the sales manager's feelings, but these products just aren't that central to people's lives. Compare the dialogue of 'Coronation Street' with the language of the commercials in the middle of it. One is about real people, the other is about cardboard figures that even an avalanche of glistening adjectives and a coating of North Country dialect can't bring to life. Or take the new slice-of-life films and compare them to the advertisement. *Midnight Cowboy, Easy Rider, Tell them Willie Boy is here* are just three of the new realistic (usage) movies. Compared to the slice-of-life that these sorts of films betray, the resemblance in advertising to any person living or dead is purely coincidental.

Talking to people who don't exist with words that don't mean anything is one way for the admen to keep themselves out of the consumer's heart. An equally good way is to trivialize important emotions and feelings by trying to link them to their products. Like Greens of Brighton who ran an advertisement for their *cake-mix* with the headline 'How to be the best mum in the world in 30 minutes'.

The rationale behind this has been provided by the British adman Ronnie Kirkwood who believes that today's woman 'is positively interested in any product that can make her a better wife, a better mother, a better cook'. All this from a can of beans, or a bottle of bleach?

The emotion which has been most used by the admen as wrapping for their products is, of course, sex. Ultrabrite is a toothpaste with sex appeal. Certs breath mints ask, 'If he kissed you once, will he kiss you again?' Badedas hint to you about the 'things that can happen after a Badedas bath'. Even gravy mixes are apparently aphrodisiac potions. The recent King Beef commercial on British television showed a young permissive wife mixing the King Beef gravy mix for the young trendy husband and ended with the memorable lines 'King Beef . . . it makes everything between us better . . . well, everything' hint, hint. One almost yearns for the Bisto Kids, for all their over-developed sense of smell.

A Tokyo psychiatrist Dr Solchi Hakozaki kept a 'sex in ads' check over a seven-year period. He found sexual expression in about 30% of the advertisements he monitored.

But how can the use of something which consumers are so fond of be a cause of consumer irritation when the advertiser uses it to tart up his wares? First, because the relationship is normally a phoney one. Second, because it's debasing an important emotion by putting it on the supermarket shelf.

Forgetting even the morality of it, the advertiser who injects sex into his advertisement is putting something there that is a lot more interesting than the product he's selling. And guess which one the consumer will remember?

The actual way the advertiser talks about sex is a further example of the distance that separates the audience from the advertiser. The coy sexual innuendo is right off key for a twenty-five-year-old girl to whom sex is something in the open, rather normal, and altogether very different from the leering wink that the wet-dreaming adman sends her as his mistaken impression of the real thing.

Presenting trivia as important, suggesting that this same trivia can do important things, and trivializing important emotions in the process are all different features of the same phenomenon : a belief that the consumer is dumb. Nothing else can explain the extraordinary achievement of grown men in trying to get consumers to buy their wares. Marshall McLuhan opined that because reading out an advertisement aloud made it sound ridiculous it must be targeted not on your conscious but on your subconscious. A more reasonable explanation, though admittedly less exotic, is that the advertisement is simply laughable.

Martin Mayer in Madison Avenue U.S.A. reports this delightful conversation between an advertising man and his young son. 'The other day the kids were watching television and one of those cartoon commercials came on. It showed two big wrestlers in a ring, one with the label "pain" on his robe and the other with the label "ordinary pain killer". The "pain" then threw "ordinary pain killer" out of the ring. Then another wrestler climbed into the ring with this brand name stencilled onto his robe, and he threw "pain" out of the ring, knocking him out completely. My own boy called me aside and said "Dad, am I to understand that a bunch of grown men sat down and said that was a good idea, and another bunch of grown men went to all the trouble to make a movie out of it?" '

No wonder that over a third of the adolescents covered in the American study of the effect of advertising on children criticized commercials because they are 'stupid ... and insult the intelligence'.

As has been shrewdly observed, the only person nowadays with a mind of a thirteen-year-old is a six-year-old. Yet the advertisers have completely ignored this. Just pick up any women's magazine, for example, and compare the editorial on beauty or the editorial on slimming with the advertisements for products in either category. The beauty editorial deals factually and simply with how to cope with real beauty problems, accepting as it must that not all its readers look like Elizabeth Taylor. But the advertisements? Listen to this piece of copy for a Revlon advertisement: 'Hear it crashing now, on the softer shores of chic. A new wave of shimmer shades. Sun glistening. Sea cooled. Trembly with the frost. The Seafrostlings.'

And the slimming editorial recognizes that dieting is a long, slow hard business. A very different impression from the quick easy and painless ways offered by the advertisers to lose inches and wipe off lbs: 'I cut down starchy foods, refused sweets and biscuits, did exercises every morning. And still I bulged out of my swimsuit! Then I started using Saxin and those extra inches soon began to go.' Over half of all women believe they're overweight and most of these have tried to diet, and failed. They know that there are no easy solutions. So why do the advertisers try to kid them? The great historian H. L. Menken once observed that 'nobody ever went broke underestimating the intelligence of the American public'. It's an attitude shared by the bulk of the advertising industry who, if they would see further than the next martini, would be listening to Bob Dylan singing 'If you don't underestimate me, I won't underestimate you'.

The advertising industry has developed a respectable theory to justify their assessment of the backward mental age of their audience. They argue, as did Colin Goodson and Burkard Frobenius in the British publication *Admap*, that as the communicators and the communicated-to have different linguistic and comprehension levels 'familiar' concepts in advertisements are better than 'original' concepts. In short, be childishly simple because you're dealing with nincumpoops. 'Original' thoughts, i.e. those involving pleasing, entertaining ideas, will simply confuse the wretched fellow.

The evidence for the 'low comprehension level' of the consumer was simple. The researchers simply asked various grades of consumer whether they undestood certain phrases. For instance 79% of the top occupation group understood what was meant by 'sterling area'. Whereas only 9% of the lowest occupation group understood this term. That's certainly proof that if you talk about 'sterling area' in your advertisements and you're aiming at the lower income group, you're likely to be disappointed. But it's not proof that you have to baby talk to women when you're talking to them about something they fully understand like detergents or dehydrated peas. You don't have to be a Ph. D. to grasp the meaning of 'Happiness is a cigar called Hamlet'. Even backward children could probably understand Avis' 'we try harder'.

The key to the talking down problem lies in the sort of people who work for advertising agencies. There are basically two types. First, the ex-public school, forty-year-old gent. Second, the thirty-year-old or under working-class kid who has 'made it' into advertising. This second group, for all their Cockney twangs, went into advertising as a conscious act of climbing onto an escalator that could take them away from their proletarian backgrounds. Consequently, they tend to adopt middle-class camouflage, like joining smart London clubs and living in places like Gerrard's Cross.

The key point about both the natural born and adopted members of the middle-class working in advertising is that they are fundamentally alienated from their audience. Through all the promotion of miracle this and amazing that, through the talking and the trivialization of values, runs a thin – but persistent – vein of contempt. The adman finds it difficult to create advertisements that respect his audience's intelligence because fundamentally he doesn't. He has persuaded himself that he has in his hands a tool which, without too much difficulty, he can more often than not persuade working-class people to do what he wants. No wonder, then, that he flaunts the symbols of the middle class at his working-class audience. No wonder he crudely and unsympathetically spreads the gospel that cleanliness is next to godliness. And parades scenario after scenario of suburban bliss, so those less fortunate souls living in their back to backs by the railway line are in no doubt as to what they're missing. And all the time with a sneer on his lips.

The extraordinary truth is that these middle-class admen are singularly unsuccessful in doing what they believe they are doing. For not only is their handiwork profoundly irritating to those who it is intended to influence. It is also extremely unpersuasive.

What the hidden persuaders have been best at hiding is the severe limitations of their persuasive powers. The following chapter will show why the day of reckoning is at hand. Because many of the advertisers themselves have recovered enough from their double Chivas Regals and their expense account lunches to realize that they're the ones who've been sold, rather than their beloved products.

The Witch Doctors
Who Lost
Their Magic

Once upon a time there was a lion tamer who, though he was a very clever man, wasn't very clever at taming lions. But because he was such a clever man he discovered a way to make the circus audience believe that he had actually tamed the lions. Every time the lion climbed onto the tub in the centre of the ring, he cracked his whip. Then, when the lion roared, he cracked his whip twice. And because he was so clever he managed to crack his whip at just about the same time as the lion performed all these things. So everyone thought that the lion had climbed onto the tub and then roared because the lion tamer had cracked his whip. Then one day the lion decided to show the audience who really controlled who. So he ate the lion tamer.

The moral of this sad little fable is, hopefully, clear for all to see. And whether you regard the advertising industry as fraudulent lion tamers or unmagical witch doctors, doesn't really matter. What is important is how the advertising industry has so long managed to conceal from itself and its clients its very real failure to deliver the goods on anything approaching the scale that has been promised. That this industry, alleged to have its hand firmly on the pulse of its audience, should have allowed itself to suffer such delusions of grandeur is folly enough. That it should in doing so provoke the ire and contempt of those it is trying to sell to, resembles nothing so much as the self-destructive urge of the lemmings as they plunge into the cold waters of Canada.

The most extraordinary point about the story to be told in

this and the next chapter is that every key fact about the way communication *actually works*, as opposed to the way the communication experts *say it works* has been published for up to twenty years. Yet for all this time the vast majority of advertisements have been constructed in a way which pretends that none of the developments in social psychology or communications theory over the last twenty years has taken place. As Harry Henry, elder statesman of British market research has seen fit to observe: 'Most of the contributions that have been made by me or my contemporaries during the past two decades might as well have been written in water.'

Before looking at these contributions further it would be as well just to recall the way in which advertising has managed to win golden opinions for itself.

It was in the years between the wars that advertising made its rise in the eyes of business – from being just a huckster selling quack medicines to becoming something else: a process with the power to persuade people in the mass to do as the advertiser said. The credit for this change belongs not so much to any new inventory of skills that the admen developed as to the First World War. This was the first war to be fought with words as well as bullets, and it was here that the foundation of modern advertising was laid.

And by the end of the 1960s J. K. Galbraith could observe without provoking too much dissent, that 'it is an every day assumption of the industrial system that, if sales are slipping, a new sale formula can be found that will correct the situation'. If you *do* wish to dissent, the Harvard professor will ask you why, in that case, the largest and most successful companies in the world keep on coming back for a second helping of this wonder drug. But there have been few dissenters. And hardly more when Vance Packard took a Cook's tour round the research departments of a handful of advertising agencies, emerging to dub them as the *Hidden Persuaders*: 'Americans have become the most manipulated people outside the United Kingdom'.

Of course, subliminal advertising was quite wrong. But try finding many comments on this book from within the advertising industry which said more than that 'providing advertising exercised its powers responsibly, all would be well'. Far and few were the *denials* of that power at that time.

And so, for example, you find a marketing man like Ralph

Glasser declaring in *The New High Priesthood*: 'All he [the consumer] can do, and it is indicative of his weak position as a buyer, is to be guided by what he is told in the advertising.'

And why this total submission? Because of motivation research: 'The greatest breakthrough in modern persuasive skills is the discovery of how to peep behind the screen that a person's consciousness erects before the world and use that vision to fix upon the thoughts and designs one is most likely to tempt with successfully.'

But despite all this, and claim from other sources ranging from Marshall McLuhan upwards, that the admen now have the power to see into men's souls, the evidence tells a different story. It shows how advertising has very often oversold its powers and underdelivered its promises.

For a start, consumers only pay conscious attention to seventy-six advertisements a day (according to the indefatigable Bauer and Greyser who ask their equally indefatigable sample to press a hand counter every time they noted an advertisement).

Whatever figure you accept for the total number of advertising messages to which a consumer is exposed in a day, seventy-six is a smallish proportion of the total.

That, in view of the consumer's defence mechanisms which will be described in a moment, isn't so surprising. What *is* surprising to those anxious to protect the laurels of Madison Avenue is that consumers find 85% of the ads they note *neither* enjoyable, informative, annoying nor offensive. They are merely indifferent to them.

In fact, according to studies done in 1971 and 1972 by Daniel Starch, the number of viewers who 'note' a TV commercial in America (i.e. remember within three hours of transmission that the commercial had been on the air) has slumped from one in three to one in four in just twelve months.

Four years before this study an enterprising Dr Charles C. Allen had set up an object called the Dynascope in a sample of American homes. This enabled him to record what the people in the room were doing while the television set was on. And going through Dr Allen's film must have been like looking at some of the Masters and Johnson clips. For he reported: 'Adults eat, drink, play, argue, fight, and occasionally make love in front of their televisions. Sometimes these activities are co-existensive with viewing.' Clearly their minds would be on the other things than the amazing flavour of Morton's cranberry pie.

And so (we find that statistics confirm what common sense suggests, that only a very small proportion of advertisements are remembered.) According to Gallup and Robinson the average for the 'featured idea' being retained for *twenty-four hours* was *under* 10% for TV set advertisements, tyre advertisements, after-shave and insurance advertisements (down to 2.6%).

Alas, worse is to follow. For if the ad. is looked at, and if the claim is remembered, it is now *more* likely to be attached to the wrong brand than to the right brand. In the last twelve months alone there has been a 70% drop in the percentage of commercials that are attached to their correct brand.

Or take the admen's great love : slogans. American Air Lines spent $15 million telling people it was the 'airline built for professional travellers'. But after spending that sum of money only one consumer in five could link that slogan with American Air Lines. So four-fifths of the benefit went to other airlines than the one who had paid the bill.

This in fact is happening every day on television in America (and there is no reason to believe that the figures in Britain would be much lower).

A vaginal deodorant, Pristeen, actually had *more* viewers associating the advertisement with its main rival, F.D.S., than with itself. And Exedrin, with the David Jansen commercial mentioned in the discussion on consumer power, actually had *twice* as many viewers associating the advertisement with its biggest rival, Anacin, than with Exedrin itself. And so on and so forth.

It is ironical in this context to read this remark from the London *Times*: 'It is now popular to turn to the claimed effectiveness of television advertising as proof that the medium is massively influential as a motivation force.' This was in relation to a report assessing the impact of television violence on people.

Now the lesson from all these studies of mass communication is that the effect of mass media is far less than Mrs Mary Whitehouse imagines. If it is this little for the content, how much less will it be for the advertisements? The facts again are at hand, and have been for several years, to confirm the limited shortterm impact of advertising. First, a study by J. Walter Thompson, the biggest advertising agency in the world. They recorded

205

what a sample of consumers bought over a thirteen-week period and compared it to the advertising they were exposed to. One can summarize their key finding in this way: imagine a group of people some of whom use product X and some of whom don't. Then expose the *whole group* to two commercials for a product X. The result is that these people are only five percent more likely to *start* to purchase the brand than to stop purchasing the brand after being exposed to two commercials. To get this number of exposures to a television commercial *between* each purchase for three-quarters of all housewives for something that's bought weekly (like butter or tea) would cost £750,000 a year in television time alone. There can be hardly a dozen brands with that money to spend.

The second study was directed by Leo Bogart, executive vice-president of the Bureau of Advertising of the American Newspaper Publishers' Association (an extremely kosher outfit anxious to prove the efficacy of advertising). This study was designed to find out the effect of just one advertisement. Well, over twenty-four brands of packaged goods, one ad. certainly *had* an effect. Instead of 0.44% of the population buying it, 0.50% bought it. But the way these ads. worked seemed to be by making some customers purchase the brand a day or so before they would have purchased it anyway. Was it for this that the copy-writer toiled and the art director sweated? Or, for that matter, that the client forked out his dollars?

The third study was a complete book, written over ten years ago by a Harvard professor J. B. Stewart: *Repetitive Advertising in Newspapers*. This studied the impact under carefully controlled conditions over a twenty-six-week period in Fort Wayne, Indiana, of the advertising for two products: a bleach called Lestare and the other a frozen food, Chicken Sara Lee.

The town was divided into areas who were exposed to the advertising and areas that weren't. And the conclusion for the Lestare advertising was that by the end of the test period more housewives had bought Lestare in the areas where the advertising *hadn't* appeared than in the areas where it had. This led to Professor Stewart's view that 'beyond any doubt some advertising is not necessarily better than no advertising'.

You can understand why the advertising industry has ignored this conclusion from one of the most carefully controlled field tests of advertising effectiveness. For the basic *assumption* behind every advertisement is that it is better to run it than not to run it. *How much better* is a matter for argument, but the other assumption has never, to my recollection, yet been questioned by any advertising agency (and quite understandably).

The effect of the Chicken Sara Lee advertising was a fifth better than that of Lestare, though still not much more than marginal.

Both these case histories relate to new products, and the launching of these is one key task entrusted by the advertisers to their agencies. And it is this same area that Galbraith uses to make his taunt against those who put forward the Edsel as proof of the limited power of advertising: 'Its notoriety owes much to its being exceptional'.

But the evidence is that precisely the reverse is true. Starting with the motoring field, very few cases suggest a power of mass persuasion that Galbraith's 'demand management' implies. For example, the Maxi failed at its first launch. The new Cortina only got half the initial market share Ford had planned. The Classic failed almost totally. The Pinto and Vega sold almost half the number that Detroit had *publicly* announced they would sell.

You step outside this particular product category and there you see further testimonials to the limited power of advertising. Heinz Happy Soups (flop), Knorr Dry Soup Mix (flop), Cue Toothpaste (flop), Reef Mouthwash (flop) are amongst the 7,500 new products that flopped in America in 1969.

And in Britain the roll-call of distinction includes Unilever (with three Spree Squash Concentrate and Lyril Soap), Beechams (Water Lily Shampoo, Mark Vardy Toiletries), Nestlé (Nestea), Cadburys (meat), Rank (Bowling), General Foods (Jello and now freeze dried coffee).

The point has already been made in an earlier chapter that many of these new products were rejected because the housewife was fed up with the new improved way of doing something that she wasn't interested in doing. But, and here's the crunch as far as the efficiency of advertising is concerned, bad advertising was found to be the reason for failure *three times* as often as bad product performance (according to Ted Angelus, who looked at the American flops). So the failures then are with 'successful' products.

How about the long term (by this is meant the period outside that which immediately follows the running of the advertising)? Doesn't advertising give 'added value' to a product by draping it with feelings and qualities to make it more desirable to the consumer?

There is certainly quite a lot of evidence that something of this nature happens. The story of Andrex toilet paper versus Delsey toilet paper is a case in point. What appears to have happened is that Andrex, by continuing to advertise heavily over a ten-year period, became a brand that was 'more highly valued by consumers than Delsey' (which after six years stopped advertising). So that relative to Andrex 'people value Delsey a little less highly' (both quotations from a J. Walter Thompson case history on Andrex).

Or take another case of a well known food product. When one sample of consumers were asked to try this product and its main competitor in *a situation where the identity of the brand was not revealed* consumers split 51 to 49 in favour of Brand A. But when another sample did the same test, this time *with the brand identity* revealed, brand A was preferred 67 to 33. A 32% increase in preference for one product just by identifying which brand people were eating.

There are other studies which may be cited to show the long-term success of advertising including the ones carried out by the Television Consumer Audit of Great Britain. Their study of fruit squashes, toothpaste, and heavy duty detergents suggests that brand loyalty to the major brands was supported by media advertising and actually eroded by promotional expenditure, particularly amongst the heavy buyers. And a lot of evidence has certainly emerged to show that money-offs and deals only create a temporary upward kink in the sales curve, caused by consumers increasing their stock of the product at the special offer price, followed by a sales decline as consumers use up the extra stock. Which shows that brand advertising is better for the brand than money-offs.

But even the more optimistic case histories about the long-term effect of advertising don't always show that it was a *cost effective* way for the company to have promoted its product.

If, for example, you had spent £300,000 to launch a dry cat food in the English market (as did Carnation Foods for their Go-Cat) and you achieved a one third market share, that might seem like a substantial success. Until you realize that the total value of the dry cat food market at that time was barely two million pounds a year. £600,000 of sales for £300,000 worth of advertising. Or take the case of Lucozade. Their marketing director revealed to the Admap World Advertising Workshop that increasing the advertising expenditure by 46% increased the sales level by 9%. And when the advertising expenditure on Ribena, its sister product, has been increased by 25% sales actually *declined* by 6 per cent. Maybe sales of Ribena would have declined more without the advertising. And maybe the sale of Lucozade wouldn't have increased at all without advertising. But this isn't the sort of stuff that would persuade me if I was a Beecham shareholder to endorse my Board's expenditure of £1,021,000 in 1971 on advertising these two brands.

Or take the case of petrol marketing. *Management Today* magazine, the prestigious British management monthly, carried in December 1971 an article that should have caused at least some tremors to be felt in the advertising industry. This was a report of a study carried out by the University of Louvain where data on petrol markets for up to a seven-year period were obtained and analysed for a representative sample of European countries. The data included sales volumes, market shares, outlet shares, short-term innovations, promotional campaigns, and measures of advertising pressure on the market place by the brands concerned. The conclusion of this study, as it was reported in *Management Today,* was: *'in all the cases studied there was no economical return on the advertising budget'*. It is true that this study has been fiercely attacked in private by both the advertising and petrol establishment. But until it is adequately rebutted it remains as further evidence that the value of advertising to a brand is certainly not something that can be *assumed*.

Cigarette advertising tells a similar tale. Between 1954 and 1965 the tobacco barons increased their annual advertising expenditure from £1,000,000 a year to £16,000,000 a year. But despite this sixteen-fold increase in the weight of advertising they were unable to persuade a higher proportion of the total population to take up the habit. Since then, of course, they have used this inefficiency to justify the continued advertising of cigarettes after the cancer scare, saying the advertisements are only designed to sell their own particular brand and not to expand the market by selling the idea of smoking. Even if one accepts this spurious plea, the fact remains that the relationship between brands' share and advertising expenditure is equally tenuous. Three brands, Embassy Filter, Benson and Hedges King Size, and Piccadilly No. 7, all spend roughly the *same* amount on advertising. But their market shares were 19.6% 6.6% and 0.4% respectively.

Even in the case of the 'relatively' successful Sara Lee campaign studied by J. B. Stewart, he was forced to conclude that 'the advertising efficiency in this experimental campaign [was] just barely enough to justify the expenditure'. If this marginal benefit is the return on a 'successful' campaign, the return on an average campaign could even be negative.

What all this shows, as much as the limits to the skills of the agencies, is the unmalleable nature of the consumers to whom they are pleading. Far from the only option being to do what the advertiser tells them (as Glasser suggests) or to become more malleable the more affluent they become (as Galbraith suggests) consumers are showing that they are becoming *less* persuadable than ever before.

The social psychologists have done quite a lot of work on this particular point and the evidence is clear. The people who are *most persuadable* are those who feel inadequate (Klapper), who lack confidence (Secord and Blackman), and are less intelligent (Hoveland, Janis and Kelley). There is also the finding that women tend to be slightly more persuadable than men (Whittaker). And the *least* persuadable, according to the same authorities, are the more intelligent and the more extroverted, the most confident and those with the highest self-esteem.

If we relate all this to the way consumers and patterns of consumption have changed, all the developments – from the emergence of individualism in product choice to the increased role of men in the purchasing of everyday items – they all point to more and more consumers having the sort of characteristics that will make them less and less persuadable.

And though this fact is recognized by very few agencies, it is being appreciated by more and more advertisers. For the advertiser is also a consumer. He knows that he's not persuaded by the vast majority of advertising, so why should the consumer he's currently trying to win over to his product be any more persuadable?

This is just one more question mark to be placed against the value of advertising by business. And the rush into consumer promotions in the last few years (the money-offs and free tights) was really a way of the companies' saying to their agencies that they'd lost faith in the advertisements themselves.

Now, having found that this approach isn't really worth the money that's spent on it, the advertisers come back, albeit reluctantly, to the wide open spaces.

The fact is the only reason why many companies advertise is because other people do. A study by the Marketing Communications Research Centre found that top industrial executives advertised 'out of fear of some nebulous, possibly dire, consequences if they discontinued or dramatically cut their advertising while their competitors continued'.

No surprise then that barely more than *a quarter* of the business executives in the *Harvard Business Review* study agreed that most of the money allocated for advertising was well spent. The president of General Motors even publicly pointed out that whereas it would cost him 45% more in 1970 to run the same amount of advertising as he ran in 1960, the average price of his cars had gone down in that time by 2.5%, despite an 82% increase in labour costs.

If industrial productivity could increase so much, why was advertising productivity so stagnant? In fact, individual advertisements differ enormously in their productivity. In America it can cost as little as 0.8 of a cent to get one message to one person who can correctly identify the commercial as yours. Or it can cost as much as 2.8 of a cent. The extra 2 cents is the price of bad advertising. Even taking a less extreme maximum/minimum position the difference in readership between the *average* full page colour advertisement and the best read colour advertisement is 136%.

And though, as will emerge later, reading and noting scores are not the most useful measure of advertising efficiency, the wide variation in one suggests an equally wide variation in the other. And all for the cost of the same media space.

The crucial point is that the advertising agency is probably no more able to pick an advertisement for the client that will help his sales than is a pin. Leo Bogart reported in *What one Little Ad Can Do* on whether the advertising experts' ratings of advertisements tallied with the performance of these advertisements as measured in the market place. Their predictions of 'recall' were no better than you get by tossing a coin. And the

H

odds were sixteen to one *against* their picking the advertisement that could get the best sales result.

Hell may have no fury like a woman scorned, but business has no fury like an advertiser misled by his agency. The resultant night of the long knives struck blindly and almost unselectively through Madison Avenue (and to some extent through British and German advertising as well).

Just when Bill Bernbachs' ideas were about to win out by showing the power of 'creative' advertising, 'creative' suddenly became a dirty word. 'Creative' was the trend and just because the clients were getting upitty (particularly under the influence of the slump) the industry had to drop *whatever* trend they were currently running on and pick one up that would be sure to mollify the irate advertisers. 'Look,' they said, 'once we get those long-haired creatures out of our office, once we stop being cute, once we get back to the sort of ads. that really shifted product, then all will be well.' So public executions of the leading 'creatives' were arranged. Even the head of Young and Rubican, Steve Frankfurt a former art director, was dutifully axed. The example was sufficient *'pour décourager les autres'*.

One of the early disciples of creativity, Mary Wells Lawrence, went over to 'product orientated advertising'. (Compare her original Braniff campaign with her latest Alka Seltzer advertisements and you will see that smart lady realizes that her bread is now buttered on a different side.)

The ill wind also blew on this side of the Atlantic. In Britain, one of the earliest creative agencies, Collett, Dickenson, Pearce and Partners started getting cold feet. Remember those zany Ford ads. of 1968 like 'When it rains it shines'? Compare that with the 'Incomparable Cortina'. Geers Gross, the people who dreamed up those delightful Flour Graders, started to churn out the sort of advertising that would have done credit to any of the flat-footed advertising giants. And these people were right, of course. The business was turning away from 'creative' just when 'creative' was on the point of making business flow.

Doyle, Dane, Bernbach, uncompromising as ever, actually *lost* billing overall in 1971 – an unheard of phenomenon. And their London office made so little headway that it had to spend a small fortune buying up a rival agency called Gallagher Smail that had found success by doing the sort of advertising that normally gave Bill Bernbach nightmares.

212

The irony of this switch back to the old safe principles of the fifties and sixties was twofold. First in the words of *Ad Daily*, the New York news sheet on advertising: 'The creative revolution brought honesty...believability...relevance...originality...drama ...respect...authority...and excitement to advertising. Stuff that it seldom demonstrated before and it sold things like crazy – Alka Seltzer...Braniff...Benson and Hedges...the original Contac...Fresca...Volkswagen...Polaroid...Clairol...Diet... Pepsi...North East Air...*Forbes* magazine and a hundred more.'

Second, even if these enthusiastic claims weren't true, even if 'creative' advertising has been as much a flop as its detractors claimed, going back to what might have worked ten years previously was no solution. In that time the consumer had transformed herself into something else. And it made no more sense to talk to the 1970 consumer like the 1950 one than it would to talk to a twenty-year-old girl like a ten-year-old one.

Nevertheless it is onto these 'tried and tested' principles that advertising has now retreated. It is almost as though an ageing comedian tried to make a comeback using the style and the jokes that brought him success in his golden years. But the old formulae no longer get them rolling in the aisles or – for that matter – rushing along to the cash register. Indeed when one examines the admens' supposedly 'successful' magic formulae it appears that when their ads *did* seem to work it was largely because of the dubious way their effect was measured. As the next chapter will reveal.

12

⚇ Putting Advertising on the Psychologist's Couch

If you asked almost any one of the 30,000 people involved in advertising in Britain exactly *how* the process of advertising works you would find them less forthcoming than their colleagues from other professions talking about their specialities. Doctors understand the physical properties of the body, engineers understand the processes of physics. Yet the process of communication is hardly discussed within the industry that spends over £600 million every year to communicate.

The annals of social psychology, rich sources of knowledge for those anxious to influence human behaviour, remain largely untapped. Instead a folklore (and it is no more than that) has grown up about how advertising, as it is practised, works. It is a folklore that is enshrined in a series of principles that stand – implicitly or openly stated – behind the bulk of advertisements on both sides of the Atlantic.

First, that 'hard sell' is better than 'soft sell'.

Second, that the more you can repeat your sales point the better.

Third, that overclaim or exaggeration is a sensible advertising practice.

Fourth, that you should aim for high recall of your advertising message (i.e. the more people who can remember your jingle the better).

Fifth, that if you can get people to look at your advertisement and understand it, your job's virtually done.

Sixth, that the greater the change of attitude you can measure about your product, the more your sales are likely to rise.

Seventh, that if you do get more sales, it's because of the advertising.

These principles have the advantage of being so simple and straightforward that even a B-stream advertising manager can understand them. The seven assumptions convert into a simple model of advertising theory that is also straightforward and commonsense.

Claim
↓
Repetition of Claim
↓
Recall of Claim
↓
Attitude Change
↓
Behaviour Change
↓
Sales

The procedure works as follows. First you make your claim, then you make sure it's attended to. Then you repeat that claim as often as your budget allows. You repeat that claim to get it into people's memories (which you measure as 'recall'). You do this because you believe that if you've got your powerful claim into someone's head, there's a fair chance of their thinking better things about your brand. And if they do this, that someone is more likely to buy your product.

The important point about this model is the suggestion that there is a simple, direct link between the advertisement and the sale. So if you manage to steer your claim through stages two, three, four and five, then six *will* happen.

Consistent with this, those who live by this theory of persuasion also believe that the *more* advertising you feed into the top in terms of money spent on buying space, the more you'll get out of the bottom in sales. So that a £500,000 campaign is ten times as effective as a £50,000 campaign.

This particular model of the persuasion process is not one you'll find in any serious study of social psychology. You won't even find many believers of it in the research departments of the advertising agencies. Why? Because over the last twenty years each of the relationships in this model have been shown to be false. And that the way a claim 'works' on people is not in any way as simple as the flow of arrows suggests.

Even without looking at the research evidence that follows, simple mathematics suggest that this cannot be the model of Galbraith's 'demand management', or Orwells' 'Big Brother', or Packard's 'hidden persuaders'. For each step in the chain can only happen if the previous step has occurred. As probability values decline as probabilities are multiplied even this simple six-step model is extremely tenuous. If, for example, each step had a 50/50 chance of happening then, when all the probabilities had been multiplied together, you find that the chance of a 'claim' leading to a 'sale' is 50:1 against.

With this background, let us wend our way through this model and see the snares and delusions beckoning the unwary. To begin with the claim. This is the kernel of any advertisement: what you say to the consumer to persuade her of the merit of your case. It can be a U.S.P. *à la* Rosser Reeves, or a brand image claim *à la* David Ogilvy.

There are two key points about the sort of claims that charge at you from the newspaper page and television screen. First, that they tend to be formulated as though they were trying to persuade someone who didn't use a product to start using it. A sort of conversion process whereby non-users of the product are converted into users by means of the advertisement. Second, that the weapon for this conversion is *either* anxiety arousal (B.O. being the classic) *or* overclaim ('whiter than white' being the classic of this).

The notion of converting people to become users of your product has, like the model itself, the blessing of commonsense. But that is all. For the fact is that for nearly all mass market, low cost, items, like detergents or baked beans, your proper audience should be the *existing* users of your product.

Take the frozen pea market. Most consumers will be 'users' of all the major brands. The examples given about the lack of brand loyalty in chapter nine have as their corollary, multiple brand usage. In fact, if you forget for a moment about the amount of product that people buy, the actual *numbers* of users of a brand vary only slightly over a year. According to J. Walter Thompson's Advertising Planning Index there's only a 1%

change in the number of users of a typical brand in a year, and the number of first-time users of a brand is rarely more than 3% per year for an established product.

Of course, for some people this average brand will be purchased once a year, for others once a week. But the task of advertising is still to make it as frequent as possible for both of them. This may involve encouraging *usage* of the product rather than *purchase* of it (i.e. eating the can of baked beans off your shelf rather than being persuaded to buy another can from the super-market).

The heavy users tend to be the guts of a brand's business. If you look at virtually any mass market low cost product you will find that about half the sales volume is consumed by about one-fifth of the users. So clearly discovering what it is that shifts people into this category and what stops them shifting out of it are relevant questions to the advertiser. But judging by the large number of advertisements that seem to be trying to argue you into *trying* the brand as though you'd never bought it before, it's not a question the typical advertisement is tackling.

The fact that the target of our advertisement is also the user of the product, albeit a light user, is of immense significance. It is also of immense significance that she is probably also a user of the product we're competing against.

To see how this affects the process of claim→to sale we must dig into the annals of social psychology to discover that the consumer who is receiving our claim is not in any way a *'tabula rasa'*, an empty tablet, on which to imprint our U.S.P. On the contrary she has a whole set of feelings, beliefs and thoughts, many of which are born out of her experience of our own and competing products, within her skull. All these feelings, thoughts, and beliefs are mutually consistent and in balance one with another. And they are all in balance one with another because it would create psychological stress for the consumer if they were at logger-heads with each other within her skull. A simple example of this internal self consistency is that you find that someone who regards a certain brand of beer as 'manly' will also think that the beer itself is stronger. Or a detergent that is advertised on a efficiency platform will also be thought of as not being gentle to the hands. One half of the attitude naturally follows from the other, even if it's not overtly expressed.

Now if we confront our consumer with a piece of information, say an advertising claim, that is out of balance or inconsistent with the contents of her mental dossier, we have created a stress causing situation for her. The feelings we're offering her about the brand are out of balance with her own feelings about the brand. The theory of social psychology that predicts what now happens in this situation is Leon Festinger's theory of cognitive dissonance, which sounds frighteningly complicated but actually is beautifully simple. 'Cognitive' relates to the knowledge in your mental dossier. And 'dissonance' simple means unbalance or inconsistency.

The theory simply says that when a piece of information is put into the consumer's mental dossier that is 'out of balance' with other information already in the dossier then she will modify her attitudes and behaviour in such a way that the two conflicting 'cognitive elements' are brought into balance. More than this, the theory also says that she will actively avoid situations which might lead to 'out of balance' pieces of information coming into her mental dossier.

For example, if you have just bought a new car, it's probable that the car you chose *not* to buy had *some* attractive features that the one you chose hadn't. The cognitive dissonance theory predicts that you will therefore find large numbers of new car purchasers reading the advertisements for that car *after* they've bought it as part of the process of seeking information to buttress their choice. And this, in fact, is precisely what occurs.

Apply the cognitive dissonance theory to testimonial advertising and you have a neat ethical problem. If the *normal* response after purchase is to modify your perception of the product so you can persuade yourself that you made the right decision, then to tell a non-purchaser that a purchaser finds a product does all that the advertising says it would is – arguably – exploiting the purchaser's need for self consistency to the possible detriment of the non-purchaser.

How does the dissonance theory affect the claim that we fired at the consumer? It simply means that the consumer is equipped with a large number of mechanisms to make sure that our claim *doesn't* create any psychological stress by becoming out of balance with any part of her mental dossier.

The first of these is *selective exposure*. This can mean that the mind may simply not receive a message that doesn't fit in with the recipient's mental dossier, in the same way that a lock will not admit the wrong key. For example, twice as many non-smokers as smokers look at anti-smoking propaganda. For the non-smoker, it fits in with her view of the world *as a non-smoker*. But for the smoker it creates tension and stress as the propaganda is in conflict with attitudes and feelings within her mental dossier. So the watchdogs in her brain will pounce on any anti-smoking propaganda as it comes in, and try to kick it out before it creates any stress. This is why the people you may want most in your audience often are least likely to be there.

After this first filter that can stop our claim getting through, comes the second. For certain sorts of message may be so powerful, for example some television commercials, that they can actually manage to batter their way past this first line of defence. If the claim cannot be accommodated into the mental dossier, it is then dealt with by the process of *selective retention*, and promptly kicked out of the brain.

The third watchdog protecting the consumer's mental dossier is *selective perception*. Instead of not admitting or throwing out out-of-balance material, the *incoming* material is recast until it fits in with the consumer's existing attitudes. This can take the form of 'ego defence mechanisms' : simply denying a communication that threatens some aspects of your ego structure (e.g. a smoker saying 'it can't happen to me'). Or it can work by an ordinary denial, saying that the relationship of the out-of-balance attitude that's causing stress doesn't really exist (e.g. denying that there is a link between smoking and cancer).

This was actually measured in the study in Minneapolis after a news release about the relationship of smoking to health. When asked whether they thought the relationship had been proved, 29% of non-smokers said 'yes', compared to only 7% of smokers.

Or selective perception can work by balancing the stress-causing incoming attitude with something that makes it acceptable (e.g. smoking may be unhealthy, *but* it does make me relax). Or, finally, the incoming material can be split into bits, one of which fits in with the consumer's mental dossier (e.g. smoking may be unhealthy, but filter cigarettes aren't so unhealthy).

So the simple act of 'making a claim' for the product really isn't anything like as simple as the current consensus of advertising practice suggests. Before our poor little claim has even reached the stage of repetition it is pounced on by a pack of watchdogs that just aren't allowed for in the theoretical model. Let us see how these watchdogs treat some of the typical forms of claim that try to gain admittance into the consumer.

Let us suppose our claim is an *'overclaim'*, i.e. it is typical of the exaggerated puffery that the advertising industry produces. More precisely, let us suppose that you are an advertiser making a 'overclaim' for your detergent called Doz. What you might say would be that it would get my clothes 'whiter than white'.

If I am a typical user of your product, I not only use Doz but I have also used most other brand of detergents at some time or another. I am thus well aware of the differences between the brands. There could be any of a dozen reasons why I am using Doz at the present moment, but let us say that I find it gets my clothes satisfactorily clean and the pack I bought happened to have 2p off. But I certainly wouldn't agree with your claim that it got my clothes 'whiter than white'. There is thus a imbalance between my attitude towards Doz (gets my clothes clean) and the attitude your advertising is asking me to accept (gets clothes 'whiter than white').

Dissonance theory predicts that I will have to modify one of these two attitudes to avoid creating stress in myself. As the 'whiter than white' claim is coming from such a low credibility source as an advertiser, I will tend to reject that one and buttress my own attitude towards the brand. So by overclaiming on me in a situation where I had an easy way of verifying the claim, i.e. I used the product, the net effect was to make me think less of the advertising claim and to rank advertising as a lower credibility source than before. This means that the next time round, maybe when the manufacturers of Doz offer me a new product, I will have an extra reason for rejecting their claim.

Let us now make another supposition about Doz. That Doz is a a good product. That it cleans my clothes efficiently. So why should I stop using it? Maybe my laundry needs will even increase, and I might even use more of it.

In short, even though I have *rejected* the 'whiter than white' claim I may very well continue using Doz. This is particularly, likely to be true if, as has been suggested (H. A. Simon in *Models of Man*), I am not so much trying to maximize as 'satisfice': that is, I have an idea of what is 'good enough' in detergents and one that 'satisfices' these criteria, as does Doz, is fully qualified to receive my money.

This fact, however, goes right to the heart of one of the

220

central doctrines of modern advertising: that if the consumer is misled once he won't come back and purchase the product again. For provided the product 'satisfices' he may well come back. But if you are the advertiser working on the simple claim→sales model and observe that I haven't deserted your brand, you will deduce that I have accepted your claim and it is this claim that has motivated me to buy Doz. You will therefore repeat this claim again and again and again and again. And the whole business of processing your claim in such a way that it fits in to my mental dossier (i.e. by rejecting it) but still continuing to use the product, will also repeat itself. So the spiral of overclaim gradually winds its way upwards into cloud cuckoo land, where the gap between claim and reality grows wider and wider.

This particular communication structure may well be the typical way an overclaim affects a consumer who is already a user of the product. But even a non-user could respond in this way, because he has his own *expectations* of how the product will perform. For instance, the car that suggests it'll make you the biggest draw for the girls since Marlon Brando may still be bought by a consumer who has rejected that claim and is buying the car on the grounds of the vehicle's superior roadholding.

Provided the product *does* satisfice then the overclaim won't – at least in the short term – makes the product less appealing to the consumer. It will just make the overclaim less appealing to the consumer.

There is just one question mark which one is bound to put against this argument. Is a 'whiter than white' claim really sufficient to create the sort of stress that'll bring all these fancy balancing mechanisms into play?

The research studies show that the *higher* the ego involvement of someone in a particular situation the *greater* will be the tension caused by introducing an out-of-balance belief into that situation. But which detergent I use, it might be argued, is hardly a very ego involving situation. It certainly shouldn't be. But the whole weight of advertising for all these trivial products is to try to make them ego involving. To make which detergent, which aspirin, which lavatory paper, I use an important part of my life. To the extent that they succeed in this, these trivia do become important to the consumer's ego. To the extent that they fail then the advertisement, as the source of a rejected standpoint, sinks even lower in the credibility stakes. So either way, the overclaim gets rejected.

But though rejected it can, in the long term, still have one remaining effect on the consumer. By continually being told that Doz gets my clothes 'whiter than white' I eventually become disappointed that my clothes are merely clean (even though I may still go on using Doz). This means that the normal overclaim, as it works on the typical consumer, is creating not sales, but simply dissatisfaction. And if one is looking for a reason why consumers are now becoming more demanding – the 'phenomenon of rising expectations' as it's been called – one reason at least is that they are simply demanding what they have been promised.

Little of this, however, crosses the mind of the advertiser who is instructing his agency to say his product is the greatest thing since sliced bread. 'Are you ashamed of our television sets?' a client once asked me when I demurred at saying that its fabulous woodprint cabinet would be the pride and joy of every home.

The effect then of the first type of claim that's in everyday use – the overclaim – is to lower still further the credibility of the advertiser even though the advertiser believes it is in fact moving his product off the shelves at the speed of light.

The second typical sort of claim, the *high anxiety appeal,* has scarcely more success in crashing through the consumer's defence barriers. Whether the anxiety invoked is by suggesting that you might smell, that your neighbour thinks your child's white clothes look off-white, that you ought to buy insurance as danger could strike at any moment, or just that smoking will kill you, the principle is the same. And the evidence of how the watchdogs respond to this sort of appeal is that the *stronger* the fear invoked by the advertiser, the *less effective* the advertisement.

First of all, these anxiety arousing appeals cause too much stress in the poor old consumer's mental dossier. Simply because they contain a lot of elements out of balance with the consumer's own feelings. So the fear will tend to be processed in such a way by the brain that the threat to the consumer is *minimized.* The Tavistock Institute found this out when they did some research on road safety: the mind simply switched off when confronted by anxiety provoking situations.

And a classic study by Janis and Fesbach almost twenty years ago shows the differing impacts of a mild fear appeal with a strong fear appeal. A fifteen-minute illustrated lecture on dental hygiene was prepared in three different forms for three groups of students. The strong fear appeal contained a powerful emotional appeal emphasizing the serious consequences (including cancer) of not brushing your teeth. The mild fear appeal simply gave a 'minimal' appeal which didn't dramatize the consequences of tooth neglect at all but gave advice about dental hygiene. The third appeal, a moderate one, was somewhere between the two. The result was that the minimal factual appeal persuaded *twice* as many students to follow the advice given (which included going to a dentist for a check-up) than the strong fear appeal. In fact, *fewer* students in this group actually looked after their teeth properly after the strong fear appeal than before.

This is really an example of what is called 'The Law of Reversed Effort', namely the more frightened people become of the consequences of an action, the more they may be impelled to continue or even increase committing it. This certainly appears to be the case with the British anti-smoking campaign. Using strong fear appeals, its greatest impact seems to be on the bodies who hand out advertising awards. According to Action for Smoking and Health (ASH) just as many cigarettes are now being smoked as before the campaign. In fact, the likelihood is that a high fear campaign would *increase* the level of smoking. For the effect of this sort of advertising would be to increase tension amongst smokers. They would be more aware of the dangers of smoking but unable, because of the addictive power of nicotine, to give it up. And to relieve the extra tension this would cause, they probably smoke more cigarettes. Certainly the famous 'Black Widow' road safety series of posters of some years back actually coincided with a rise in the number of road accidents.

So, to revert to our claim→sale model, if a fear appeal is to get anywhere it needs to be the very opposite of what the advertising agent tends to make it : it needs to be a *mild* fear appeal which can be relatively easily absorbed into the consumer's mental dossier without causing too much mental upset.

Partly as a result of the overclaiming, and the high anxiety, the sort of claim that spins off the standard claim→sales model is also one that tends to be actively disliked by consumers. This is not a matter of concern for the majority of advertisers. They are not in the business to make friends, so goes the argument

223

but to make sales. 'If there were any correlation between liking and effectiveness in advertising Proctor and Gamble would not be the great marketing company it is today,' said the head of research of the London office of the BBDO agency. But as we shall see in a moment, the main measures made by Proctor and Gamble are not with effectiveness but with the extent to which their commercial has been *remembered*. And the relationship is that the most remembered commercials are *either* the most liked *or* the most disliked.

But in the same way that you'd be more likely to buy from a door-to-door salesman with good manners and a friendly smile than a rude one who bellowed at you from the doorstep, it would be natural to expect the same to be true of advertising. And it doesn't take much of a search of the literature to find evidence for this. As long ago as 1949 a study for N.B.C. by Thomas Coffin amongst 1,600 people in New York found that 'those who saw and liked a commercial advertising a product were found to be more apt to buy the brand than those who saw the commercials but did not like them'. There's also been no shortage of studies to show that communicators are more effective when they are 'liked' by their listeners.

Treasure and Joyce in *As Others See Us* written for the I.P.A. found that almost eight times the percentage of people who liked a commercial a lot shifted brands after seeing it compared to those who disliked the same commercial a lot. (But despite this, they finally concluded that liking and effectiveness were not related in any simple way.)

The detergent companies have a great mass of evidence on their files on the subject of liking and effectiveness, and the commercials that are made on the basis of it are prima facie evidence that in the selling situation liking and effectiveness are *not* twin brothers.

Even supposing that this is correct (and the theory of cognitive dissonance suggests that you will be less willing to look at an advertisement which you dislike than one you like) the question remains as to *why* liking and effectiveness have become such a discussion point amongst the admen. Is it the suggestion that in order to sell something the price you must pay is to be disliked by the person you sell it to? What has surely happened is that the admen have neglected the finer feelings of their audience in a way that would shame a common street pedlar and they have *then* set out to justify this dislike on the grounds that their product is still selling. Maybe it is. Maybe you can bully, cajole and nag people into buying your product. But why do this, when you can influence people by winning friends just as easily?

As well as an unconcern with dislike, the advertiser working on the traditional claim→sales model also feels he is immune to any bad effects that might arise from the consumer disbelieving his sales message. Faced with the massive incredulity that confronts the agency's handiwork when it reaches the market place, the 'irrelevance of belief' is the only response it can logically offer to their client to persuade him that their advertisement is doing a good job for him: 'If the consumer says your advertisement is completely believable, it probably means you have nothing in the advertisement which will get him to try your brand'. (Nahl).

Going even further than this, the motivation researchers have developed an approach to the subject of belief which is accepted with apparent alacrity by Professor Galbraith when he observes: 'Failure to win belief does not impair the effectiveness of the management of demand for consumer products. Management involves the creation of a compelling image of the product in the minds of the consumer. To this he responds *more or less automatically* (my italics) under the circumstances where the product does not merit a great deal of thought.' In this model, an ounce of powerful fantasy is worth a lb. of circumstantial evidence of the truth of the claim.

If all this is correct, advertising has a good deal less to worry about as a proven low credibility source than the earlier discussion of the growing disbelief in advertising implied.

But the believers in the unimportance of belief still owe us an explanation of why, contrary to the impression given by Galbraith and others, the majority of advertisements don't normally work in the way their creators had intended. Does disbelief really have no part to play in this?

Of course, the less rigorously you define 'advertising working' the easier it is to show that it works either in conditions where people don't consciously look at it or where they don't consciously believe it. The head of research at General Electric in America, Herbert Krugman has, for example, written about advertising 'working' in the sense of 'being repeatedly learned and repeatedly forgotten and then repeatedly learned a little more'. This process over a very long period of time can alter the way you think about a brand in a manner that 'may fall short of persuasion or attitude change'. 'Learning without involvement' is the way Krugman describes the process whereby this can happen. Belief isn't important because you're not sufficiently involved with the message to either believe or disbelieve it. The question simply doesn't arise. (A humbling side discovery by Krugman was that the 'learning curve' for advertising resembled almost precisely the 'learning curve' for nonsense material).

If most advertising restricted itself to being this sort of low profile, non-challenging 'mental wallpaper' (which, as we shall see, has quite a lot to commend it) then maybe belief wouldn't be important. But the majority of advertisements *do* try to smash into the consumer's consciousness. And they do so by arguing vigorously for *belief* in their proposition ('Builds strong bodies twelve ways' 'Sweeps as it beats as it cleans' etc.)

Can one accept the dictum of the motivational high priests (and their strange ally from Harvard) that in this situation the new, aggressive, questioning, cynical, critical consumer can be motivated to act in a way that goes contrary to what she believes? She may, and she does, disbelieve the advertisement even though she buys their product (for example detergent advertising).

And there's also the interesting half-way point between belief and disbelief called 'curious non-belief'. Here uncertainty is aroused in the consumer: 'I wonder if that *would* be a better product after all'. This uncertainty creates a type of imbalance within the mental dossier, and to restore the situation the consumer may well try the product as a form of 'tension reduction'. These sorts of claims would need to be ones that were verifiable by consumer experience of the product. Like 'end scuffed up floors', 'the margarine that spreads even when ice cold', 'the dog food that ends dog odour' – all of which arouse considerable 'curious non-belief' but apparently improve sales.

But the paper that developed this concept (Maloney) also stated quite categorically, if circumlocutedly, that a *disbelief* response was 'generally predictive of inhibited consumer interest to interact with the product advertised'. The simple explanation of this goes back to the concept of the mental dossier. A claim you 'disbelieve' is simply one that doesn't fit in. So to reduce the tension that its arrival creates it will either be processed in such a way that it can fit in or simply be rejected.

Funnily enough, it is this same mental dossier which, working on the advertiser, persuades him that disbelief of his message won't harm its sales impact. For, fortified by a conviction of the massive power of advertising (that is quite at odds with all the studies of the impact of mass communication) he is convinced that advertising, like Double Diamond, works wonders. So logically it *cannot* matter that the claims aren't believed. Nor can it matter that the advertisement is fear-arousing, overclaiming or disliked. The advertiser's mental dossier finds these notions uncomfortable so it is not prepared to countenance them. And until he begins to question the fact that advertising has the sort of strength that Galbraith's 'demand management' implies, then these huge hurdles to persuasion seems to be no more than bumps in the pathway to success.

Should but a shadow of doubt creep over a client's face, and if a good dinner at the Caprice can't wipe it off, the instrument that keeps the tottering edifice in the upright position is 'research'. 'Well, we did research it' is a phrase that a client will use to you to justify the latest irritating inanity that his agency has just spent half a million pounds exposing to the great British public.

This extraordinary process of the measurement (and justification) of the claims produced by the traditional advertising model requires a little analysis.

Most admen will admit that they know very little about how the process of communication works in advertising. There is no general theory which satisfactorily explains the various stages of the mental processes that are involved. So faced with the odd situation of believing that their advertising works but being unable to say much about *why* it works, the admen have chosen to build a series of stages between claim and sales which act as mile posts along the route. These show how far the 'message' has gone towards its ultimate destination of getting those cash registers ringing. If you don't accept the simplistic claim→sales relationship, then the intervening process of measuring to see how far you've got can be of very little interests. But the advertising industry as a whole has accepted all or most of them without substantial reservation. And the conclusions it draws from the investigations it makes into the campaigns it runs for its clients

I

are treated with the sort of numerate lunacy you might expect from a computer gone berserk. This particular formula, was developed by Warren Twedlt in 1952 to predict advertising readership. Advertising readership = 10.456 + 8.2 (size of advertisement in pages) + 3.869 (number of colours) + 0.181 (square inches of illustration).

The slide rule worship that produces this sort of mathematical creature is reared on the erroneous belief that if you express something in numerical form then you are 'measuring' it. But Stanley Pollitt of Boase Massimi Pollitt publicly conceded when discussing the sort of research techniques that the advertising industry used: 'We are not dealing with something which is at present just a little bit imperfect, or with existing techniques not working properly, *but of them not working at all*'.

Just to begin with, the testing situation is normally so remote from the real buying situation as to make assessments in the former of dubious application to the latter. Those sessions where they test television commercials bear little relationship to the environment in which you normally watch television commercials, stuck between boiling the kettle and going to the loo.

Forgetting even the technical inadequacies of this and other types of research, there's another sort of bias that's involved. The bias of the agency who prepared the advertisements and who tries to show the client that it's working like clockwork.

A sad example of this occurred during the F.T.C. hearings on Firestone tyres described in chapter three. A study by Firestone's agency, Campbell Ewald, was cited during the hearing which reported that 81% of consumers had got the impression from the advertising that Firestone tyres were safer than others. But another study, done by Hans Zeigel, professor of sociology and law at the University of Chicago, told a rather different story. This found that only 15.1% of consumers had felt that Firestone tyres were absolutely safe after seeing the Firestone advertisement. Professor Zeigel dubbed the Campbell Ewald study 'the sloppiest type of survey' and when asked by one of the attorneys why advertising agencies spend so much money on this sort of worthless research, he replied 'You and I know the answer'.

But even if the environment of testing was realistic and the motivation was pure the techniques of measurement just don't stand up to serious examination. The first of these are the measures of how much of the claim (for all its exaggeration or anxiety-arousing qualities) has been attended to. The way of assessing the extent to which an advertisement is consciously attended to ranges from watching people look at test advertisements to observing how much their pupils dilate when exposed to the advertisement.

After you've done a fair number of these studies, you can then deduce the general principles that will get your advertisement a high 'attention score'. Babies, dogs, naked ladies, big pictures generally covering three-quarters of the page, shortish headlines and so on. The net result is a whole string of advertisements which look like a 1960 Ivy League student: well-groomed but dull. For the art of getting attention is no more prone to such simple formulae than the art of writing sonnets. In fact, the key variable in attention – if you want to measure it – is the number of people who use your product already. These people will wish to read your advertisement in order to reassure themselves that they're buying the right product. But despite this fact you never find in the Gallup reading and noting studies (one of the most popular tests of attention) any index of the market shares of the brands whose ads were checked and so make their data in any way meaningful. Add to this the problem that about 40% of the people who say they look at your advertisement, don't actually do so and you can see the sort of problems that face even this fairly basic sort of measurement.

Is it worth all the palaver? Certainly, the more of your target audience who attend to your advertisement the better. But the very careful study by Leo Bogart found that *'sales results have only a chance relationship to the advertisement's ability to win attention'*. Yet this thing with the chance relationship to sales is the object of more veneration within the advertising industry than any other single measurement.

If one does want to find a relevant measure for the persuasive impact of an advertisement, it's not attention or comprehension that is the key, but the *credibility* of the source of the message (and this has been known for twenty years). For instance, in one carefully controlled study where precisely the same communication on four topics was used, first when linked to a high credibility source (Robert J. Oppenheimer) and then to a low credibility source (*Pravda*) the *identical* text was judged almost twice as convincing for Oppenheimer as for *Pravda*. There was no correlation between the attention to or comprehension of the message with persuasiveness.

This being the case, you might have reasonably expected the advertising industry to have looked how it could raise the credibility of itself as a source of information. You would expect it to discuss some of the different credibility levels of the various media in which it can place its advertisements. In one sense, for example, television should be credible because it is 'now'. But it isn't because most commercials are prerecorded.

Most important, the rhubarb noises that greet the commercial provide group pressures which reduces the credibility of this information source still further. The effect of group viewing by an audience, in front of the television or in the cinema, is something that can reduce the credibility of an advertisement in a way that the private viewing of that same message when reading a printed advertisement or a poster would not. The group situation provides the social support for distrust that isn't present in the private viewing situation.

Even within the same type of media there can be differences in credibility. The so-called 'presenter effect' is a direct descendant of the difference between having your message delivered by an Oppenheimer and delivered by *Pravda*. One study done by the I.P.C. showed that an advertisement for Armstrong cork floors was 27% more persuasive in the *Sunday Times* magazine than in *Ideal Home*, and that a television commercial with the same message was 10% less persuasive than the advertisement in *Ideal Home*.

Before moving away entirely from the matter of whether it's right to look at the measures of credibility instead of the measures of attention and comprehension, the 'sleeper effect' deserves an airing. You may recall that the 'sleeper effect' was used by SOUP in developing the 'rotten apple concept' where an advertiser was argued to receive some benefit in year four from the advertisement in year one. Technically speaking, the 'sleeper effect' is the phenomenon of forgetting the source of the message over a period of time and, if the source is a low credibility one, it may mean the message will be actually more persuasive eight weeks after it was delivered than when it was delivered. This certainly showed when during the last war researchers who had shown American troops a film about the Battle of Britain (in an attempt to make the American troops believe their British allies) found that nine weeks after the showing of the film it had *increased* in persuasiveness.

If you apply this to advertising, you have a mechanism that might suggest that Professor Galbraith and his allies are right in saying that belief isn't important. For eight weeks after you've run your advertisement the consumer has forgotten *where* the message came from, and will then lap up your opinion like a cat taking to cream.

The only snag with this argument is that advertising, by the way it functions, makes it very hard for its audience to forget that the source of the message was a low credibility, highly despised advertisement. After all, there's quite a wide range of people who might have spoken to the American troops about the Battle of Britain following the film. They could even have chatted amongst themselves about it, read articles in the newspapers etc. Gradually the exact source of any particular attitude could have become fuzzier and fuzzier until the message remained alone, unsullied by its carrier. But in the case of advertising, there aren't many alternative sources for the information that Radiant has the whiter white. You know that any message you have stored in your brain about the whiteness of Radiant *must* have come from an advertisement because nobody else talks about such things. Just to make sure that we don't 'disassociate the source from the message' the advertiser is continually repeating his claims, continually reminding us that the 'whiter white' message is coming from a low credibility source.

This isn't a new point. It was in 1953 that Hoveland Janis and Kelley showed that while with a high credibility source the effect of reminding the recipient of the message after three weeks *added* to its persuasiveness, the effect of 'reinstating' a low credibility source was simply to wipe out the 'sleeper effect'. Once more the message was *reduced* in impact because of the low credibility of the source (namely an advertisement).

It's perhaps worth enquiring why the advertiser is so resolved to destroy any possible benefit he could receive from the 'sleeper effect' by persistently repeating his message. It is because he's resolved to get the maximum 'recall' for his sales message. He's been persuaded that the purpose of advertising is 'to make the consumer learn and retain the association between the two elements of an advertisement – the product and the brand name' (Kanungo, *Journal of Applied Psychology,* 1969).

If that brand name comes wrapped in a snappy phrase like 'The Esso sign means happy motoring', and then is further encapsulated in a musical form (otherwise known as a jingle) perfection is nigh. For then, the more he repeats this memorable expression of his product's virtues, the more virtuous the product will appear to become. Just how persistent is this belief is shown by the fact that the jingle is just about the most common form of television message. And almost the only reason for using a jingle is to make your sales message so 'catchy' that it will be self repeating, i.e. every time you hum 'a million housewives every day pick up a can of beans and say, Beanz means Heinz', you're giving the advertiser a free showing of his commercial inside your cranium.

'Recall measures' are thus a measure of the extent to which, through repetition, you have got your parcel of information about the products safely delivered into the consumer. Those who believe in using repetition for this purpose, ought to study the psychological concept of 'semantic satiation'. The standard way of arousing annoyance in an audience for experimental purposes is to repeat the same word or phrase twenty to thirty times over a brief period. So the psychologist's tool for creating annoyance is the advertiser's tool for creating sales.

However, even if you do manage with parrot-like repetition to embed your claim in the consumers' memory, it probably won't make you richer.

For there is twenty years of evidence to show that there is precisely no relationship between whatever measures of recall you take and whatever measures of attitude and behaviour change that you make. The parable of the three mirrors, as told by researcher Alfred Politz (*Journal of Marketing*, 1960) explains why. One of the mirrors was cracked, the second was perfect and had a beautiful gilt frame, and the third was perfect but unframed. These faced an open window and a visitor was asked to look at the mirrors on the wall and say what he could see. Of the first mirror he said, 'I see an old cracked mirror'. Of the second, 'I see a mirror in a beautiful frame'. Of the third, 'I see a beautiful view out of an open window.' The third mirror was Politz's description of good advertising: in reflecting the product favourably without drawing attention to itself. 'Recall' is paying attention to the frame instead of looking at the view through the windows. But whatever recall of sales points does correlate with it isn't sales. For example, though the higher the recall does *not* mean the higher the attitude change recall *is* highest for those who have shown the greatest attitude change. This is the result of the consumer's mental dossier looking for pieces of information which buttress its current position. That being so, the greater the proportion of the market the higher will be that brand's recall scores. So once your client's brand has obtained a hefty share of the market, then you can 'prove' how good your advertising is just by showing him the high recall scores which it is achieving.

With this built in bias for the larger brands advertising, it's understandable that the agencies handling these brands have stuck with recall measures. Sophisticated agencies like Ogilvy & Mather and sophisticated clients like Proctor & Gamble still chase high recall scores like Sir Lancelot sought the Holy Grail.

Agency documents abound with boasts about high recall scores. And case histories use recall measures to prove the 'success' of the campaign. For example, the 1971 I.T.A. Annual Report commented on the Scottish anti-smoking campaign: 'The campaign...has pleased the unit as regards public response and a recent survey carried out by the University of Strathclyde ascertained that the advertisement had reached and stayed in the minds of nearly 70% of the I.T.V. audience in Glasgow.'

One reason for all this is that throughout David Ogilvy's book *Confessions of an Advertising Man* are continual admonitions to do things like use captions under photographs, or use large type for the first paragraph of the copy in order to push up the *readership* by X%. Or mention the brand name in the first ten seconds of a television commercial because it increases the *recall* score by 14% (this last suggestion by the head of Ogilvy's agency in Canada). But all this leads to is a crazy numbers game with all these figures being used as fodder to keep the client happy.

Of course, information may have a big role in an advertisement. But you can't measure how much of that information has been *communicated* by asking someone to parrot it back at you. Of course, an advertisement needs to be looked at if it's to affect a consumer. But that doesn't mean the most looked at ad. is the most effective one. But the belief that in parroting there is communication and in readership there is riches are two of the foundation stones of modern advertising practice.

The other central belief is that the more I can make you change your attitude in favour of my product, as measured by various techniques, the more likely you are to buy my brand. The classic study on this subject (again almost twenty years old) is the Janis and Fesbach mentioned previously. It involved testing different sorts of appeal to persuade people to clean their teeth. You may recall that it was the strong (horror) appeal which got the least behaviour change and the minimal (factual) appeal got the most. But in terms of *attitude* change the result was exactly the other way round. For while the *factual* appeal got 79% more behaviour change than the horror appeal, the *horror* appeal got 64% more attitude change than the factual one. And since this discovery, a lot more evidence has emerged to suggest that there is not *necessarily* a relationship between favourable attitudes and purchase.

In 1965 Dr Anthony Greenwald found he could get junior high school children to change their beliefs about the importance of learning vocabulary but still not get them to change their behaviour (by doing difficult vocabulary problems). This occurred when the children had previously stated they were anti-vocabulary. The effect of this 'prior commitment on behaviour change after a persuasive communication' also worked in reverse. An anti-vocabulary child could be persuaded to learn more vocabulary with a 'behavioural incentive' (e.g. giving him money for extra words learned) but that didn't stop him having an anti-vocabulary attitude. This second point helps explain why 'behavioural incentives' to buy groceries, e.g. 2p off, don't do anything to strengthen a brand's image.

The first point is also demonstrated in the way people respond to propaganda about wearing seat belts in their cars. For manifold reasons, some to do with the fact that wearing a seat belt is to deny your masculinity, less than one driver in six wears a seat belt *despite* the fact that five out of six drivers believe they could well be involved in a serious accident at some time. So the propaganda has persuaded them that they might have an accident but it has still not persuaded them to wear their seat belt.

Even without a 'prior commitment' operating, there can still be a change of attitude without the expected change of behaviour. I may have a favourable attitude towards wearing trendy clothes but it may be that my wish to dress as others expect me to keeps me wearing pin stripes. Or my wife may have a favourable attitude towards a brand of soap but actually buy another brand which she feels less favourable towards when her mother-in-law visits, in her desire to conform with what she believes the mother-in-law expects her to find.

In both these cases, simple prediction of how one would behave based upon attitude measurements would have proved wrong. And an extra reason for these sort of predictions proving wrong in the case of advertising is that there is normally quite a gap in time and space between the attitude measured and the behaviour expected.

Some time ago R.C.A. did a survey which demonstrated this exact point. People who thought they might buy a television set within the next twelve months were asked to say which set they liked best or were most likely to buy, and rank other sets in order of likelihood of purchase. Later on the interviewer returned to these homes to see what actual brand of television was bought. Twenty-two per cent had bought one of the four brands they had listed as possibilities. But 59% had bought a brand which they had marked out in the first interview as being most unlikely for them to purchase. It could be argued that all that had happened was that these consumers' attitudes simply changed after the first interview. However, as long ago as 1954 a study by Du Pont amongst 5,700 women showed that only three out of ten actually purchased the brand they expected to buy before they entered the store. And that seven out of ten changed their minds in the store.

An ingenious theory which explains this phenomenon has been developed by Dr Herbert Krugman of General Electric. He suggests that the supermarket provides a catalyst which brings out all the potential shifts of attitude that have been accumulated up to this point by the consumer. Though nothing could or would be verbalized prior to *that* moment if the consumer was asked about his attitude. The attitude change that results *after* this purchase would be two-fold. First, bringing into balance the expectations of the product and the reality of the product's performance. Second, the balancing of the act of purchase with other elements in the mental dossier (rationalization).

Interestingly, Dr Andrew Ehrenberg has shown that once you know the penetration of a brand into a market you can predict with uncanny accuracy the likely response of consumers to most attitude questions. But researchers are still having great difficulty in making the prediction in the other direction. And the fact that it may not be possible to predict choice of brands or type of product purchased knowing a consumer's previous habits, beliefs, or attitudes is a fairly tough one for the crystal ball gazers of the market research industry to have to stomach.

The full impact of these theoretical doubts has not yet sunk home to the mass of the advertisers and their agencies who, for the most part, are still merrily measuring people's attitudes before exposure to the advertisement, measuring the attitudes after exposure and deducing from that the sales effectiveness of the advertisement. As though the past criticisms of this approach had never been penned.

The only real alternative to measuring attitudes as a predictor of behaviour which has emerged is to measure what is called the 'behavioural intention'. This tries to shift the moment of measurement much closer to the act of purchase. For instance, if you asked a woman who was standing in front of the soap section of the supermarket which brand she was going to buy, your correlation with behaviour would probably be much higher than if you asked the same question just after she had seen a commercial for your brand of soap. But, despite the brave hopes of the supporters of this notion, it doesn't at present amount to a lot more than saying 'once you know what someone's going to do, you know what someone's going to do'. This leaves the poor advertiser stranded like a whale on a beach. He's spent his huge advertising budget. His agency has told him that the recall scores are tremendous. But then he learns he can't believe in recall scores. So the agency tells him that the promotion produced a tremendous shift in attitude by consumers in favour of the product. But now he learns that this doesn't mean that they will also be buying his product in droves. How, then, can he go to his managing director to justify the expenditure of this enormous sum, when all the other departments in the company, can't wait to get their hands on what they regard as a conspicuous way of putting money down the drain? In this situation he will fall back on the final link in the chain: 'Well', he can say to the Board looking the R. and D. man straight between the eyes, 'your wife may think our commercial stinks, and maybe I haven't got any convincing research measures to prove the ads. were right. But I can tell you one thing' – he pauses here – *'it sells'*.

These two little words have been the justification of much of the advertising that has helped to build up the consumerist backlash. (Perhaps one should add that the relationship is expressed slightly more subtly: if sales go up, it's because of the advertising but if they go down it's because of something else.)

Every advertiser who visits a new agency will be told about the campaign that lifted sales 40% or of an advertisement that took this brand out of the dustbin and turned it into a brand leader.

Isn't this a fair measure of an advertisement's success? As we shall see, the proper function of an advertisement may well be to create sales. But sales are not normally a proper measure of how well that function has been carried out.

For a start, there's a huge number of other variables, many of which the agency has no control over. Like the efficiency of the sales force, the company's track record with the trade, the price of the product, its distribution, the packaging, the quality of the product, the competitor's share of the market, the competitor's activity in the market, the consumer's attitude towards the product itself. But, more than this, the way cognitive dissonance theory suggests people respond to overclaim shows how – despite total *rejection* of the advertisement – sales of a product may still go up subsequent to the claim, even when all the other variables are held constant.

A case in point is Fairy Liquid. The depth interviews reported earlier on people's attitudes to advertising also showed that these commercials were irritating. (You will doubtless 'recall' they involved children playing with bubbles and their mother cooing to the accompaniment of massed choirs singing the 'hands that do dishes can feel soft as your face' jingle.) To this, many of the consumers I spoke to reply, 'children don't behave like that', and 'it's silly to make such a song and dance over washing up', etc. Yet the product is a brand leader, and that despite having entered the market later than its main rivals.

Can the undoubted sales success of this product be attributed to its hard sell advertising? Well, the Fairy Liquid company, Proctor and Gamble, had a lot on their side – like an ultra-tough sales force and a good track record with the trade. But they've also had flops in their time so these alone couldn't explain the success of Fairy Liquid. What *is* revealing, however, is to look at the actual performance of this product against other brands of washing up liquid. The *News of the World* did a study, for example, which showed that because Fairy Liquid contained the highest proportion of 'active ingredients' (i.e. the solvents that get rid of grease) it gave 20% more 'washing up power' than the next major brand. And a study by *Ideal Home* found that, compared to the retailers' own brands, Fairy Liquid could absorb three to four times as much fat before the washing up water went flat (you'd need four drops of a retailer's own brand of detergent to get the same sudsing power as one drop of Fairy Liquid). In short, it is Fairy Liquid's *performance* in cleaning dishes that explains its success.

Many consumers have tried a retailers' own brand because they have a low pack price. But after finding that they actually worked out more expensively they have returned to Fairy Liquid. (And recently there have been more Fairy Liquid commercials using disc jockey Tony Blackburn that reflect the reality of this situation.)

What is certain, however, is that the housewives are not buying Fairy Liquid because they believe the advertising claim that 'hands that do dishes can feel soft as your face with mild green Fairy Liquid'. For even if they tell the researchers from Young and Rubican, Fairy Liquid's advertising agency, that they think the product is amazingly mild, they are voting with their hands to show they think nothing of the sort: 57% of all housewives use rubber gloves regularly for washing up (according to London Rubber Industries who make Marigold gloves). Unless all the non-rubber glove wearers are skewed towards Fairy Liquid, this fact can only mean one of two things. That either the mildness claim is not relevant, as housewives use rubber gloves because of the effect of water on their skin. Or they find that as Fairy Liquid is such a strong detergent, they need rubber gloves for protection. (Certainly, though Proctor and Gamble were unable to supply any evidence that Fairy Liquid is as mild as the advertising claims.) All of which makes the link between Fairy Liquid's advertising and the success of the brand an extremely tenuous one. Nevertheless, this case history is often used in the advertising industry as proof that schmaltzy hard sell is the thing that moves mountains of groceries.

So does that mean that Fairy Liquid would have been just as successful as a brand without the many million pounds in advertising that they have spent telling people about its mildness? It's not impossible.

238

Certainly, in the case of the world's largest animal food producer, Ralston Purina, advertising played an insignificant role in their success in the British market. They launched their Seanip dinners into the British dry catfood market in 1968. Within three years they had over a third of the market nationally and half the market in the key London area. But they achieved that without spending a penny on advertising (even though at the same time their main rival spent over half a million pounds on advertising). If, however, Purina had appointed an agency and if that agency had spent large sums of money running commercials for Seanip they would have pointed triumphantly to the 30% market share as indication of the cost effectiveness of their advertising.

This naïve *post hoc ergo propter hoc* relationship is not only misleading, it is very dangerous for the advertising industry itself. For once a company starts to judge its advertising by a measure that may well be a false one, then the agency is in trouble if it dares to adopt a new approach to its advertising.

Suppose a big agency, recognizing the scientific reality, decides to chuck out recall studies, to boot out attitudes measures and to concentrate on some of the techniques of persuasion which are described in the following chapter, it becomes very vulnerable if it's being judged on sales alone. Sales may go down. Or they may rise less faster than previously. And for no reason at all to do with the advertising. (In the same way that their earlier rise may have had very little to do with the advertising.) Then the client will be complaining that the advertisements 'aren't working' (as happened, in fact, when several agencies tried to move towards the so-called 'creative' approach).

In short, the advertising industry is hoist on its own petard. It can't change its ways easily because it's chained itself to a method of judgement that makes any innovation, even if it's an improvement, vulnerable to attack.

The other reason why the advertising industry finds it hard to change, even though most of their measures have been found to be built on sand, is that they have nothing else to fall back on. If a manufacturing company decides to write off some capital equipment because it doesn't work properly, it can simply dispose of it by putting in new capital equipment instead. But the advertising agency can do no such thing. Remove the data bank of twenty years of recall studies and they have nothing. Rob them of their pre- and post-exposure attitudinal measures and they are naked in the boardroom. And always not just the agencies who feel the need for props. A company like Proctor and Gamble finds recall studies useful as a management tool to keep their brand managers up to the mark, quite apart from any marketing importance it might have. Take all this away and the advertising industry is left with a whole battery of techniques for selling products without any method, which any professional scientist could accept, of measuring whether these techniques function as their makers claim or not.

It is this tremendous void that advertising has to quickly fill if it is to avoid becoming no more than a memento of the golden days of the sizzling sixties. A not-so-glorious future where little children ask their fathers 'Daddy, what was a commercial?'

13
As Not Advertised on TV

Is it really so fanciful to suggest that signs carrying the words of this chapter heading should spring up in the shop windows of affluent societies? I, as a practitioner of the advertising industry whose mortgage payments hinge on the relative prosperity of this business, hope so. But the evidence presented in the earlier chapters suggests that already the mere act of advertising a product puts it at a disadvantage, and then the communication has first to make up for this *before* it can add any plus points to the product.

Trapped within a pincer attack – from the consumerist hostility on one side and the revelations of its limited power on the other – advertising seems seriously in danger of going out of business; and the continued practices of the industry only increase the odds of its own extinction.

There are certainly many who would be happy to see it go the way of sky projection and quack medicine : 'The destiny of our civilization', writes Arnold Toynbee, 'turns on the outcome of the struggle with all that Madison Avenue stands for.'

Only if Madison Avenue (and the equivalent avenues and strasses on this side of the Atlantic) start to stand for something else does the advertising industry appear, to this writer at least, to be able to look forward to much more than increasing hostility, reducing budgets, and an eventual long slow withering away.

The first change that is required to ensure the survival of this species is that it recognizes the sorts of change amongst consumers that have occurred over the past ten years. That it actu-

241

ally looks up from its double whiskies and thick carpets to see past the bunny girl receptionist and the chromium plated doors to look at the people beyond – yes, those funny objects you sell to have actually *changed*. They don't worship materialism in the way the advertisements suggest. The housewives don't worship housewifery as the advertisement suggests. And a new ethos is growing up amongst the under-twenty-fives who wonder why so much money is being spent on selling trivia when half the world is dying for a meal.

If the admen can appreciate all this, they will soon see that they are living and behaving in a way that is quite out of keeping with the times. If, as seems likely, the advertising industry is still unable to lead the parade of reform itself, then it will have to be dragged along behind.

First, as chapters three and four showed, the rules controlling advertising on both sides of the Atlantic have a laxness that is unacceptable in the age of militant consumerism. No advertiser, for example, should be permitted to make a claim (even a trade puff) unless he can fully substantiate it. And the judgement of what claim has actually been made should be based on communication research (which actually measures what people get out of a communication). This would both allow those humorous claims that aren't really claims as well as eliminating those claims which cunningly use verbal hair splitting to get themselves on the air, but are actually implying a lot more than they're saying.

The restrictive practice of not allowing comparisons between yours and a rival products should be dropped. Strangely enough the prohibition of comparisons is strongest in Germany, where otherwise their advertising controls tend to be in the best interests of the consumer. The only restraint on comparisons should be the laws of libel.

The same rules that govern television advertising should also govern all other sorts of advertising. A dual standard of truth is not acceptable any more.

Remembering how much lower was the hostility to advertising in those countries where there was less television advertising, it would be in the advertising industry's interests to *reduce* the amount of television advertising. A lower figure of the minutes of television advertising per hour is required. And commercials should not be allowed to interrupt programmes, as this is one of the major causes of hostility.

The loss of revenue that this would cause the television programme companies could be replaced by increasing the rates at which they sell television time to advertisers to a level where the total revenue obtained was the same as previously. The price-elasticity of television time is probably sufficient to allow this increase of price to be made. And by making companies pay a lot more for their advertising, it would also serve to make them think much more carefully about the efficiency of the way they spent it.

If putting up the price was insufficient to bridge the income gap caused by the reduction in advertising time, tax concessions to the programme companies might be used as compensation. (And in Britain the return of the television levy to the programme companies in 1970 would have given back to them an extra profit of £20 million.)

The final draconian measure that would actually be helping the advertising industry is a *maximum* budget level for advertisers. The fact that cigarette sales were maintained both in Britain and America after banning the advertising of cigarettes on television suggests that a lot of advertising expenditure is simply self-cancelling. A high proportion of the £500,000 I may spend to advertise my brand is cancelled by the £500,000 my rival spends (and my expenditure also serves to cancel a lot of his). But though the advertising may have been neutralized in a commercial sense, from the consumer standpoint there is still a great deal of unpleasant noise going on around him. If a maximum ceiling was placed on advertising budgets (and I can see that it would be difficult to arrange) it wouldn't stop new companies from coming into the market (though it would discourage the build-up of monopoly positions by the established companies). But it would slice off the top end of the giant advertising budgets and so eliminate some of the self-cancelling advertising.

These measures would *start* to restore to advertising a modicum of tolerance from the public. They would also, by eliminating most of the puffery and unrelated comparitives, *help* to turn advertising from a flabby amalgam of words and pictures into an effective selling tool. But in order to regain the respect of their *clients,* two further reforms are necessary.

First, agencies should endeavour to have a slightly higher standard of whose account they will handle. They should ask potential clients questions about the satisfactory performance of the product, the safety of the product, the value of such a product in a consumer society, as well as the routine questions of brand shares. And they should refuse to take on products that don't give satisfactory answers to such questions instead of the current practice of jumping into bed with virtually anyone. If agencies *are* ever fussy it is more often because they're worried their customers can't pay the bill than because there is is anything wrong with what the customer has to offer. And to have no higher standard of client selection than a common prostitute is not the way to obtain the respect of the business community.

Second, the 15% commission payment system for agencies should be ended. This is a system where for every £100 of media space an agency books, the media only charge £85 – though the agency bills the clients for the full £100. Quite apart from its stifling effect on price competition, this system focuses the agency's attention on producing advertisements rather than on the wider, non-15%, areas of problem solving. It also has the disadvantage of making clients feel that they're getting the services of an advertising agency for free: if they prepared the advertisement and placed it themselves in the media it would still cost them £100. If clients had to pay for their agency's services in the same way that they pay for other services the effect on the whole advertising industry would be salutary, though perhaps unwelcome for the lame ducks. In any event it hardly helps the agency's relationship with his client to be always supplying something for nothing. If nothing is what you pay, nothing is what it's worth. But when a company pays McKinseys, the management consultants, £1000 a day for their advice they think twice before rejecting it.

The next result of the changes proposed so far would be to improve the quality while reducing the quantity of advertising, as well as improving the lord and vassal client/agency relationship. But all this only makes it *possible* for advertising to have a future, it doesn't provide it with one. For that to happen it needs to redefine its role.

First, it must cease to regard itself as the *prima donna* of the marketing process. Yes, advertising *can* have an effect on sales. But the relationship of the two is by no means the simple casual one of the traditional claim to sales chain.

Overleaf is a more realistic assessment of the advertising to sales relationship. This shows that advertising is a very small part of a very big picture. And reminds one that there are a great many intervening stages between claim and sales that can stop the claim stone dead in its tracks.

In fact, in many of the experiments where it was possible to keep the 'other things being equal' variables under control, advertising was shown to be far less effective than many think. The case histories which show advertising's relative success tend to be ones where these other variables were far less under control than the cases showing its relative failure.

If advertising's place is not necessarily in the centre of the stage, does it still have a role to play in the drama of consumer choice? Its prime job is to help consumers solve problems in the consumption area. The problem solving consumer is an intelligent animal who's faced with needs to fulfil. She seeks out as much information as seems to her necessary (that is more for buying a car than for buying a packet of chewing gum) and relates this information to the purchasing problem. She acts consistently within the confines of her mental dossier (though not always rationally). And the flow chart model overleaf shows conceptually at least the various stages she will go through in making a product choice.

To pass each of the hurdles the advertising message will have to be constructed in a way that is quite different from the typical hard-nosed, hard-sell U.S.P. (which is quickly chewed up and spat out by the watchdogs, selective exposure, selective perception, and selective retention).

Instead of over-claiming, *under-claiming* offers the advertiser a better chance in the seventies. Under-claiming is exactly the opposite of over-claiming. In some ways similar to that much maligned concept 'soft sell', but while this is an intuitive feeling amongst some perceptive admen, under-claiming is an analytical response to a particular communication situation.

Under-claim, to revert to the theory of cognitive dissonance, creates the *minimum* amount of cognitive dissonance necessary to persuade the consumer to act as you suggest. Just enough to get the 'curious non-belief' described on page 226 but *not* too much to get rejected because the claim doesn't tally with the contents of her mental dossier.

There is considerable evidence, including one experiment try-

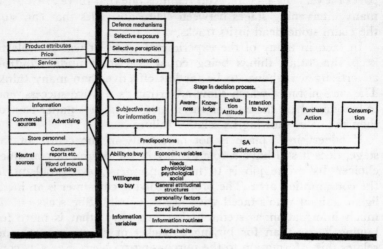

Source: Arndt

ing to persuade American soldiers to eat grasshoppers, that this sort of minimal appeal is more effective. One amusing, if unscientific, anecdote of the success of under-claiming is reported in Sam Baker's *The Permissible Lie*. He related the tale of a New York department store which couldn't sell a consignment of green neck ties. They tried every advertising gimmick, even cutting the price by two dollars, but nothing worked. In the end the celebrated Ira Hirschman tried an advertisement with the headline 'Our buyer made a bad mistake'. The copy told what had happened and concluded 'if there are 207 men who'd like a green tie, you can get these magnificent $7 dollar imported ties for $5 because very few men like green neck ties'. The ties sold out like hot cakes.

Volkswagen ads generally use under-claim. So also did the Campari ad that ran in America with the headline '9 out of every 10,000 Americans prefer Campari' to present it as a status drink, instead of using the (unbelievable) photograph of a room full of (unbelievable) smart people drinking (unbelievable) nothing but Campari. Or take Ronson in Britain, who ran an ad for their new hair dryer with the headline 'Ronson announces a slightly better hair dryer'. No nonsense about a new-improved-hair-dryer with-30%-more power. Just the truth. Because not only is honesty the best policy in the seventies, it is probably the *only* policy for an advertiser trying to sell things faced by the new consumers' defence mechanisms.

In the same way that under-claiming is a *stronger* claim than hard selling in the new customer environment, equally admitting that there are two sides to the story you're telling can make your advertisement *more* effective. When your audience initially disagrees with you or when it's probable that they will hear the other side from someone else (as is generally the case with advertising) a two-sided argument will stand you in better stead. Better educated men, in particular, are more influenced by two-sided communications. Probably because they feel that as there must be two sides to the point in question, a one-sided presentation is treating them like nincompoops.

In one study in America one-sided and two-sided commercials were made for cars, gas cookers and floor waxes. They were tested on 500 people and it was found that the two-sided commercials produced significantly more attitude change in favour of the product. (One has of course, reservations about this sort of measurement but still it may be revealing something.)

Another study (Mcniven) on Marlborough cigarettes also confirmed in practice what communication theory had suggested in principle. In this case the researchers produced advertisements which gave the standard one-sided version available in most print ads, saying that Marlborough cigarettes were the mildest, best-tasting available. And they also produced advertisements which said that everybody knows a filter cigarette can't be as nice tasting as a plain cigarette. But Marlborough is still the finest-tasting filter cigarette you can get. The second appeal was clearly negative, as it admitted that filter cigarettes didn't taste as good as plain, but in discussions it emerged that smokers responded better to the two-sided argument: 'He's giving us the straight scoop,' was one typical comment.

All these forms of under-claiming take into account, in a way that current advertising practice does not, the low credibility of advertising as an information source. And the evidence of the social psychologists is that the lower your credibility, then the *more* you attempt to influence people, the *greater* will be their resistance.

Strangely enough, the advertiser receives one side benefit from being such a low credibility source. Raymond Bauer of the Harvard Business School has found that the best defence *against* counter propaganda is a *low* trust *high* competence source. So if you make your advertising, say very factual and informative then *just because* you are a low credibility source the consumer will tend to think the matter over carefully. This process of weighing up the pros and cons serves to inoculate the consumer against the rival advertising counter propaganda.

One implication Bauer draws from this is that if you are selling something with a long shopping period, like a car, and the rival brands are coming in with counter messages to your own, this inoculation procedure can be used to help you. However, if you can try and borrow 'a high credibility source', like Chevrolet borrow Bob Godfrey, then this source though excellent is more vulnerable to the counter propaganda (because the consumer has taken the word of the source and not thought the matter out for himself).

On the other hand, if you are selling a product with a short shopping period, maybe hiring a high credibility source to deliver your message would be sensible. Certainly, the Norman Ross discount chain found it successful in Australia. They signed up three clergymen as pitchmen for their commercials, all of which ended with the same words: 'The offers of Norman Ross are genuine. I wouldn't do their commercials if they weren't.' And then was superimposed on the screen the following message: 'Norman Ross discounts pledge 2% of net profits to the Aid of Humanities Foundation.'

As well as renting vicars, another way an advertiser can raise his credibility is by presenting his message *before* revealing his identity as a low credibility source. This doesn't mean hiding your advertisement in an editorial style, which may only irritate the consumer. But it does suggest that a client who insists that his agency sticks an enormous logo in the advertisement, dominating the whole page, is actually making the agency's handiwork *less effective*.

As well as taking its credibility (or lack of it) into account, the advertisement also needs to take into account its audience, in a way that is rather different from the conventional aiming of the message at 'young marrieds with 2 children'. You can classify differences in your audience on the basis of their defence mechanisms, on how close they are to a purchase decision. On what they think about the brand. And each of these different segments may need a different sort of message. Then as the consumer 'progresses' from one segment to another segment you will need to modify the type of advertising that now reaches him. What this is effectively doing is making your advertisement fit your target consumer's predispositions. And there is plenty of evidence to show that if, for example, the advertiser expresses some views that are also held by his audience he'll find it easier to persuade the audience towards his view point on another (and maybe quite separate) issue. This is a phenomenon described by one social psychologist as 'flogging a dead horse'.

As an alternative to making your proposition acceptable to the consumer by *adjusting it to him*, you can also make a message bespoke by constructing it in such a way that the consumer *adjusts himself to it*. This is something that goes back to McLuhan and the participatory nature of television. Applying this thinking to advertising he observes: 'The need is to make the ad. include the audience experience.' One way of doing this is to leave the message incomplete, like just saying, 'You can take Salen out of the country but …' Or you can make your claim incomplete by leaving the brand name out, as in 'I'm only here for the beer'. The 'zargonic' effect this causes encourages the consumer to complete the phrase or add the brand name, and by so involving himself in the message it becomes more acceptable than if it was thrust upon him in a complete form.

What you are encouraging the consumer to do by leaving the message incomplete is simply to improvise. And improvising is, again, a proven way of increasing the persuasiveness of the message. In one study (King and Janis) two groups were shown a script. Those in one of the groups were then asked to read the script out aloud, while those in the other group had to present the contents of the script without relying on the script. It was this second group that were most persuaded by the arguments in the original script. They had been forced to 'hand tailor' the message to fit themselves, and so they were more influenced by it.

In fact, one of the latest research measurements tries to assess a number of 'connexions' a consumer makes with your advertisement. Developed by Dr Herbert Krugman of General Electric, it suggests that the more 'connexions' a consumer makes, the more unstructured is the advertisement, and the more unstructured is the advertisement, the more the consumer can fit himself into it. And so the more persuasive it becomes.

But all these techniques (and I don't say new techniques because many of them have been lurking in the annals of social psychology for some time) are no more than a better way of doing the traditional advertising agency job. They're still treating the function of an advertising agency as the production of advertisements, albeit advertisements that get past the consumer's watchdog.

Given the state of information technology there is no reason why carrying out this function should require the advertising agency structured as it is today. All the advertising factories are doing is to churn out their hardware to the appropriate formula (and this would still be partly true if the old formula were replaced by some of the guiding principles just enumerated).

There is no particular reason why the agencies should not take the next step forward (or is it backwards) and go the whole hog over to Dial-an-ad. Why don't they just feed all their headlines with proven pulling power into the I.B.M. computer, along with the clinch words like *new, free* and *amazing* (or whatever the formula prescribes), add their tested marketing plans, their key emotional buying triggers, and their optimum media schedules. Then they could simply give each client a computer terminal. When he wants anything, from a eight-inch double column in the *Barnsley Gazette* to a new product launch with all the trimmings, he simply taps out the instructions down the line. If the computer is kept fed with all the latest market shares and information about competitors' activities, this could probably do the same as the factory agencies are currently doing, but in a matter of seventeen seconds.

If agencies want a more meaningful role in the future perhaps they should extend the area of their concern far beyond the business of churning out advertisements. They should look at the product and see how, using their communication skills, *extra value* can be added to the product in the same way that the production engineer adds extra value to the product. The values which can be added by the agency will not, needless to say, be the phoney ones so beloved in the fifties and sixties – the neighbour approval and heightened sexuality syndrome. Nor will they arise just by shuffling the permutations of a pack's shape, colour

250

or size as David Bernstein's new style 'business consultancy advertising agency' has started to do for Rowntrees. No, the new added-value concept goes further than seeing if a bright blue on the box will stuff more liquorice allsorts down the consumer's throat than a bright yellow. Instead, it turns the agency into a pastoral 'social information broker' who tries to act as both a *sensor* in the market place picking up tremors (like the man who saw people mixing vinegar and olive oil to stop sunburn and then himself brought out a commercial suntan oil) and also a *modifier* of products based upon these soundings. Following in the footsteps of Dr Banzhaf and his bandits, the acronym C.O.N.T.A.C.T. seems a fitting way of summarizing this function; it stands for Consumer Orientated New Thinking And Communication Techniques.

C.O.N.T.A.C.T. is the antithesis of Dial-an-ad, always looking for new ways to add value to its clients' products with concepts that are based on communication techniques and communication insights rather than technological insights (though there is no reason why a C.O.N.T.A.C.T. agency shouldn't sit down with the technical people and go lateral).

Unit pricing and open dating show clearly the difference between C.O.N.T.A.C.T. and Dial-an-ad. C.O.N.T.A.C.T., as a social information broker, would have dreamt up both these ideas *on behalf of* its supermarket client. But Dial-an-ad is programmed to *fight* these questions on behalf of its supermarket client.

There are already some advertisers and some agencies which are carrying out, to a greater or lesser extent, part of the C.O.N.T.A.C.T. philosophy. Mary Wells, before she slipped backwards, acted as a social information broker when she painted Braniff's planes bright colours. And she did the same, in a different way, when she enhanced the function of TWA by the 'million dollar bonus' improved service scheme. Ford's 'we listen better' concept is a clear expression of social information brokering on the C.O.N.T.A.C.T. lines.

One company which has gone further than any other in the direction of C.O.N.T.A.C.T. is Hunt Wesson. They have shown that they are fully aware of the way a communicator (in this case within the company) can add value to their products. For example, in 1970 they began their 'We'll help you make it' programme to help families live healthily within their food budgets. They simply invited housewives to send off the number

251

and ages of the people in their family and the amount of their weekly food budget. The housewife then got back a personalized letter plus a special computer printout of menus for her family for an entire month, though tied to her budget (as well as the recipes for preparing the things on this menu). Over $1\frac{1}{4}$ million housewives have sent off for this menu so far. The sort of goodwill that this type of activity builds may not be easily measurable, but then neither is the goodwill listed in a company's annual report.

Or take the other Hunt Wesson added value concepts of 1971. In conjunction with the U.S. Forestry Service, it buys and plants a tree in the name of those who send in labels from its Big John's Beans'nFixin's product. It also started an 'Operational Ecology' programme to recycle all their packaging, and their Canada Dry division has even offered to recycle the bottles of rival drink manufacturers. As a final touch, the company publicly announced that they would not try to capitalize on relatively irrelevant differences in their food advertising.

The advice of a social information broker acting on the C.O.N.T.A.C.T. philosophy can go even further than this. Dr Joe Juran has suggested that in the future a manufacturer may have to undertake responsibilities for the service of a product for the whole lifetime of that product (in the same way that the village craftsman performed the task of design, manufacture, sale and service with a clear undivided responsibility). This is the sort of suggestion that a C.O.N.T.A.C.T. agency might make to a client to give their products an added value over rival consumer durables in the market place.

If this philosophy were to grow, and not be trampled underfoot by the men in grey flannel suits with minds to match, then I *can* see a future for the advertising industry. It can cease to be the irritator, the deliverer of half truths, the uninformer, the disrespecter of persons, the social blackmailer. And instead it can become a problem solver for consumers, a bridge between consumers and manufacturers carrying two-way traffic, and a way of adding genuine, not phoney values to its clients' products.

Despite all its failings, blindness, folly, ignorance and stupidity advertising still has one more chance. For the Consumer Revolution is not vengeful. It does not demand the death of the old and fraudulent magicians. It merely wishes to turn them into useful human beings.

Index

253